CROSSING CAIRO

A JEWISH WOMAN'S ENCOUNTER WITH EGYPT

The author with her husband Reuven Firestone
and Arabic teacher, Zayna, in Tahir Square, July 2011
Photo by Mohamed Hawary

CROSSING CAIRO

A JEWISH WOMAN'S ENCOUNTER WITH EGYPT

Ruth H. Sohn

Gaon Books
www.gaonbooks.com

For permissions, group pricing, and other information contact
Gaon Books
P.O. Box 23924
Santa Fe, NM 87502
or write (gaonbooks@gmail.com).

Manufactured in the United States of America.
The paper used in this publication is acid free and meets all ANSI (American National Standards for Information Sciences) standards for archival quality paper. All wood product components used in this book are Sustainable Forest Initiative (SFI) certified.

Library of Congress Cataloging-in-Publication Data
Sohn, Ruth H.*Crossing Cairo : a Jewish woman's encounter with Egypt / Ruth H. Sohn.*
pages ; cm.
ISBN 978-1-935604-50-1 (pbk. : alk. paper) -- ISBN 978-1-935604-51-8 (ebook)
1. Egypt--Description and travel--Juvenile literature. 2. Sohn, Ruth H.--Travel--Egypt--Personal narratives--Juvenile literature. 3. Jews, American--Travel--Egypt--Juvenile literature. I. Title.
DT56.2.S64 2013
305.48'892'406216092--dc23
[B]
2012042842

Cover and interior photographs are by Ruth H. Sohn
unless otherwise noted.

Contents

Acknowledgments

الكلمة في فمك ـ أنت سيدها، خرجت من فمك ـ هي سيدتك

While the word is yet unspoken, you are master of it;
once it is spoken, it is master of you.
~Arabic Proverb

THIS BOOK COULD NOT HAVE COME INTO BEING WITHOUT THE support and encouragement of my family and friends. First, I want to express my gratitude to all the people in Egypt, named and unnamed, who reached out to us in many different ways. In particular, to those who became our friends, who gave so generously of their time and never tired of our questions, and who were eager to share "their" Cairo with us. In particular, I want to express my gratitude to Zayna, my Arabic teacher, and to Mahabbah, our housekeeper, both of whom helped me learn Arabic and offered me unique and invaluable windows into Egyptian life and society. In their case and in most other cases, I have changed the names of the people with whom we interacted in Cairo and Israel, out of concern for their privacy and in some cases their security. This is not the case with public figures including the following:

My thanks to Elie Antebi, who served as the Israeli Consul General to Alexandria and was living in Maadi during our sojourn there, who, from our first phone conversation proved a most helpful source of information and soon became a friend.

My appreciation and thanks to Carmen Weinstein, President of the Jewish Community in Cairo, who graciously met with me and shared some of her perspectives and experiences working on behalf of the Jewish community of Cairo, including her efforts to preserve the Bassatine Cemetery and remaining synagogues of the city. My gratitude also goes to Mohamed Hawary, Professor of Religious Jewish Thought and Comparative Religions at Ain Shams University in Cairo, for his warm friendship with Reuven and our family over many years and his irrepressible humor and love of word plays in any language. Mohamed was always ready to answer my questions about Egyptian politics and religion, and he provided insightful assistance identifying the original Arabic of certain proverbs I could only find in English, and offering translations back into Arabic for others. Unfortunately, when we lived in Cairo in 2006, Mohamed was away, teaching in Saudi Arabia. We made up for his absence then, by taking full advantage of his generous hospitality when we visited Cairo again in 2007 and 2011.

I am grateful to Yona Sabar, linguist and expert in Semitic languages of UCLA, for his help also, translating certain proverbs that I only found in English, back into Arabic.

Samir Rafaat's book, *Maadi 1904-1962: Society and History in a Cairo Suburb*, and his numerous articles in the Egyptian English press and on the Cairo Jewish Community Center's website, *Bassatine News*, proved an invaluable and delightfully rich source on Jewish life in Cairo past and present. Michael M. Laskier's *The Jews of Egypt, 1920-1970: in the Midst of Zionism, Anti-Semitism, and the Middle East Conflict*, and Joel Beinin's *The Dispersion of Egyptian Jewry: Culture, Politics, and the Formation of a Modern Diaspora*, both provided important documentation of the last decades of active Jewish life in Cairo, and insightful analysis of this period.

Bonny V. Fetterman, my editor, challenged me time and again to clarify my thinking and articulation, and with her honesty, forthrightness, and untiring attention to detail, helped me grow as a writer. I am deeply grateful.

To our sons, Noam and Amir, for their spirit of adventure and for their unfailing good humor, my admiration and appreciation. My appreciation also goes to our daughter Rachel, who supported us enthusiastically from college in Connecticut.

And to the love of my life, Reuven, whose adventurous spirit first led us to Cairo and who encouraged me to think about writing this book even before we left for Egypt, my deep gratitude. Reuven's patience and support throughout the writing process were unwavering. I dedicate *Crossing Cairo* to him.

Prologue

رحلة الألف ميل تبدأ بخطوة

A journey of a thousand miles begins with one step.
~Arabic Proverb

I AM A RABBI MARRIED TO A RABBI. MY HUSBAND AND I ARE ON A
plane bound for Egypt with our two sons, Noam, 17, and Amir, 12—not
just for a family vacation, but to live in Cairo for six months.

9

A Jewish family moving to Cairo for half a year? Why, you might
ask. I had asked this question too—and a few others—when Reuven first
broached the subject of spending his next sabbatical in Cairo.

"Why Cairo?" I had asked, stomach tightening. "I can think of a
hundred places I would rather live. Can't you study Arabic in Istanbul?"
I was only half-joking.

"Or," I asked, more realistically, "maybe in an Arab town in Israel?"
Israel was a second home to us. We had spent many summers and on two
different occasions, a full year with our children, teaching and studying
in Israel and we had a whole network of friends there. Returning to Israel to live in or near an Arab community was an option I could imagine
much more easily than living in Cairo. It would also be easier for me to
justify a leave of absence from the Jewish high school where I taught if I
was doing something in Israel.

But for years already, Reuven had wanted to live in an Arab country.
A rabbi and academic in the joint fields of Judaism and Islam, Reuven
had devoted most of his scholarship to the historical development of Islam. He had no idea when he first went into this field in the 1980s that
twenty years later Americans would be straining to understand the difference between Sunni and Shiite and "Islamic" and "Islamist."

9/11 not only changed the course of history, it changed the course of
Reuven's career. Suddenly he found himself called upon to explain Islam
to Jews and Jewish communities all over the country. As a rabbi, Reuven
was someone who could make connections between Islam and Judaism,

and someone Jews could trust. The growing number of speakers bashing Islam made Reuven stand out even more in the Jewish community, as someone who appreciated the richness of Islam and who could offer intelligent, nuanced analysis of contemporary and historical trends affecting Muslims.

Now, at this point in his academic career, Reuven felt even more strongly the need to live in an Arab country. He needed this experience in order to deepen his understanding of the contemporary Arab world and to establish credibility with some of his critics. He also wanted to improve his Arabic in order to gain freer access to contemporary Arab writings of a political and religious nature. I understood and wanted to support him in these efforts.

But at the same time, I was deeply apprehensive. What would it be like for us as Jews to live in Cairo? Would we be safe? While 80,000 Jews had lived in Egypt in the early 1940s, today there were almost none. Anti-Jewish sentiment and persecution after the creation of the State of Israel as well as Nasser's nationalization and exile of foreigners had sent most Jews packing from the late 1940s through the 1950s. Almost all the remaining Jews left after the 1967 war. Israel was still vilified in the Arab world. How much did this carry over to Jews in general, I wondered. It was one thing to visit Cairo, as we had briefly four years earlier, but quite another to live there.

"Cairo is amazing," Reuven said, hoping to persuade me. "It is the intellectual and cultural center of the Arab world. And there are thousands of American ex-pats who live there …all kinds of people doing really interesting things." I knew this was important to Reuven and I tried to be open to the idea, but I kept coming back to my memories of our earlier trip to Cairo. There was no question, Cairo was a fascinating place, rich in history and culture. I loved that aspect of it. But unlike other Middle Eastern towns and cities I had visited, like Istanbul, I had found Cairo uncomfortable and alienating rather than exotic and romantic. Where Istanbul conjured up memories of deep reds and blues and gold, when I thought of Cairo, the pictures came up in gray.

Cairo, with its ornate old buildings and splendid circles and squares downtown still carried hints of grandeur, but now the old European style buildings were tired and dirty. And even more off-putting than the grime was the presence of military police and security guards at every corner and in front of virtually every building. Seeing so many armed men in uniform might make other people feel more secure, but they made me feel nervous. Was this simply a way for the government to keep thousands of men employed and content, or was the government trying to keep the lid on something that might otherwise explode? Reuven was not sure himself.

And then there was the memory of walking together as a family on a quiet Sunday morning, on a deserted street between several prominent and strikingly beautiful old mosques near the well-known Citadel. Reuven stopped three young men, "Is this the way to the Mosque of Sultan Hassan?" he asked in Arabic. The tallest of the young men nodded, and then asked where we were from. "The U.S.," answered Reuven. This clearly did not satisfy the young man. "Where did you learn Arabic?" was his next question, and then: "Why do you have a nose like *this*?" he asked in English, not just pointing, but actually lightly swiping Reuven's nose with a brush of his fingers. Reuven's nose is the most prominent feature of his face, and gives him the chiseled Semitic look I so love. But for this young Egyptian, the "Jewish Look" rang different bells and his tone and gesture were clearly hostile.

"I guess for the same reason you have this nose," Reuven answered, looking the young man right in the eye and gently swiping his nose in response. "It's no different."

I liked that Reuven was not intimidated, but I did not like where this conversation might be heading. "Come on, let's just go," I said quietly, hooking my arm in his. "I don't need to see the mosque." And we turned and walked away, the kids by our sides.

"Relax," Reuven said quietly and calmly under his breath. "They won't do anything, they're just acting stupid." But I only began to relax when we reached the end of the block and I turned around just enough to see that the young men had made no moves to follow us.

That experience was not one I had dwelt on but it came back to me now. How typical was the antisemitic feeling of that young Egyptian, and how might it manifest itself if we lived in Cairo? Were we being adventuresome or naive? How could we knowingly choose to put our two sons in a situation where there was a high likelihood that they would experience hatred just for being Jews? The thought repelled me, especially as the child of German Jewish refugees. Thank God we live in a world where we have choices, I thought. We live in a country where, like most places in the world today, we can contemplate living without fear of an antisemitic attack. My parents had not always had that choice, but we did. Why would we choose to live somewhere where we might have to fear for our safety as Jews?

My father, born in southern Germany, was sixteen when Hitler came to power. He managed to finish school and because of a family connection, he was able to secure a job in a leather tannery before finally fleeing Germany for England after *Kristallnacht*, "The Night of Broken Glass" on November 9-10, 1938. In two days, hundreds of synagogues were burned and ransacked, and thousands of Jewish homes as well as stores and businesses, schools, and hospitals were vandalized and torched, and between 25,000 and 30,000 Jews were arrested and sent to concentration camps. More than windows were shattered during these two days of state-sanctioned and well-planned violent attacks against Jews that were simultaneously launched all over the country. Shattered as well were any remaining hopes that the anti-Jewish measures and violent rhetoric of the last several years in Germany might soon pass.

Never one to complain, and wanting to put the past behind him, my father said very little about those last years in Germany and England before he came to the United States. He preferred sharing stories about making ice cream as a young boy and cycling with his older brothers through the Black Forest. He probably saw no value in visiting upon his children the frightening and painful experiences of his past. I did know, however, about his hardships in the war years, even after he fled Germany. One night in 1940, officials had come knocking on his door in London; he soon found himself crowded onto a ship called the *Dunera* with 2500 German refugees, most of them Jewish. As German-speaking immigrants, they had been arrested as enemy aliens and possible Nazi spies. The British soldiers refused to tell the men where they were being taken, but by looking at the stars over the next several nights, the men determined that they were on their way to Australia. Over the next two months, the men aboard the *Dunera* suffered severe crowding in a ship loaded to more than double its capacity, and such harsh treatment, that when they landed in Sydney on September 6, 1940, their weakened condition prompted an investigation and created an international scandal.

"The Dunera Boys" were all transferred to the DP Camp in Hays, near Sydney, immediately upon landing and released a year later.

In 1948, my father was able to reunite with his parents and brothers in the United States. They had also managed to escape from Germany to safety before the genocide, but some of their extended family did not. I learned about my father's aunts, uncles, and cousins, murdered at Auschwitz, Dachau, and other death camps, in later years. My father simply did not talk about it when we were growing up. He would sometimes speak lovingly of Seders and other occasions with his mother's siblings and their families, but these were isolated fragments of a story without an end. I was left to fill in the blanks.

When I was in my late twenties, my father suddenly started having "night terrors." He would bolt upright in the middle of the night screaming "Help!" in German, not knowing where he was when my mother gently woke him. A family doctor advised two ways to end the nightmares—therapy or medication; my father chose medication, and I was left wondering what memories were too painful to be discussed or recalled.

My mother's family also came from Germany, but where my father's father simply could not believe Germany would ever turn against its Jews—and ended up among the last Jews to get out of Germany alive in 1940—my mother's father decided already in 1931, before Hitler even came to power, that Germany was no longer safe for Jews. He moved his family to Switzerland and opened up a branch of the family manufacturing business. In 1933, he invited his three brothers and their families for Passover, and when they arrived, he told them that they could not go back to Germany. Most of them listened and relocated to Switzerland and Italy. In 1938, those in Italy were forced to flee and several of the men ended up in concentration camps. My grandfather wore himself out in his efforts to save his and his wife's extended families; tragically, he succumbed to a serious infection in 1939 and died. My mother was thirteen.

As the various parts of the family eventually all fled Europe for England and the United States, my grandmother did not want to be left behind with her two daughters, so in 1941, she, my mother and her older sister sailed to Cuba, where they waited six months for a quota number to legally enter the United States.

13

Neither of my parents was in slave labor or concentration camps but both of them had experienced fear, dislocation, and loss. In our comfortable home in Teaneck, New Jersey, where my parents put their children's well-being first in every way, I grew up knowing that the world had real dangers in it and protecting one's children was everything.

Our different backgrounds—mine rooted in the European experience and Reuven's in the American West—rose to the fore as we talked about Cairo. Reuven's roots were also German-Jewish, but his family had been in America for generations, with ancestors first arriving in the mid-nineteenth century. He was raised in northern California as the youngest of three boys by parents who loved to go the Sierra Nevada mountains for skiing in the winter and backpacking in the summer. Where Reuven was raised to push himself physically—sailing, scuba diving, skiing—and to test his own limits again and again, violin lessons and academics were the arenas in which I was encouraged to push myself and excel. To this day, anytime I do something physically challenging or the least bit dangerous, "be careful!" are the words I hear in my head. Now Reuven was asking me to make a temporary move with our two sons to Cairo, where the possibility of antisemitic encounters, verbal or physical, was a real fear I had for them.

14

When we started to tell our friends and family that we were thinking of moving to Cairo for half a year, their reactions were mixed, but every conversation started with "Cairo?" Living in Egypt was just not something people in our world contemplated doing. Our friends' reactions ranged from total lack of comprehension and anxiety on our behalf, to genuine excitement at the adventure of living in Cairo. The worst reactions came from Israelis. "Why would you want to live in Egypt?" one Israeli teacher at the Jewish high school where I taught asked with a visible shudder. "All the Jews have left. Aren't you afraid?" Others didn't say much, but their silent disapproval was clear. "Be careful," they said again and again, with genuine concern. I could only hope their fears would be proven wrong.

Strangely, and to my great surprise, when we mentioned the possibility to my parents, they were supportive and encouraging, knowing what it meant to Reuven and his career. Looking back, I think their endorsement of the project helped me realize that this choice, as well as my fears, needed to be explored rationally.

As Reuven continued to try to pique my interest in the cultural richness of Cairo, I also wondered, what would it feel like for me as a woman, to walk around this Muslim Arab city on a daily basis? On our visit four years earlier I had gone everywhere with Reuven and the kids. Would I be able to walk around on my own? Would I, as some friends had asked, have to cover up with a *hijaab* (headscarf) to avoid people's stares? And if I found I had this privilege as a foreign woman, at what cost would that privilege come? Would I ever feel "at home" in Cairo?

And yet, I knew that what Reuven was proposing presented unique opportunities for all of us. What most attracted me to living in Cairo was the flip side of my fears: if we could tolerate the emotional discomfort and push ourselves a little, we would have the chance to experience a very different world, one that was often at odds with our own. We would have the chance to listen to and get to know people with points of view markedly different from our own. The chance to see the world through the eyes of the other—this exerted a strong attraction and pull for me.

Six months in Egypt, I realized, offered us opportunities that related to several of my own long-standing interests. I had been an active supporter of dialogue and co-existence projects between Israeli Jews and Israeli Arabs for many years. During the 1980s and 90s I had worked as a campus rabbi and developed a number of projects promoting Black-Jewish relations and creative interfaith projects. I had always been drawn to the challenges of building relationships across the divides of ethnicity and religion, so I found myself drawn to this aspect of the experience, even while I was apprehensive.

In the end I decided to take the leap and go because it was unlikely we'd ever have this opportunity again. I won't say I didn't have second thoughts. One of those occasions was when we got a call early one morning from the American International School (AIS), the school we were hoping the boys would attend. While there are many schools in Cairo where the language of instruction is English, only two schools follow an American curriculum, and we had selected AIS over the better known Cairo American College because the student body was predominantly Egyptian, and the boys would have more opportunity to make Egyptian friends. But that morning we learned that the more Egyptian school might be too Egyptian.

"*Ahlan w'sahlan*! We want to welcome you to Egypt and to the American International School!" The school's director spoke warmly from the other end of the phone. "We are very happy to have your boys study at our school for a semester. There are just a couple of things we need to talk about." He went on to tell us that AIS prided itself on being pluralistic and its population, while predominantly Muslim, included Coptic Christians, the largest group of Egypt's Christians, as well as Christians of different denominations. While students came to the school with different degrees of openness, the values of tolerance and mutual respect were actively taught and cultivated at the school. "But," he continued, "AIS has never had any Jewish students. Your sons will be the first." I couldn't believe my ears. In over ten years, they had never had a Jewish student, even with 20 percent of their students coming from the U.S. and Europe?

The director went on in a kind but businesslike manner. In order to test the waters, he had gathered a small group of student leaders in the high school and had discussed the situation with them to see what they thought about Jewish students coming to the school. The students' reactions were positive, but they had two suggestions he wanted to share with us.

"First, it will be best for Noam and Amir not to tell the other students that they are Jewish." Not tell anyone they are Jewish? Was he serious?

"It is particularly important for Amir," he continued, "who will be with younger students who have had less time in our school to learn from our efforts to impart the values of tolerance and pluralism. After a few months, when your sons have made good friends, then it will be fine for them to share with these friends the fact that they are Jewish. But it is probably better for it still not to be general information. Second, when Israel comes up in conversation the boys should listen and not argue."

The director tried to sound encouraging; he said that he hoped we would enroll the boys in AIS and he thought they would have a wonderful experience. "We are all very excited about your boys coming. We just wanted you to be aware of the situation and think about it," he said, drawing the phone conversation to a close. We thanked him and said we would be in touch soon. Then we hung up the phone.

No way! I wanted to shout. We're finding another school.

But it was more than the school that worried me. If this was the American International School in Cairo, what would the rest of the city be like? Images of our boys being taunted and bullied and pushed floated before me. What was I agreeing to?

A few days later Reuven and I had another conversation that helped us better imagine living as Jews in Cairo. Reuven had met Ari Alexander, the co-founder and co-director of "Children of Abraham" at a recent conference and had invited him to come over for coffee when Ari was visiting Los Angeles. "Children of Abraham" is a project that enables Jewish and Muslim teens from all over the world to share photographs and discussion about their religious lives over the Internet. We had a wonderful talk with Ari over an extended cup of coffee in our home about his experiences living in Beirut and Damascus as an American Jew and his experiences visiting Cairo. Ari strongly agreed with the advice we had been given by the boys' school—not to openly share the fact that we are Jewish.

"I generally don't tell people I am Jewish when traveling or living in any of the Arab countries," Ari said.

"Really. What would happen if you told people you were Jewish?" I asked.

"You would probably get an angry tirade against Israel and an invisible wall would go up between you and the other person. It's not so much a question of physical safety, but it's just not a good idea," he answered. Ari was very enthusiastic and encouraging about our moving to Cairo and promised to send me some names of people to get in touch with there. His enthusiasm was contagious and as we talked, I felt more confident and excited about going myself.

Later that evening, we brought up the conversation we had with the director of AIS with the boys and asked them how they felt about it. Did they want us to look into other schools or did they want to stick with this school? They were both surprised but kind of excited at the thought of being the only Jews and the first Jews ever in the school. They wanted to go ahead with the initial plan of attending AIS. I had a rush of conflicting emotions. I felt their sweet innocence and trust, and their vulnerability too, and I felt the weight of responsibility as their parent, wanting to protect them, even as I wanted to join in their sense of adventure. At the same time, their enthusiasm and readiness to commit to the experience probably tipped the scales for me too.

In the weeks before our departure, we occasionally tried to speak some Arabic with Reuven at dinnertime, to give us a head start on some basic vocabulary. We started with greetings.

17

"How do you say good morning?" Noam asked.

"*Sabah al khayr*," Reuven responded and we all repeated the phrase several times.

"But the response is different—you don't just say the same thing back. It's like Hebrew: *boker tov* ("good morning") is answered with *boker or* ("morning of light"), right? In Arabic, the common response is *sabah an-nur*. It even means the same thing as *boker or* in Hebrew—'May you have a morning of light.'

"You can also answer '*sabah al fuul*—may you have a morning of beans!'" We laughed, remembering that cooked beans is a favorite breakfast item for Egyptians. "May you have a morning of beans!" the boys repeated, laughing. But the best was still to come.

"Or," said Reuven, "you can respond '*sabah al yasmin*—may you have a jasmine morning.'"

"*Sabah al yasmin*." I said the words myself, and suddenly—it was as if fairy dust, tiny specks of glittering silver light—floated slowly down over the four of us sitting there at the dinner table. The poetry of the words reached deep into my soul. I repeated the sequence of greetings a few times, enjoying the feeling and the sounds of the words rolling over my tongue. In the days ahead I found myself enthusiastically sharing this greeting with friends and colleagues and even my students, and realized that something profound had altered in me. "*Sabah al khayr, sabah al yasmin*, may you have a jasmine morning."

"I think I actually know all the letters," I said, turning to Reuven on the plane bound for Cairo. I was holding a single sheet of paper with the Arabic alphabet in large print before me, the exotic swirls of each enlarged letter—twenty-eight in all—identified in smaller English print by name and by the sound it makes. I was hoping to at least learn the alphabet before we landed in Cairo. Our sons were behind us—Noam, sprawled out as best he could and fast asleep, while Amir, wide awake, was engrossed in his third movie for this flight.

"That was fast," said Reuven as he looked up from his reading. "Really great. Now you can learn the other forms."

"What other forms—you're joking," I responded. Just when I was feeling like maybe I could do this.

"What you just learned are the forms for the Arabic letters when they stand alone. Each letter also has three other slightly different forms, depending on where in the word the letter comes—the beginning, the middle, or the end. It's not as hard as it sounds."

No way, I thought to myself, but I looked at the next sheet, curious to see how different the new forms were. Most were minor variations on the theme, but I could see that this would take time... more time than even the seemingly interminable plane ride to Cairo. I worked at it for a few more minutes and then sat back in my seat and closed my eyes to rest. I had made a good start, I thought. With the ten Arabic numerals and the twenty-eight letters I had started with, I might be able to make out some street names—or at least the house numbers—when we arrived in Cairo.

The low humming drone of the air conditioning was lulling me to sleep. I found myself listening to the men across the aisle speaking Arabic. The gutturals sounded harsh and ugly to my ears, I sadly realized. I pushed these thoughts away... after all, I had just committed to learning Arabic and spending six months in Cairo. And what about the poetry of Arabic I had so recently discovered in "May you have a jasmine morning!"

"Maybe I am just tired," I tell myself, disappointed with my immediate reaction to the Arabic I hear around me. I close my eyes again and allow my thoughts to drift. After a few minutes I realize that I have slipped into a daydream and I am walking alone on a crowded Arab street with streams of men, women and children walking past me in both directions. I know this has to be different than the reality I will soon confront, but I suspend all disbelief and allow myself to drift with the images. Suddenly I realize my chest is constricted and my breathing more rapid, as the images I am spinning are evoking strong feelings of apprehension and anxiety.

Startled, I wonder, what is so scary about these people walking the crowded streets of my mind? Arabs, Muslims, judging from appearances, but nothing else is clear. Why this emotional reaction, I gently wonder, hoping to coax out whatever lies under my buried feelings, instead of chasing them away by my disapproval. Is it that I am so different from them? No, it is more... they hate us, I find myself thinking...they hate Israel, they hate Americans...they don't really understand what the West is all about, and they hate us.... I am shocked and even embarrassed at

19

the raw fear and the unsavory stereotypes I carry so deep within me. I thought I was above such feelings. But it seems I am not.

The daily barrage of images and ideas in the media and our culture at large takes its toll. Even if my rational mind rejects the view of the Arab as "the Enemy," I have absorbed some of these sentiments that swirl around me, deep into my own psyche. And if I am honest, even with my left-leaning politics, my own understanding of the recent history and politics of the Arab world, particularly in relation to Israel, also contributes to these deep-seated emotions.

Personal experience, I remind myself, can broaden our views and change even our deepest feelings about the other. Wasn't that part of why we were going to Egypt? I remembered how in Israel too, especially during the Intifada, I had felt fear in relation to Arabs I saw around me on the street. This had saddened me, though I understood where the feelings came from, given the tensions and real threat of terrorist bombings that were part of daily life. Still, it is a terrible thing when members of a nationality or ethnic or religious group are all automatically suspect.

My personal experiences with Israeli Palestinians, however, had always been different. Almost every interaction had opened up a human connection for me, not just to this individual, but towards other Arabs I saw later on the street. What would it be like in Cairo? In just a few hours I would begin to find out.

Chapter 1
Crossing Cairo

صدّق ما تَراه، ونحي جانباً ما تُسمعه

Believe what you see and lay aside what you hear.
~Arabic Proverb

IT WAS LATE EVENING WHEN OUR PLANE LANDED IN CAIRO. We were met at the airport by a driver sent by Reuven's fellowship program.

"Dr. Robert…Madame…*Ahlan w'sahlan!*" he said warmly, using Reuven's English name. (Robert, I mentally noted. I would have to get used to calling him that in public instead of Reuven, his Hebrew name.) Without waiting for a reply, the man quickly grabbed as much of our luggage as he could manage and proceeded to push us through the customs line. I was grateful. The lines were long and we were tired. The airport terminal was new and strikingly modern—it had clearly been rebuilt in the last five years since our last visit. Was this indicative of a new building trend in Cairo? I had no time to speculate. Waved through by the Customs official, we were on our way.

Soon we were outside making our way to our driver's cab. When we found the car it was tiny—barely large enough for the four of us, let alone our bags. While Reuven and the cab driver went to find an additional taxi, the boys and I busied ourselves reading aloud the Arabic numerals on the various license plates all around us, correcting each other and vying for speed. We were really here, and this time, we would be *living* in Cairo, not just visiting as tourists. I was aware of the difference not only in my attitude, but also in the boys'. We were all ready to adapt to this new culture and we hadn't even left the airport parking lot. Reuven and our driver were suddenly back with a second driver and in minutes we were on our way.

On the hour's drive to the hotel, we passed several military academies. Hewn into their stone walls were larger-than-life images of soldiers from Pharaonic times — poised in their chariots, spears raised, engaging their enemy in battle. The soldiers were standing tall and proud in the side-view pose we have come to associate with the art of ancient Egypt. Successive images of other battle scenes from different periods of Egyptian history up to the present whirled by us, and the message was clear: the line was clearly drawn from the glory of ancient Egypt to the modern state, with a strong military securing Egypt today and linking her to her glorious past.

Our driver pointed out President Mubarak's well-guarded, stately residence before we left the fashionable suburb of Heliopolis and headed south for downtown Cairo. Soon we were greeted by the best-known sights of Islamic Cairo — the imposing walls of the Citadel, the twelfth-century fortress built by the Muslim warrior, Salah ad-Din, and its crowning jewel, the Muhammad Ali Mosque. This striking mosque, with its tight cluster of multiple silver domes and tall minarets, was dramatically lit up against the night sky. Salah ad-Din had the wisdom to recognize the strategic advantage of building his fortress on a hill overlooking the city and surrounding valley, and in so doing, established what would prove to be the home for Egypt's rulers for almost seven hundred years. Despite the fact that the Muhammad Ali Mosque is a relatively recent addition to Cairo, dating from the nineteenth century and built entirely in the Turkish style, it is today one of the most famous sights of Cairo, second only to the pyramids.

The drive proceeded through Cairo's "City of the Dead," the sprawling Northern and Southern Cemeteries where poor people live in and among the tombs. While their "neighborhood" officially does not even exist, as many as five million people call these and the three nearby cemeteries home. Even in the darkness we could see laundry hanging on clotheslines and men making change for their last minute customers as they closed the shutters of their grocery stores.

Continuing along the eastern edge of downtown Cairo we finally reached Maadi, a neighborhood south of downtown and east of the Nile River, where we hoped to live. Maadi was popular with American and European ex-pats because of its proximity to downtown Cairo, a twenty-minute ride by subway. Even though we would be pushing ourselves to speak Arabic as much as possible, Maadi was a place we would be able to find shop owners who spoke English (as well as French and German) and where we would be comfortable as foreigners.

Until we could find an apartment, we would be staying in a residential hotel. As we pulled up outside the hotel, two men came out to help us with our bags. They showed us to a large, three-bedroom apartment on the ground level, a welcome surprise over the small, cramped quarters I had imagined. The wooden floors, worn Oriental rugs, and older furniture were markedly different than we would find in an American hotel of this sort. The rooms had a slightly worn but comfortable European flavor, along with a layout that was typically Egyptian, with two sitting areas in the living room that seemed designed for intimate conversation. The four of us made our way from room to room, exclaiming about how nice it all was, and deciding who would sleep where. After we moved our bags into our respective rooms, we found the essentials and fell into bed.

23

The next morning, we went out for a walk to explore the neighborhood. Sunshine greeted us through the slight haze. We appreciated the warm shirtsleeve weather for a day in late January, not so different what we had left behind in Los Angeles. One difference we noticed immediately was the armed security guards sitting in front of the buildings on both sides of the block. They all seemed friendly and greeted us, "*Sabah al khayr, Ustaz, Sabah al khayr, Madame* (Good morning Sir, Good morning Madame)" as we walked by. I couldn't respond fast enough, so I just smiled and nodded as Reuven answered with the appropriate response. I made a mental note that the first phrases I needed to master were the greetings and responses.

Following the instructions from the men at the hotel, we turned right and made our way towards Road Nine, the "Main Street" of Maadi, passing an open square dissected by a few different streets filled with small old fashioned black and white taxis. They looked like little bumper cars, most of them a bit battered and worn. A boy in a white *jalabiya* (long robe), or as they pronounced it here in Egypt, *galabiya*, darted past us carrying a round brass tray filled with small glasses of hot black tea. He disappeared into a shop, apparently bringing the tea to the men working there.

Two young women in dark blue *galabiyas* walked by, effortlessly balancing packages of fresh pita bread wrapped in plastic bags on top of their heads. Looking around, I noticed that all the women were wearing the *hijaab* (pronounced *higaab* in Egypt), the headscarf, but there was quite a range of styles. There were young women, stylishly dressed, some even in tight-fitting pants and sweaters, with bright colored scarves to match their outfits. Other women, like those I saw carrying the pita bread on their heads, wore plain head scarves together with the long dark colored *galabiyas* over their clothes. For those women, modest dress was clearly the essential goal. Only occasionally did we see a woman wearing the full *burqa*—the sweeping black robe and headscarf that covered everything, leaving only narrow slits for her eyes. Even hands and wrists were covered with black gloves. The majority of women, regardless of age, were wearing headscarves together with modest western clothing. I did not see any women with their hair uncovered. I was the only one, marking me as a non-Muslim. I was glad I had chosen to wear pants and a long sleeved cotton shirt, rather than short sleeves, with modesty in mind. I wondered how acceptable it was for women to wear short sleeves in the intense hot weather we could expect in the next few months and made a mental note to ask someone.

24

The streets radiating from the square were lined with small shops, some of them very simple, with subdued lights to save electricity, like the butcher and the stores selling electronic goods and house wares. Others seemed to cater to a wealthier clientele, with stylish European clothes, perfumes, and skin products on display. I was surprised and a bit disappointed to see a small supermarket with "Metro" gleaming in red English letters on a sign above the store. But the streets were also dotted with smaller food markets and produce stands with a more local feel to them. We crossed the square and made our way up Road Nine slowly, looking at the shops, buying a map, and stopping in a small Internet Café to send quick messages home to let our parents know we had arrived safely. Most shopkeepers seemed to speak English as well as French and German. They greeted us warmly and encouraged our efforts to speak Arabic.

By the time we were ready for breakfast it was almost noon and we decided to go for an Egyptian breakfast of *ta'amia* (falafel) and *fuul* (beans). We were now on a part of Road Nine that seemed more like a working class area, with smaller, less flashy shops. We chose the most crowded *ta'amia* restaurant in the area. After putting in our order and paying for the food, we joined the clamoring crowds waving little slips of paper to get the attention of the men behind the counter. These men were moving as quickly as McDonald's employees back in the States, filling the small pita breads with *ta'amia* or *fuul* and chopped vegetable salad — Egypt's version of fast food — and stuffing them into plastic bags. We exchanged our ticket for our food and made our way back up the street looking for a tea shop where we could sit down and have some tea with our breakfast.

We found just the place in a small alley off the main road. Across from us were four middle-aged men smoking *shishas* (water pipes) and drinking tea and iced water. The air was decidedly relaxed, especially for the middle of a workday. Cairo, or at least Maadi, seemed to wake up slowly. There were no other women in the tea shop and I wondered if that was typical. I knew I would not have felt free to sit down and order a glass of tea if I were alone. But no one was looking at me funny and I felt comfortable sitting there with Reuven and the boys. We all happily sipped our glasses of strong, sweet tea and ate our *ta'amia* and *fuul* sandwiches.

The alluring smell of fresh bread wafted in, and when we were finished eating, we followed our noses to a small alley bakery around the corner from where we were sitting. We were just in time—a young man in work clothes and apron was pulling large trays of rolls and baguettes from the oven, and setting them on the counter. We bought a sampling of each, and then set out for the main activity of the day—a visit to the boys' new school.

Back in the States, we had already explained to the boys that we would not be telling people that we are Jewish until we knew them better. "Amir" was an Arabic name as well as a Hebrew one, so he would continue to use it, but Noam, who had a modern Hebrew name, had to change his. He had tentatively decided on "Noaman," an Arabic name, and had been "trying it on" by introducing himself as "Noaman" since our arrival.

The American International School was about a half-hour drive away so we found a taxi and headed for the new Ring Road that encircles Cairo. Soon the urban congestion gave way to larger and larger stretches of sand and sky. We were surprised to see so many little clusters of apartment buildings in various stages of completion, standing isolated and lonely with empty stretches of desert in between. Cairo, we learned, was now a city of eighteen million at night, with about twenty million during the day. Universities, private schools, hotels, and even government agencies were beginning to move out of the city in increasing numbers as new suburbs were rapidly being built.

Finally we saw a sign for the American International School. Other than the school and the Mubarak Police Academy across the street, the area was utterly desolate. It was a striking contrast with the dense congestion of Cairo. There were no buildings of any kind — no office or apartment buildings or stores or even a gas station. The Police Academy was surrounded by barbed wire and was set back from the street. In contrast, the obviously new red brick and white plaster buildings of the American International School seemed more friendly and inviting, with a small area of newly planted grass and palm trees in front of the school. Uniformed security guards greeted us politely when we stepped out of the taxi and asked us whom we wished to see.

Inside, the highly polished marble floors gleamed in the sunlight streaming through the large glass windows of the central high-ceilinged foyer. We met some of the administrators and school counselors of the middle school and high school who all welcomed questions, particularly from the boys.

Amir wanted to know if he and Noam would be in the same building. At twelve, five years Noam's junior, Amir often looked to Noam to take the lead. They had always been close, and even though Noam increasingly spent time with his own friends at home, he continued to spend significant chunks of time with Amir, playing computer games and building ever more ambitious Lego projects. I was not surprised that in these new surroundings Amir would welcome having his older brother close by. It turned out that the boys would in fact be in the same building, just on different floors.

The school counselors helped the boys finalize their class schedules. They would both be taking Arabic and Noam chose to take Egyptian History and Environmental Science for his electives. At seventeen, this was the middle of Noam's junior year of high school and he would soon be applying to college. I was concerned that he was overloading his schedule with too many academic classes, but Noam seemed very confident about the course load.

In the middle school office, Amir was introduced to Abdul Aziz, a fellow sixth grader who would be his special buddy the first few days, to help make Amir's transition into the school as smooth as possible. Within a few minutes the boys had discovered that they both played soccer and were comparing notes on what positions they liked to play.

Amir and Noam both seemed more animated than when we had arrived an hour earlier. We said our good-byes and headed back to the street to find a taxi to take us back to Maadi — or so we thought. There were hardly any cars at all on the street and no empty taxis. This was not surprising given the general isolation of the area, but still something we hadn't anticipated. Finally one of the security guards motioned us toward the school buses that were just leaving to take support staff home and asked a bus driver to drop us off at the nearest metro stop. I saw an empty seat next to a young Muslim woman and sat down quietly beside her. Suddenly I felt shy. Uncomfortable with the silence, I turned to her and asked, "Do you speak English?"

"No," she answered, shaking her head, smiling slightly. She asked me something ending with the word "*Arabi*" that I assumed meant "Do you speak Arabic?" and I also shook my head no. I told her that I wanted to learn Arabic, and between our desire to talk to each other and my phrase book, we actually managed to have a little bit of conversation. We counted to ten in each other's language — that much we knew — and we exchanged names. She taught me how to say, "I want to learn to speak Arabic," and was encouraging of my efforts to pronounce the words correctly. By the time we left the bus, I had made my first attempt to bridge the language gap in Cairo. Already I felt a thrill at being able to initiate a conversation on my own that included a little bit of Arabic. I knew with sudden certainty that the more energy I invested in learning Arabic, the more I would be able to connect with Egyptians without Reuven by my side.

It was rush hour when we reached the Metro station and everyone in downtown Cairo seemed to be hurrying home. We found ourselves swept along by the swelling throngs moving slowly forward like a single organism, with vendors on both sides of us barking out their lowest prices for the fresh pita bread and oranges they were pointing to with exaggerated animation, competing with each other and the blaring horns for our attention. But it was the brightly colored oranges themselves that caught my eye—they were the only spot of color in a sea of browns and grays. Reuven must have felt the same way, because he handed a man some money and took a bag of oranges from him. "*Bortugal*," Reuven said, smiling at me. "Isn't that cool—that's the word for 'oranges' here." It was cool. At some point the oranges in Egypt must have been imported from Portugal. This little shard of history buried in the Arabic language excited me. Learning Arabic would allow me to connect with the people and the culture of my new home in ways that I couldn't even imagine and I resolved to make this happen. We pushed our way forward to the ticket booth, together with the crowd.

Eventually we made it onto the Metro and as this was the first stop, we even got seats. A few minutes into the ride, an Egyptian teenage boy sitting across from us leaned over and started talking to Noam. He attended another English-speaking high school, it turned out, and spoke beautiful English. He and Noam talked together until we arrived back in Maadi. These little conversations seemed to bode well for our Cairo adventure and all of us were in good spirits even though we were tired.

Before heading back to the hotel, Noam asked if we could go out for *kusheri* for dinner. Great idea, we all agreed. *Kusheri* is a kind of people's stew—a hearty mix of rice, small macaroni noodles as well as spaghetti, lentils, chickpeas, tomato sauce and crispy, fried onions, all served in layers in one bowl. It is very popular in Egypt, and there are restaurants all over Cairo that serve just *kusheri*—for about 20 cents a bowl. We had fond memories of many *kusheri* meals from our visit five years ago and the boys especially had been looking forward to more.

"Where is the best place for *kusheri* in the neighborhood?" Reuven asked the man next to us as we walked down the steps from the Metro. "Salah. You want to go to Salah," he answered, smiling broadly. He pointed us to the other side of the Metro tracks, a working class area, and told us where to go. We made our way through the bustling outdoor market and after asking a few more people, someone walked us to a simple little restaurant of just a few tables and old chairs, with sawdust scattered on the ground. We sat down at a table in the corner and in minutes, the owner had wiped down the table and placed before us our four steaming bowls of *kusheri* with hot sauce, garlic sauce, and the unique blend of tastes and textures we remembered. Our first day in Egypt was complete.

Friday night was fast approaching. *Shabbat*, the Jewish Sabbath, is an important part of the rhythm of our family life. We normally ushered in Shabbat by lighting candles on Friday night and enjoying a special dinner that almost always included guests. We hoped to do the same thing in Cairo, even though most of our guests, we assumed, would not be Jewish. Since we did not yet have a home of our own, we were not sure how we would celebrate our first Shabbat in Cairo.

On Friday morning we got a phone call from Kathy, a friend of our friend Maureen, who was living in Cairo, welcoming us in Maureen's absence and inviting us for dinner that night. Kathy and her husband Paul, both teachers, were Americans who had lived in Cairo for over a decade. Even though we knew it was not intended to be a Shabbat celebration, we were happily surprised and quickly decided to accept their invitation.

We spent a good part of Friday afternoon looking at apartments. The school had referred us to a realtor who was named Muhammad, who showed us a variety of apartments ranging from old and almost shabby to new and quite elegant, all located in different parts of Maadi. We saw nothing that we really liked and ended the day feeling discouraged. Muhammad seemed almost hurt that we did not see anything we were interested in, but he offered to try to find more apartments to show us on Sunday.

As the sun began to set on Friday evening we decided to welcome Shabbat as a family by singing and chanting the beautiful Friday night *Kabbalat Shabbat* service, as we sometimes did at home. We would not be lighting Shabbat candles, however, because we were in a hotel and going out that evening. Since the whole wall of the living room and dining room facing the street consisted of floor to ceiling windows I went to close the curtains to insure the privacy of our Shabbat ritual. As I pulled on the cord, feeling the resistance of the heavy curtains dragging against the force of my effort, the act felt deliberate and dramatic. I had not closed the curtains on other evenings and I was startled to see how quickly the room around me was darkening as the curtains closed out the light from outside. In a single moment, I was aware of standing on the border between inside and outside, between darkness and light. I felt sad that we needed to hide what we were about to do, but I also felt a surge of strength with the sudden recognition that this simple act of pulling the curtains closed linked me in a profound way to the thousands of Jews who had come before me in towns and cities all over the world who had pulled the curtains shut on Friday nights to hide their Shabbat practice from the judging eyes of the outside world. I hoped we would find a way tonight and in the weeks ahead to cast our own light as a family and live as Jews, even in the shadows of our curtains here in Cairo.

I need not have worried about that, I realized, as I looked up to see the beaming faces of my sons. I turned on a few lights and we settled into the overstuffed chairs in the living room to sing a few *nigunim*—wordless Hasidic melodies. Our voices tentatively mingled together and slowly filled the room as we moved on to our favorite melodies for the psalms that make up the opening part of the service to welcome Shabbat. First the slow melodies of longing, meant to reawaken inside of each of us the longing for a connection to God, then the livelier melodies of joy and celebration that are unique to Shabbat. Gradually, judging from the clapping, tapping, and smiles, we all relaxed into Shabbat in a way that felt familiar, even here in our new surroundings. We finished the prayers and happily embraced each other with "Shabbat shalom!" and got ready to go to dinner.

We were all wearing *kippot*, traditional head coverings that some Jews wear all the time and others, like us, just for prayer, study, and Shabbat and holiday meals. We consciously removed them before we left the apartment. That was another first that made me feel a little bit sad. At home, the *kippot* would have stayed on our heads when we left home to walk to someone else's house.

But taking off the *kippot* also reminded me that I had not always felt comfortable announcing my religion publicly, even in the United States. When I was thirteen, I had received a Bat Mitzvah gift of a gold necklace with a simple and delicately shaped *Magen David*, or "Star of David." I thought it was beautiful and at the first opportunity, I wore it downstairs to breakfast. When my mother saw the *Magen David* she made a face. "Religion isn't something you wear around your neck," she said dismissively. "It should be more of a private thing." I remembered feeling sad and a little bit confused at the time, as this simple, joyous expression of identity was interpreted in a way that would forever awaken ambivalence in me. Later, the undercurrent I sensed in my mother's words came to the surface.

"Why don't we have a *mezuzah* on our front door?" I asked one day, years later. A *mezuzah* is a small scroll with several verses from the Torah that is placed in a decorative case and affixed to the upper right hand side of the entrance to a Jewish home. It serves to remind us of God's presence as we enter and leave our houses.

"I don't know, it's like putting up a sign that Jews live here. Is that necessary?" she responded. Even in Teaneck, New Jersey, where more than half the community was Jewish, my mother who immigrated from Europe at age fifteen still did not feel completely safe as a Jew in full public view. And here in Cairo, neither did I.

The thirty-minute walk to Kathy and Paul's took us through a very pretty residential neighborhood along "Canal Street," where what once had clearly been a canal was now filled in with grass and trees. The apartment buildings lining the street were generally only three or four stories tall. The walk was pleasant and soon we reached a more commercial boulevard where we easily found the apartment building where they lived.

31

Paul welcomed us into a warm and colorful apartment with oriental rugs, wall hangings, and Bedouin embroidered pillows scattered generously on the couches, overstuffed chairs, and the floor. The ethnically rich decorations drew me in and I found myself wanting to explore the apartment almost as much as I wanted to meet and talk with our hosts. A few moments later, Kathy came into the room, wearing a hand woven long peasant shirt over pants, and barefoot. Kathy's short-cropped red hair framed her wind and sun weathered face, and her blue eyes sparkled as she greeted with "*Ahlan w'sahlan!* Welcome! It's so good to finally meet you!"

The evening had a warm informality to it, combined with delicious food and a gracious tone, supplied by our hosts with the help of Jeanie, a woman from Singapore who had worked for them for years, and who had helped cook the meal. Bright orange carrot soup, saffron yellow Indian curry with cauliflower dotted with small dark lentils, and an old fashioned American egg custard for dessert made for a feast for the eyes as well as our stomachs. Kathy and Paul knew that we were Jewish, and before we started to eat, they asked if we would like to say a blessing. We chanted the Hebrew blessing over the wine as well as the blessing over the bread, and offered our hosts brief English translations. Kathy and Paul seemed genuinely delighted and we felt warmly welcomed.

Kathy and Paul, we learned, had together served in the Peace Corp in India in the sixties and lived in Tanzania for a number of years before moving to Cairo. The move to Cairo was prompted by Paul's work as an education consultant. Kathy had started off working in Cairo, but now devoted her time to her art and writing projects. As practicing liberal

Catholics and politically left-leaning activists, Kathy and Paul came from backgrounds that were in some ways different from, and in other ways similar to our own. Underneath our different life experience, we seemed to share basic values and found we had a lot to talk about. Kathy asked me what I was hoping to do while in Cairo and I explained that my first priority was learning Arabic. She responded enthusiastically, suggesting several places I could study either colloquial or classical Arabic, offering her views on the strengths and limitations of each program. If Paul and Kathy were any indication, it was clear that in Cairo we would find unique opportunities for friendships with American ex-pats with interesting experience and perspectives on Egyptian life.

Saturday was a relaxing Shabbat day of sleeping late, reading, and eating simple meals of cold salads in our hotel apartment. Reuven and I took a walk, exploring more of the residential part of the neighborhood away from Road Nine. There were beautiful single-family residences along with small apartment buildings along the tree-lined streets that radiated from traffic circles that seemed to appear every few blocks. This neighborhood was a sharp contrast to most of Cairo, I knew, and I felt a little bit uncomfortable about our choosing to live here. At the same time I knew we would be pushing beyond our comfort zone on an almost daily basis and it would be nice for all of us to be able to come home at the end of the day to a place of comfort and beauty.

Saturday night, after Shabbat had ended, we went with the boys to Road Nine to buy school supplies. There seemed to be excitement in the air and in front of most of the shops people were huddled around televisions that had been moved out unto the sidewalks. They were all intently focused on watching what turned out to be a soccer game, a match that could qualify Egypt for the Quarter Finals of the African Cup competition. We headed down the road to a stationery store where we had already met the owner, Muhammad, who had been especially helpful and kind in our first interactions. We bought our supplies quickly and then joined the small crowd gathered outside the store. People were sitting amphitheater style, on several rows of wide steps sloping down from the sidewalk to the store entrance, with a good view of the television sitting on a little table right next to the door. Spirits were high and every few minutes, collective moans or cheers rippled up and down the street depending on which team had scored a goal. It was a real community event and we loved feeling part of it. When Egypt won the game, we were on our feet cheering along with everyone else.

One of the first people we met by name and started to get to know was Muhammad, the owner of the Internet Café. (Almost every man we had met so far was named Muhammad. We had taken to calling them Internet Muhammad, Stationery Muhammad, and Real Estate Muhammad.) Until we would be in our own apartment and arrange for an Internet hookup, we would see Internet Muhammad almost daily and he was especially nice to Noam and Amir. He spoke Arabic clearly and more slowly than most people, sensitive to the fact that we were not native Arabic speakers, and he was happy to answer all our questions about Maadi. One evening after the boys went to bed, Reuven and I returned to the Internet Café to check our email. As we were packing up our laptops to go, Muhammad asked us where we were from. He looked unconvinced when we said we were from the United States.

"But where are you *really* from? What are your *roots*?" he asked Reuven pointedly. Reuven smiled and said we were really from the States. We knew what he was asking. Whether it was Reuven's Semitic looks, the boys' names, or Reuven's Arabic, several times people had already pushed us on that question, not satisfied with our answer that we were American.

"You speak Arabic so well, and you speak a Palestinian-Syrian dialect… it made me think maybe your background is Palestinian, or Israeli, I don't know…," Muhammad shrugged, trying to appear casual in his interest. Reuven shook his head no, and explained that actually his family went back several generations in America. Muhammad dropped the subject and we stayed a few minutes longer, chatting, before we said good night.

Part of me really wanted to tell Muhammad that we were Jews, especially since he was openly wondering and, I thought, trying to politely hint that he had already guessed. If we told him, I reasoned, however he treated us, at least we would know it was in relation to who we really were. I did not like the feeling of enjoying his warmth while still wondering, "If he knew, would he act differently?" I knew we had to take it slow, but I hoped we would find we could tell people sooner rather than later. Surely, I felt, we would find some people who were open, as I imagined and hoped Muhammad would be.

During our first few days in Cairo, our "Noam-Noaman" spent much of his free time talking with the young men, Umar and Seif, who sat behind the desk at our hotel. The men clearly had the time and they seemed to enjoy it. Noam always had a special gift for striking up a conversation with strangers. Amir did not immediately initiate conversations the way Noam did. He was shy and tended to be the observer before joining in with others in new situations, but he was also easygoing and quick to make friends. I anticipated this would be the case in Cairo too. Within days of our arrival, Amir was happy to go out on his own to buy bread at the bakery or lunch at a falafel stand. Our part of Maadi had the feel of small town more than a city. I was sure that the shopkeepers' friendliness and some already familiar faces in the nearby shops helped Amir feel at home.

After a few days of apartment-hunting in vain—even knocking on doors of apartment buildings in our neighborhood to see if any apartments were available—Reuven and I asked Umar and Seif, the two men Noam had befriended at the hotel desk, if they knew of any apartments in the area for rent. They spoke with their friend Imad, the *bowab* (door man and building caretaker) for the apartment building directly across the street, and the next day, he showed us two apartments in the building. The one on the first floor was perfect for us and nicer than anything we had seen. It had three medium-sized bedrooms, and was furnished tastefully and freshly painted. There was even a small walled-in garden accessible from all three bedrooms. And the location was even better than we had hoped for. We liked that it was so close to Road Nine and the Metro, and in the other direction adjacent to a beautiful, relatively quiet residential area. My only hesitation was that it was a ground floor apartment and quite dark.

"I have a feeling we'll be grateful for the shade in a couple of months when it gets hot," said Reuven and I realized he was probably right. We contacted the owner, "Madame Basima" and made plans to meet in the apartment a few days later. Basima and her husband, Maagid, lived nearby in an apartment on the *El Corniche*, the fashionable street lined with high rises overlooking the Nile, and they rented out this apartment which had belonged to Basima's family and now belonged to her. As it turned out, Basima had graduated from AIS, the same school our boys attended, and she and Maagid both spoke excellent English.

Basima and Maagid were clearly pleased that we liked the apartment and appreciated the work they had just put into it. They had only one hesitation: they had been looking for a lease of at least one or two years. In the end they were persuaded that we would take good care of the apartment and agreed to a six-month lease. We were thrilled and over the next two days we worked out all the arrangements and moved our things from the hotel across the street into our new home. It was an extra bonus and a big one, we all felt, to be able to stay in "our neighborhood" where we already felt surprisingly connected.

There was a reason why this part of Maadi was one of the nicest. We learned that we were actually living in "Old Maadi," the original neighborhood that was first established in the early 1900s. The town had been meticulously planned to be one of Cairo's most beautiful, and today's residents still enjoyed it as such. Old Maadi's planners drew inspiration for the town's layout from the design of Khartoum, the capital of Sudan, which featured avenues radiating in many directions from a central square, leading to other squares from which more avenues sprang. They adopted this model for Maadi, in combination with the more typical grid pattern to allow for the easy laying of water pipes and electric cables. This plan accounted for the maze of narrow streets that often made it a challenge to find our way back home even after a short walk.

Flowering trees were originally planted all over the neighborhood with the plan of providing coordinated color patterns of pink, white, and lavender in the spring, followed by lush summer and fall blossoms of purple, yellow, and red orange. Most trees were selected for their beauty; others with the goal of providing barriers to wind and sand. Eucalyptus trees from Australia, it was hoped would provide natural repellent protection against mosquitoes and flies along the Khasab Canal that bisected Maadi, (now only a grassy and wooded strip down the same Canal Street we had discovered on our walk to Kathy and Paul's apartment our first Shabbat in Cairo). Sparing no expense, spectacular red orange poincianas (flame trees) from Madagascar, purple jacarandas from South America, along with local *lebbek* and red *tekoma* trees were purchased and planted before any actual plans for housing were drawn up.

The concern that Maadi be a beautiful community distinguished by its gardens and substantial green space dominated all the early building regulations. There were rules for everything. Houses could not rise any taller than

35

fifteen meters and could not occupy more than half the land on which they were situated. The distance between houses and between houses and the street was also carefully regulated to prevent any sense of crowding. Garden walls could not be more than two meters in height and other than a small base, had to be formed entirely by shrubbery. While many today might find this degree of regulation objectionable, today's Maadi residents still enjoy the benefits of these plans and regulations made over a century ago.

While some gardens were truly lush and green, through much of Maadi we found ourselves gazing upon green covered with a thin layer of brown. Ironically, while water runs plentifully in Cairo because it is situated on the Nile, the city is surrounded by desert and literally covered with a very fine dust that finds its way everywhere, even indoors. Any breeze adds to the general grit and grime, and the city often seems veiled in a thin layer of brown. Only where gardeners hose the plants down daily do the lush green leaves and bright colored flowers attract notice and delight the eye. In such cases, passersby may even notice that the air itself feels different—moist and refreshing instead of the stifling heat more commonly associated with Cairo. We were lucky— Imad, our *bowab*, hosed down the trees and plants in front of our apartment building every morning.

In the meantime, we had been finding out more about our neighborhood. Maadi meant "ferry boats," and the town was apparently named for the ferry boats that frequently made their way from Maadi across the Nile and back. Ferries carrying goods and people across the Nile were important at the time of modern Maadi's emergence at the beginning of the twentieth century and as far back as ancient times, when Cairo was a pivotal point for traders between Africa, the Middle East, and Far East. While "the banks of the Nile" conjures up pictures of palm trees with the pyramids visible in the distance, the fashionable and bustling thoroughfare along the Nile, *El Corniche*, is lined with luxury high-rise apartments. You can still have a lazy float down the Nile on a *felucca*, an Egyptian sail boat—something we'd treat ourselves to on occasion—and there are still plenty of palm trees among the yachting clubs and restaurants that line the western bank of the Nile, even as smoke stacks across the way signal industrial development.

In addition to being an easy fifteen-minute walk from the Nile, our apartment was only two blocks from Maadi's main square, *Midan al-Mahatta*, or Station Square, as we discovered on the first day. The Metro stop was just across the square. Cairo's Metro system—still the only subway in

Africa— is generally seen as the single ray of hope for easing the choking congestion of car traffic in Cairo. With a combination of trains above and below ground, the system has only two lines but is impressive in its efficiency and boasts over two million riders a day. By law, every train has women-only cars. I sometimes chose to ride in these cars to avoid the crowds as much as to avoid men's stares.

Next to the metro station was a mosque from where we heard the call to prayer five times a day. There were many other small local mosques throughout the area, each offering its own amplified recording of the traditional call to prayer. With competing amplified voices coming from all directions at slightly different times and tempos, the blaring, raucous call to prayer sounded anything but spiritual. One Cairo resident quoted in a newspaper article described the call to prayer as "a daily torture to the ears." This is such a problem in Cairo — home to over four thousand mosques — that in the previous year the government had announced plans to replace the mosques' individual calls to prayer with a single citywide system of prayer calls. A huge public outcry prevented this plan from being put into effect.

Every time we went downtown, I was reminded of our experience in Cairo five years earlier. Crossing the streets of Cairo—more than the presence of so many gun-bearing policemen, security guards and soldiers—was what had most unnerved me. In other respects, walking in downtown Cairo was a unique, if intense experience. Walking around the city in a moving sea of people always made me feel like I was entering a kaleidoscope of different colors, smells and sounds, with horns honking and people hawking their wares, donkeys and taxis competing for their space on the road, and the swell of pedestrian traffic taking on a life of its own. People spilling off the sidewalks into the streets seemed to almost rub elbows with the taxis and buses zooming by. The few traffic lights that worked were completely ignored. It was amusing— unless one needed to get across the street. How to get across six lanes of quickly moving traffic with our three children? (Our daughter, now in college, had been with us on that trip.) At times I couldn't bring myself to step off the sidewalk and I would keep walking straight, hoping to find a better place to cross further on, only to discover it was even worse up ahead.

"Is it really worth risking our lives to cross the street?" I would yell to Reuven.

"You just have to do it!" he would yell back in response. These street crossings brought us both as close as we ever came to a divorce. But I later found my fears justified by our guidebooks that described crossing the streets of Cairo as being just as harrowing as I thought it was. Even for a short distance, one of them suggested, it was probably better to take a cab than to walk.

When it came to driving, Maadi was a scaled-down version of downtown Cairo. There were no traffic lights or even stop signs in Maadi. While the streets here were also crowded with old battered black and white taxis, private cars, buses and mini-buses, men on bicycles and even an occasional donkey, pedestrians seemed to prefer the streets to sidewalks. The roads were very narrow and met each other at odd angles, given the dominance of traffic circles with six to eight streets radiating from their center. Whether traffic was heavy or light, cars wove in and out of traffic, defying others' efforts to drive straight ahead, sometimes even daring to drive into oncoming traffic if that turned out to be the direction the driver wanted to go. It was a little bit like the bumper car rides I had enjoyed as a child, only here you were supposed to threaten but not actually bump. And these bumper cars had horns.

Horns, in fact, seemed to provide the only working traffic control system in the city. Drivers honked their horns continually, warning other drivers of their approach at intersections, or that they wanted to pass. There was a language of sorts, of single short honks letting other drivers know they were approaching, and more rapid honks to express irritation or more urgent warning. For the most part, drivers seemed to know how to threaten but avoid actual collisions, though we witnessed several accidents in Maadi.

On my trips downtown, especially after Reuven began his work and the boys started school, "Crossing Cairo" emerged as a metaphor in my mind of the fears and fascination with which I approached Cairo. It pointed to my deep desire to make the most of this opportunity to experience life in Cairo and get to know its people and places. At the same time, the phrase conjured up my fears of simply crossing the street, as well as my questions about how successful I would be in stepping over the barriers that separated me from Egyptian culture as an American, a woman, and a Jew.

Chapter 2
Settling In

يوم عسل ويوم بصل

One day honey, one day onions.
~Arabic Proverb

THE NIGHT AFTER WE MOVED INTO THE APARTMENT, NOAM 39
spent about an hour talking with Umar and Seif across the street and the
inevitable question was raised, "So, are you Christian or Muslim?" They
had asked Noam this once before and he had answered that he believed
in one God. They apparently wanted to know more.

"I don't really like to talk about religion," said Noam. "In the United
States it is more of a personal thing." Umar and Seif seemed disappointed
but dropped the subject. Noam too was unhappy with the conversation.

"I want to be able to tell people I'm Jewish and just be open about
who I am," he said in frustration. "This is really awkward. I don't like
being on guard all the time and trying to avoid the issue like this." As we
anticipated, this was quickly proving to be the hardest part of living in
Cairo, especially for the boys.

A few days later Amir came home announcing that Farag, a boy in
his class, had invited him to a party to celebrate the end of the first semester exams. Amir wasn't sure he should go, since he hadn't taken the
exams. Noam straightened him out real fast.

"Are you kidding? An Egyptian party! — you have to go!" Noam told
him. "You're so lucky—you get to go to a party and you didn't even take
the exams!" Farag lived out in Heliopolis, one of Cairo's newer suburbs,
near the boys' school. We did not have a car, but since Farag's mother
thought it would be a 20-30 minute cab ride, we decided why not all go
for the ride? None of us had been to Heliopolis before, and we liked the
idea of going to a different part of Cairo.

Even before we were out of Maadi, we found ourselves in the tangle
of a Cairo traffic jam. "What's going on?" we asked the cab driver. "Nothing," he said, "just Thursday night." Thursday night was the big night out

in Cairo, like Saturday night in the States, because the next day, Friday, was the holy day for Muslims and the one official "day off." The later the hour, the cab driver explained, the more traffic there was. This was not encouraging. We eventually made it out to Heliopolis only to find ourselves surrounded by cars blaring their horns. A wedding? Our driver was not sure, but soon it became clear that either this was an unusually big wedding or something else was happening. As it turned out, the cause for celebration was a big soccer match at the stadium just beyond Farag's apartment building. The drive ended up taking an hour and 20 minutes instead of 20-30 minutes. But Amir was very happy when Farag came to the apartment door and welcomed him in, and Farag's mother assured us it was not too late to be dropping him off. We then set out on foot to find an Internet Café, feeling like our energy for exploring had been spent. Despite frequent inquiries to people we passed on the street, thirty minutes and many blocks later, no Internet Café had materialized. We settled for a cup of coffee in a local café.

While we were walking around Heliopolis, I noticed a Kentucky Fried Chicken restaurant up ahead and my heart sank a little bit. I had been similarly disappointed to find a McDonald's on Road Nine a few blocks down from where we lived. It was bad enough that in a little town in Maine or Alabama or North Dakota on Main Street you would find the expected McDonald's, Denny's and Burger King, along with Starbucks, CVS, Toys-RUs, Home Depot and Walmart, with anything resembling local flavor having disappeared. Was the curse of globalization going to be that cities and villages in disparate corners of the world would also come to be indistinguishable from one another? Wasn't there anything better in American culture than KFC and McDonald's for Egyptians to emulate?

But when we walked by, I was startled to see that this KFC was different than any I had seen before in the States. The restaurant was jam-packed—I did not see one empty seat—and the main visual impression was—headscarves. Most of the restaurant's patrons that evening seemed to be women — women sitting with men and women relaxing together with other women. Women were leaning back in their seats, and leaning over the tables talking animatedly with each other. Most of the women were young but some were middle-aged and older, and every woman—every single one—was wearing a *higaab*. It was a carousel of color and a wonderful snapshot of contemporary life in Cairo. KFC with an Arab Muslim accent.

When we came to retrieve Amir, Farag's mother, Samira, invited us to come inside, brushing aside our concern that it was after 11 p.m. We did not yet know that for many Egyptians, even children, the night was still young, with dinner often put on the table, even on weekdays, only at 10 or 11 p.m. As we walked through a dining room into the living room, I was immediately happy we had accepted her invitation to come inside. We found ourselves in a lavishly furnished living room crowded with chandeliers, Oriental rugs, highly polished wood tables, and European style upholstered furniture. Typical of an Arab home, there were several different sitting areas in the large living room, so that a fair number of people could be accommodated with everyone sitting in an intimate setting for conversation. Samira, guided us into a smaller, more down-home family room with smaller oriental rugs on the floors and a very large flat screen television that Farag's father, Mahmud was intently watching while munching on toasted sunflower seeds.

41

We sat down on the couch and joined Mahmud in watching the soccer game on television. When Samira returned a few minutes later with glasses of fresh orange juice for everyone, Mahmud turned off the television.

Mahmud was Palestinian from the Muslim quarter of the Old City in Jerusalem. He had left with his family in 1948 when he was six years old. Some of his extended family still lived in Jerusalem, "within the green line," he said, referring to Israel's pre-1967 borders, noting that this made it impossible for him to go back to live there himself. He looked much more like us than the typical Egyptian, I noticed—lighter skin and with a Semitic nose not unlike Reuven's.

I was interested in learning more about Mahmud's experience as a Palestinian living in Egypt. He told us that he owned several clothing stores in Cairo and, judging from the lavish apartment and the fact that his son had his own horse, he was doing quite well. Still, Samira told us, Mahmud felt that he suffered significantly as a Palestinian in Egypt. Palestinians were not looked upon with favor here and Mahmud was not even an Egyptian citizen. Mahmud nodded, concurring with Samira's answers. The Egyptians might rail against Israel for its treatment of the Palestinians, she said, but then they would turn around and treat them like second-class citizens themselves.

Many Egyptians viewed Palestinians with suspicion, assuming their loyalty lay elsewhere and fearing that they might prove to be a destabilizing faction. This in fact was what had happened in Jordan in 1970, when Palestinians started a revolution that almost succeeded in overthrowing the government. Palestinian refugees had also contributed to the destabilization of the Lebanese government in Lebanon in 1975, which led to the civil war between Palestinian Muslims and Maronite Christians.

This attitude towards the Palestinians was not new in the Middle East. While Arabs throughout the region outwardly supported the call for an independent Palestinian state and regularly attacked Israel for its treatment of the Palestinians, they have never been willing to absorb the Palestinian refugee population themselves. While the purported reason for this policy has been the unwillingness to give up on the idea of a Palestinian state alongside or in place of the state of Israel, Palestinians are generally viewed as a discontented minority and treated as second-class citizens in most countries in the Arab world.

I wanted to know more about his experiences and those of his family, and yet I knew I could not ask too many questions. Even with the few I did ask, I soon found myself needing to make a quick retreat. "Have you been to Israel?" he asked in surprise when I wanted to know what part of Jerusalem he was from. "I have friends you have been and they tell me Jerusalem is very beautiful," I answered, grasping for an answer that would not be an outright lie.

Again I had to wonder, were we doing the right thing in following the advice of the people who had so strongly advised us not to tell people we are Jewish? If Mahmud knew we were Jewish, would he want to talk further, or would that end the conversation? And what about Amir—would he allow his son to become friends with him? Caution seemed the wiser choice, at least for now. After a few more minutes of conversation Mahmud and Samira walked us over to the balcony to admire the twinkling lights of nighttime Heliopolis.

We had not yet stocked our kitchen and needed to buy fruit and vegetables for Shabbat, so the next morning while the boys were sleeping in, Reuven and I decided to explore the outdoor market on the other side of Road Nine. I happily wrote a shopping list, looking up as many words as I could find in my phrase book so that I would be able to ask for things myself and not rely on Reuven for everything.

We crossed over Road Nine and the Metro track on a pedestrian bridge that would have been condemned long ago in the States. I found myself hugging the sides, where the steps were slightly less worn and the metal strips in better shape. On the bridge we passed several women with young children who were sitting and begging, offering small packs of tissues for a guinea, or just asking for money. Their children trailed after us, tugging at my arm and not willing to let us go by so quickly. Following the advice of friends, I forced myself to shake my head no. We would have to find another way to help, some organization, I realized, but not this way.

Now approaching the second set of stairs that would take us back down to street level, we could see minarets rising from several mosques and hear the soothing melody of Quran recitation from tapes playing in people's stalls in striking contrast to the men's voices ringing out, hawking their wares.

43

On the other side of Road Nine, we found ourselves in a colorful and lively market, with people selling their wares from wooden carts and small stalls. The produce looked fresh picked, some of it still with caked mud, and the prices were lower than on our side of Road Nine, where many of the shops catered to foreigners. There was a small open area in the middle of the market, with ducks and chickens, and even a few goats and rabbits for sale. For the same price, you had the choice of taking them home live, or having them slaughtered on the spot. Further along there was an egg shop, a store selling nothing but eggs. The walls were lined with bins and boxes of eggs of different sizes and colors. This was different from food shopping in Los Angeles in more ways than I could count.

We passed by some women sitting on the ground, selling only lettuce and fresh herbs. Either these came from their own garden plots, or this was all they could afford to buy and then sell again for a few pennies more. Everyone tried to arrange their produce in an attractive manner, hoping to win the notice of passersby in the face of the heavy competition.

Earthy and sweet aromatic smells competed for our attention — fresh bread and deep fried *ta'amia* (falafel), fresh ground Turkish coffee and cardamom. The smell of worn leather advertised the shoe repairman sitting at an old sewing machine, fixing an old pair of boots. A moment later I found myself gagging at the sudden overwhelming smell of raw meat, from what I soon saw were gangly limbs of freshly slaughtered calves and lambs hanging in uncomfortably recognizable full body form from large hooks in the ceiling of the small butcher shop we were now passing. With gratitude and relief, I sucked my breath in greedily as the smell of newly ground spices won out and met us head-on as we finally made it past the butcher.

We arrived at a small spice shop with a dazzling variety of spices and grains. The walls were lined with old wooden drawers marked with the names of different spices, with boxes and clear plastic bags of spices on top of them, filling every inch of space from floor to ceiling. Burlap sacks of different kinds of rice on the floor left little room to walk around. Boxes of incense and packages of dry yeast, dried fruit and nuts and candy crowded the counter. This sure beat shopping for spices in little jars on supermarket shelves.

Two young boys in *galabiyas* were helping their father on their day off from school. Almost everything we asked for, they had— somewhere. Cumin, coriander, cinnamon… they expected us to buy a kilo or at least half a kilo (one pound!) of each and were surprised but accommodating when in almost every case we wanted less. The boys ground the spices for us and put them in plastic bags. They were patient with my Arabic and were clearly pleased that I was making the effort. With good humor and smiles, they corrected my pronunciation and guessed at the spices for which I didn't know the Arabic name. In addition to the spices, we bought dried apricots and walnuts, flour, sugar, and rice, and a sampling of different kinds of incense. We also bought two new treats to try—tamarind in the form of a round ball that the man said you boil in water for a tasty drink, and *fenugreek* seeds for a popular tea called *hilba*. When we left, I found myself hoping I would be back soon.

That afternoon I thoroughly enjoyed cooking for our first Shabbat dinner in our new home, with my new pots and pans and fresh spices. I didn't have a cookbook, so I improvised a dish of red peppers stuffed with rice cooked with tomatoes, mushrooms and chopped walnuts. Soon the apartment smelled like Shabbat.

A few hours later, with the setting of the sun, I once again pulled closed the drapes in the living room and dining room, this time in our street level apartment directly across the street from the hotel where we had been the week before. Reuven, Noam, Amir, and I gathered around a low table in the middle of the living room to light the Shabbat candles. We covered our eyes and chanted the blessing together and then we sat down around the candles and *davened* the Kabbalat Shabbat service as a family. Even though we had done the same thing the week before at the hotel, this felt different. Lighting the candles and ushering in Shabbat together in our new apartment, we all sensed it: even though we might still feel like strangers in a foreign land, here in our apartment, we were home.

Saturday morning, to our surprise we were all awakened at 7:20 a.m. by an incredible amount of noise coming from behind our apartment. It sounded like hundreds of children yelling...and it was. What we hoped was a special event turned out to be simply the first day back at school—we had not realized there was an elementary school just behind us, and while most schools were off on Friday and Saturday, this was a Christian school closed on Fridays and Sundays, but open bright and early on Saturday mornings. We tried, with varying degrees of success, to go back to sleep.

Tuesday night was the African Cup Semi-Finals and we made our back way to Muhammad's stationery store where once again we joined the dozen or so men of different ages, sitting on the steps sloping down amphitheater style to the front of the store. Some people were sitting on small cushions and a young man next to us insisted that I take his. I first shook my head no, but at his continued insistence, I accepted and thanked him. The pavement was hard and I had to admit I appreciated his generosity.

Muhammad's television was again sitting on a small table in front of the door to his shop. Reuven and the boys passed around bags of cookies we had picked up at the grocery store. Egypt was playing against Senegal and the men around us were pretty pumped up. The game proved very exciting with the outcome still unclear, when about ten minutes before the end of the game, an Egyptian player, Amr Zaki, who had just been substituted for one of Egypt's most popular players, made a spectacular goal that put Egypt in the lead. The crowds went wild, including the men in our mini-stadium. We practically held our breaths for the next ten minutes, and despite a couple of close calls, the Egyptians held off the Senegal team and captured the victory that moved them into the Finals. The Final match would take place on Friday night, the men told us as they got up to go home.

Even though at home none of us would ever think to watch a soccer or football game live or on television, we all wanted to see the game the following Friday night. We decided on our way home that we would *daven* Kabbalat Shabbat and eat an early Shabbat dinner next time so we could watch the game in front of Muhammad's store again. I wondered how many others in this crowd had televisions at home, as we did, but preferred watching the game outside with their buddies and neighbors on Road Nine. For us, being part of the neighborhood scene had an obvious appeal. The open pride and enthusiasm of the young Egyptians sitting next to us had been contagious. We appreciated being welcomed so openly and we were grateful for the running commentary on the game and the players. Watching the game in our living room would have missed the whole point.

The following Friday, after our Shabbat rituals and dinner, we headed out for Muhammad's stationery store as planned. Walking toward Road Nine, the streets were strangely quiet. Where was everyone? Had we made a mistake with the date, or was the game already over? Had we missed it? A little bit disconcerted, we walked quickly. As we approached the square we suddenly heard a cry that rose from all around us like a cresting wave before exploding into cheers. Relieved that we had not made a mistake after all, we walked even more quickly.

"I wonder what the score is," said Noam, speaking for all of us. Still a few minutes from the stationary store, we now heard a collective groan, and we worried aloud that maybe the Ivory Coast team had just scored a goal. When we arrived at Muhammad's stationary store, there were about fifteen people gathered on the steps. Some people recognized us and smiled, motioning for us to sit. Most were too intent on the game to even look up. To our surprise, despite the cheers and moans we had heard and the fact that the game was well into the second quarter, the score was still zero–zero.

This remained the score until the end of the second half but the score was deceiving. This proved to be an exciting game, with the teams so well matched that neither team succeeding in getting the ball past the other team's goalie until they went into overtime. Tension was already high but gradually moved higher and higher, as both teams scored penalty kicks bringing the score to 2-2. Suddenly Egypt's team made another penalty kick and the game was over. Egypt had won! Everyone around us was on their feet cheering and whistling, and we were cheering along with them. In minutes, people were singing and dancing in the street, with young men leaning over from the balcony above, adding their voices and drumming to the high-pitched celebration. Cars appearing out of nowhere roared up and down Road Nine, horns blaring, with people hanging out of the windows waving Egyptian flags. With this victory, Egypt had become the only country to ever win the African Cup five times. It was a moment of national pride, the pure pleasure of celebrating their athletes' accomplishment, and once again we enjoyed being part of it.

Several people had advised us to join one of Cairo's athletic clubs. "Everyone belongs to a club," we had heard on more than one occasion, from Egyptians as well as ex-pats. I assumed that meant "everyone" of only a certain class. But Kathy told us that today's clubs were not the exclusive reserve of the wealthy and were very popular among members of Cairo's middle class. In fact, some of them catered to particular professions such as the police and schoolteachers.

Early one morning I walked over to the Maadi Sporting Club, *Al Naadi* or "The Club," as it was commonly called, a few blocks north of where we lived, in order to look into our becoming members. I had walked by the walled-in area several times, wondering what it was before learning this was the "Maadi Sporting Club," as there was no identifying sign.

Walking through the club, I was immediately impressed by the beautifully maintained grounds. Flowering red and yellow trees and an abundance of wicker tables and chairs created an atmosphere of luxury. Never having belonged to a country club or an athletic club of any sort, except the local Y or Jewish Community Center, and associating country clubs with people of a different class and religion intent on keeping people like me out, I found myself looking around at my surroundings, curious to see how "the other half" lived.

The attractive two-story white clubhouse overlooking a grassy area set up for croquet, the running track and soccer field and the multiple clay tennis courts all seemed well maintained and contributed to the impression of comfortable elegance. The 10-lane Olympic-size pool was stunning and just next to it construction was underway to rebuild an old equestrian track and stable. Uniformed gardeners carrying a rake or a bucket, walked by me, unhurried. I was eager to be running laps on the track, swimming in the pool, and most appealing at the moment, sitting in one of the cushioned wicker chairs, sipping an iced drink in the shade of the flowering trees.

This could be the country club experience I had never had. I suddenly recalled how growing up, every summer my Jewish friends' parents all joined the local "Jewish" swim club, but my parents—either because of finances or their European background—always refused. Instead we drove forty minutes, sweating in the hot car, to swim in a lake—"So much better than a chlorinated pool, isn't it?" they said—where my brother and I knew absolutely no one and where I hated to wade into the water with the mud squeezing between my toes. Looking at this tranquil pool surrounded by beautifully landscaped grounds gave me an instant feeling of a forbidden delight.

The Naadi was clearly a leftover from a different era Cairo—the colonial British flavor seemed to hang in the air—and yet it did not seem stiff or stuffy in any way. The slightly worn feel of the place made the elegance less imposing and more inviting, promising ease and cool respite from the hassles and crowds of the city. I wanted to just wander and explore, but pushed myself to find the membership office. Asking directions again, I rounded a corner and found myself in front of a small, domed brick mosque. By the door were wooden cubicles, some of which had shoes in them, and through the door, I could see a few people praying. A country club with a mosque: the blend of cultures was complete.

I finally came to a small nondescript building and went inside, looking for the membership office. There I found two tired, unsmiling men behind a desk who seemed reluctant to answer any of my questions. I finally determined that Reuven and I both needed to come in person, with our passports and cash to pay for a six-month membership. I returned home to tell Reuven and before heading back to the *Naadi*, we walked over to our local bank, to withdraw the money we would need. At the bank, we watched with some amazement as two men waited in line with two medium-sized suitcases. Were those suitcases really for the money they were planning to withdraw? While I had heard about the practice, I had never witnessed it before. This was what people here did when they bought a car or a house. While some restaurants and stores accepted credit cards, many did not, and nobody accepted personal checks. It was largely still a cash-only economy, especially when it came to large purchases. As we stood in line waiting for our turn, I marveled once again at how similar and how different our two societies were.

Twenty minutes later we had our money and walked the few blocks to the Naadi. The same guard was there and he waved us in.

"This is really beautiful," said Reuven, as impressed as I was with the Naadi's grounds and ambiance.

Unfortunately, the men in the membership office were no friendlier than before. In fact, their coldness verged on hostility as they counted out our money and took our photos for the ID cards. Was it that we were foreigners, or that we were Americans in particular? What would be their reaction if they knew we were Jews? I felt suddenly uncomfortable applying for membership where I knew I was probably not welcome. I could not remember ever having done something like this. Where was my pride? Back in the United States, if I had ever faced the threat of closed doors because I was Jewish, I would never have tried to "pass." I would have fought the racist attitudes head-on, probably joining forces with other Jews and non-Jews to do so most effectively. Here in Cairo, knowing we were short-term visitors, this felt different. We did not feel like we could effectively challenge anything. But was this more compromising than we were admitting to ourselves? I was not sure. Eventually we finished our business, received our temporary ID cards, and headed home, mission accomplished, but with only an ambivalent sense of success.

The next day I returned to the Naadi, determined to make a go of it, and looking forward to a real swim. To my delight, I saw that except for one other woman I would have the whole pool to myself in the early morning sunshine. I walked into the dressing room, and was a bit taken aback at the state of disrepair and gloom, incongruous with the modern pool just outside. I changed quickly and smiled at the heavy-set Egyptian woman sitting at the entrance, trying to ignore how uncomfortable her gaze made me feel. I assumed that this woman, who apparently kept the dressing room clean and guarded people's belongings, was not earning a true living wage and the gap between us felt enormous. I was suddenly uncomfortable with the juxtaposition between Egyptian poverty and wealth, and even more, with my own place in it. I felt like a colonialist. My discomfort and the morning chill propelled me to move quickly to the pool. I put down my towel and water bottle and eased my way into the water. The temperature of the water was perfect and soon, any lingering discomfort had melted away. This was delicious. Here, with the sun already warming the cool morning air, I felt myself blissfully happy to be alive.

Half an hour later, I emerged from the pool and headed back to the changing room. After a quick shower, I was back in the dressing room and so was the other woman I had seen in the pool. She was from Paris and had been living in Cairo for years. Divorced from her Egyptian husband and caring for their eight-year-old son, she had considered moving back to Paris but had decided to stay. "I can live a better life here in so many ways," she admitted. "I have a nicer apartment and more time with my son. And I feel safer walking around at night here than I would as a single woman in Paris." I saw that she had a one-pound note in her hand and asked her if she gave the woman working in the dressing room something every day she swam. "Yes," she said. "She cannot be making much money here and it's a little something I can do. I usually give her a pound or fifty piasters (half a pound). It is not something you have to do, but it is appreciated." I liked the idea, and a few minutes later, when I left, I also gave the woman a one-pound note. "*Shukran*," she said, smiling at me. I knew one Egyptian pound, or 20 cents could buy a few pita breads or a bag of tomatoes, but I felt the same discomfort as earlier. I did not like playing the part of the rich foreigner.

Over the next few months, I saw this same woman working at the dressing room almost every day, most days accompanied by a younger woman who also worked in the locker room. While I often exchanged a few words with the women and we smiled at each other in greeting, I never got over my initial discomfort. I always was aware of the tremendous gap between us. The fact that I regularly gave each of the women fifty piasters or a pound only emphasized the gaps between us, but I knew they needed the money and it seemed like the right thing to do even if I was uncomfortable doing it. All of this persisted as the "underside" of my enjoyment of a good swim and the deliberately slow walk through the Naadi with which I sometimes started my day.

As we later learned, Cairo's sporting clubs had not always been the clubs for the people they are today. In fact, these athletic clubs were exactly the exclusive colonial British institutions we first imagined them to be. When Cairo's best known athletic club, the Gezira Sporting Club, was established in 1882, it was built as a club for British Army officers. The club was built on choice real estate —150 acres of the Botanical Gardens in Zamalek, downtown Cairo's most upscale neighborhood — leased to the British army for this purpose. Over time, the membership expanded to include non-military British colonials, and a bit grudgingly, even non-British members of prominence. It was only in 1952 that the Gezira Sporting Club was nationalized under Nasser's rule, and turned into a "Public Club for the People." It is still today one of Cairo's most popular attractions.

The Maadi Sporting Club also had a long history. Established in 1921, the Maadi club was never "British only" in its membership, but was by all measures an exclusive club that catered to the British. Membership required sponsorship of two club members and one's chances of admittance were much improved if one's sponsors were British. In its early years, the few non-British members of the Maadi Sporting Club were almost exclusively northern Europeans and the occasional British-educated Egyptian of wealth and status. It was only in the 1930s that central and southern Europeans, including many Jews, became members. The Maadi Sporting Club became the central address for athletic, social, and cultural events in Maadi.

On Shabbat afternoons, we often went to the Naadi as a family. This was when I got to sit at one of the wicker tables, reading or reviewing Arabic vocabulary, luxuriating in having no demands placed upon me while Reuven and the boys played soccer nearby. I went without the iced drink, as we did not spend money on Shabbat, but I still fully enjoyed the luxury of the moment. Saturday afternoon was a popular time for families at the Naadi and it was almost always crowded. Most of the people we saw on Saturdays were Egyptian, while on weekday mornings when Reuven and I came to the club for a run or a swim, the Naadi was almost empty, and the people using the track, tennis courts, and pool were a mix of Egyptians and ex-pats. The Maadi Sporting Club did seem to cater to the middle class, with the atmosphere of elegance still about the place for all to enjoy. At the same time, there had been some popular features added—small playgrounds and trendy eateries such as a Sbarro's Pizza restaurant, which would undoubtedly have been seen as a huge step down by the Club's founders.

I went to the Naadi two or three times a week in the early mornings to swim or go jogging. One morning while running I was startled to hear the bleating of a goat from the other side of the club's walls. Grazing goats in Maadi? I had to laugh out loud. When I came around the bend the next time though, it seemed to me that the sound came from somewhere above. I looked up, puzzled, trying to imagine where the sound might be coming from. Maybe, I thought, the sound waves were just bouncing off of a structure and creating the illusion of the bleating coming from on high. But I saw that two young women had also stopped running and were looking up in the direction from where I thought I heard the goat still bleating. I asked them where they thought the goat actually was.

They pointed to a balcony of the apartment building across the street, visible over the club walls. Sure enough, there was a goat, tethered to the railing — an unhappy goat, judging from her cries. Was this a pet goat missing its young child companion away at school? Or more likely, was this next Friday's family dinner, unaware of its fate, and just hungry for its own next meal?

The little goat with its lonely cries touched something deep in me and I hoped it would still be there when I came later in the week. Its bleating tugged at more than my usual maternal feelings for a helpless animal. Perhaps it echoed my own feelings, even in this beautiful place, of being in unfamiliar territory far from home.

Chapter 3
Learning Arabic

التكرار يعلّم الحمار

Repetition teaches even a donkey.
~Arabic Proverb

"GUESS WHAT I LEARNED IN ARABIC TODAY?" NOAM ASKED ONE 53
night at dinner, clearly eager to share something with us. Amir started laughing and couldn't help chiming in: "Oh yeah, Abba, listen to this!"

"This morning in Arabic class, I said something about how cool it is
that you can answer 'Good Morning' in Arabic with *sabah al fuul* —'May
you have a morning of beans!' and then everyone started laughing. My
teacher looked at me funny and said 'What?' I repeated myself and he
started laughing too. It turns out you were wrong, Abba! It's *full*, not *fuul,*"
he said, with slightly different pronunciation. "*Full* is a kind of flower—
fuul is beans! So it's not 'May you have a morning of beans' at all! It's more
like, 'May you have a jasmine morning'—only it's a different flower!" We
all laughed, amused at how we had seized on the "beans" understanding as
so fitting, given how popular it was in the Arab world, or at least in Egypt,
to eat beans for breakfast. And we thought it was funny that Reuven, our
resident expert in Arabic, had been the source of the error. This was one to
remember, we all decided, in our family adventures learning Arabic.

Notwithstanding the fun that Noam had in class, we were all disappointed in the boys' Arabic classes at school. The pedagogy for teaching
Arabic seemed very undeveloped. We also could not understand why
foreign students at AIS were learning *Fus-ha*, Classical Arabic, which
would be useful for reading the newspaper and Arabic literature, if they
learned enough of it, but would not help them much when it came to
speaking with their Egyptian friends. Every Arabic dialect was a little
bit different from the others but Classical Arabic was very different from
'*Amiyya*, spoken Egyptian Arabic. Reuven was experiencing frustration
with this as well. He was surprised at how different Egyptian Arabic was
from the Palestinian-Syrian dialect he had learned, which was closer to

Classical Arabic. While people could understand him, he was frustrated at how often people used vocabulary and even common expressions that were unfamiliar to him.

For the students at AIS who did not already speak Egyptian Arabic, teaching only *Fus-ha* seemed a strange choice to us as well as a missed opportunity. Why not give the children the tools to speak with their Egyptian friends in the *Lingua Franca,* enabling closer friendships and the ability to take in more of the popular culture surrounding them? While we initially saw this as a failing of AIS, we soon learned that the school was simply following the national educational policy that required them to teach Classical Arabic to foreign students.

I too had faced the question, what should I study—Classical or Egyptian colloquial Arabic? The administrator at AUC with whom we discussed the question on our first visit to the university, was definite: I should learn *Fus-ha,* she said, without a moment's hesitation. It was portable and it would allow me to eventually read Arabic literature. But my main hope was not to read literature but to talk to people. I was here in Cairo, so why not learn Egyptian? I wondered. Reuven agreed and encouraged me to learn Egyptian colloquial Arabic. I decided to begin with 'Amiyya and then perhaps later on also learn *Fus-ha.*

But finding the right class was not so easy. I started calling different language schools in Cairo, beginning with those Kathy had suggested, and eventually landed on a small school I first saw advertised in the Naadi. I would be able to take a small class that met for two hours twice a week, or I could study privately with a teacher. After two weeks of working on my own with my phrase book and Reuven's help, I took the placement exam and tested at the high beginner level. The director was trying to find me one or two other students with whom to have a semi-private class, but this too was taking time and I was getting impatient. I could see my six months slowly slipping away like sand in an hourglass. I couldn't wait much longer, I decided. If I did not hear something definitive from the school in the next few days, I would have to look somewhere else.

In the meantime, I was enjoying speaking as much Arabic as I could, asking for things in the market and making very limited small talk. My enjoyment of these early efforts was largely the result of the encouragement I encountered almost everywhere I went. Shopkeepers, women on the Metro whom I asked for directions, taxi drivers, all responded warmly to my efforts to speak Arabic. Their friendliness made me want to speak more.

One woman with whom I chatted for only a few minutes on the Metro was particularly friendly and clearly pleased with my efforts to speak Arabic. When she realized her stop was next, she hastily wrote down her name and phone number on a piece of paper and gave it to me before stepping out at her stop. "It was so nice to meet you. If you have any questions or I can help you in any way—call me! Really," she said, slowly in Arabic, before getting off the train. These interactions, superficial as they might be, were frustrating when I failed, but a thrill when I succeeded. They helped me feel like I belonged where I was, even as the foreigner I so keenly knew myself to be at every moment.

Surprisingly, it was easier to find a housekeeper than an Arabic class for me to join. Basima, the owner of our apartment, recommended a woman named Mahabbah who had worked for her family for years. She called her for us and told her when to come.

When the doorbell rang I knew it was Mahabbah and opened the door. There she stood, completely covered from head to toe in a full *higaab* (head covering) and a large navy blue *galabiya* (robe) draping loosely over her body, with only her face showing. She was smiling back at me, her dark eyes dancing.

"*Issalaamu aleikum!*" I greeted her, motioning for her to come in, a little bit nervous but curious about the warm and friendly woman standing before me.

"*W'aleikum issalaam,*" she answered, her smile widening.

She started to chatter to me in Arabic, and without seeming to pause for a breath, she swept into the kitchen and started removing layers of clothing. With one hand she pulled her large *higaab* over her head and with her other hand she started to unbutton the top buttons of her *galabiya*, her long over garment. Then, with both hands, she lifted her *galabiya* up over her head, talking to me all the while. When she was finished, she stood before me barefoot, having left her shoes just outside the apartment door, still modestly dressed in a long-sleeved house dress. She was, even without all the layers, a big woman. I finally managed to get a word in and told her I didn't speak Arabic but that I was trying to learn.

"*Mish mushkila* — no problem," Mahabbah smiled again. She continued to talk to me, a little bit slower now, looking around the kitchen.

"*Inti 'ayza tishrabi shay* — would you like a cup of tea?" I asked her.

"No thank you, Madame, I already had tea at home. I just drink just one cup a day," she answered, holding up one finger. Yes—this much Arabic—with the help of a little sign language, I could understand. Mahabbah had cleaned our apartment once before we moved in and she seemed ready to jump in and get started. She motioned to the kitchen closet, asking, I assumed, if the cleaning materials were still there. I nodded and opened the closet door and she took out the bucket and rags. She started cleaning the kitchen and I went off to do other things.

A few hours later, our apartment was clean and Mahabbah was disappearing again under her layers, pulling her *higaab* over her head. At Mahabbah's suggestion, we had agreed that she would come and clean twice a week. With Reuven's help, I asked her if we could sit and speak Arabic together for half an hour or an hour each time she came, as part of her work time. She liked the idea. As she was preparing to leave, she asked if I would like her to buy groceries from the market on the way to our house when she came on Sunday. She told me she could buy fresher and cheaper fruit and vegetables at her market than we could find in Maadi. I wasn't sure what I would need, so I thanked her but declined the offer this time.

The following Sunday morning, Mahabbah walked in balancing a large pot on her head.

"*Mahshi*," she said with obvious pleasure. "You need to taste Egyptian food, so I made you *mahshi*." She carefully lifted the pot off her head and proudly placed it on the stove. *Mahshi*, it turns out, refers to stuffed vegetables of all kinds, an Egyptian favorite. Mahabbah had made us one of her specialties—stuffed cabbage—little rolls of cabbage about the size of stuffed grape leaves. The cabbage was stuffed with rice mixed with a little bit of tomato sauce, chopped onions, and fresh parsley, dill, and coriander. Knowing that we were vegetarians, Mahabbah had made the dish without meat, even though it was, she said, much better with meat. The small rolls were arranged attractively in spiraling circles, filling the whole pot. Mahabbah mixed together some water with a little bit of oil and salt and pepper, and poured the liquid over the *mahshi*, and let it cook over a low flame for about an hour. Soon the smell of the cooking cabbage and herbs wafted through the apartment and I found my mouth was watering. I was very happy when Mahabbah came back to the kitchen, pronounced the *mahshi* done, and offered me a small cabbage roll to try. It was delicious. I asked Mahabbah if she would teach me how to make *mahshi* and she agreed, clearly pleased with the idea.

After she had finished cleaning, Mahabbah and I sat in the dining room over a cup of tea for about an hour.

"*Andik kam 'ayil?* — how many children do you have?" I asked her.

Mahabbah balancing a large pot on her head

"I have three children," she answered. "My daughter, Aziza, is twenty-two." Mahabbah spoke slowly and held up her fingers in case I didn't understand. "Omar is nineteen and Muhammad, the youngest, is eight." Aziza had finished college and was certified as a teacher. She wanted to teach Arabic and Islamic studies at the middle school level but had not been able to find a job. She was teaching kindergarten for now.

Mahabbah asked me about our boys and when she heard Amir's name, her face lit up. Aziza, she told me, was engaged to young man also named Amir, and they were hoping to get married next February. Mahabbah's husband had died a few years ago and she was raising her children on her own. I knew that must be a challenge. I felt even better about the fact that Mahabbah was working for us twice a week, even though once a week would have been fine for us.

"When do your boys come home from school? When do you eat dinner?" I asked. Mahabbah explained that Muhammad went to the mosque

57

and studied the Quran everyday for an hour after school and that he and Omar both came home at about five. They usually all ate lunch then.

"You eat lunch at five?" I asked. I was sure I had misunderstood. Maybe I was confusing the Arabic for lunch and dinner and they actually ate dinner at five. No, Mahabbah assured me, they ate lunch together at five p.m.

"Then when do you eat dinner?" I asked, puzzled.

"Usually at ten, maybe a little later," she replied.

"When do you go to bed?" I asked, thinking of Mahabbah's eight-year-old, Muhammad.

58

"Between midnight and two." No way, I thought.

"Every day?" I asked, incredulous, "even Muhammad?"

"Yes, she answered with a laugh. They all got up at seven in the morning, Mahabbah told me. "When do you sleep?" I wondered out loud. Mahabbah laughed again, clearly amused by my surprise at all this obvious information.

Later, when I told Kathy about this conversation, I asked her, when do people sleep?

"When do they sleep?" Kathy responded in surprise, "Are you kidding? Just look around...you see when they sleep!" Her words called forth a stream of images of people with their heads down resting on their folded arms, or just leaning back in a chair dozing, behind the cash register, or at a desk, or outside by the side of their cab. She was right—I saw people sleeping all the time during the day. What I had viewed as catnaps in response to boredom was probably for many people a critical portion of their daily sleep. This was such a different world, in ways I had not expected—even the flow of daily routines.

This new revelation about Egyptian culture explained a number of things that had puzzled us. Store hours, for one. We had gone to our favorite local bakery one morning at about eight, in search of fresh bread for breakfast and were surprised to discover that it did not open until ten. When we learned that these were the regular hours, I was baffled. What about people on their way to school and work, or simply wanting to buy fresh bread for breakfast at home—wasn't this a big enough market for bakeries to be open early in the morning? Apparently for our local bakery, the answer was no. It had not occurred to me that most Egyptians ate breakfast several hours later. On the plus side, we frequently enjoyed the fact that late into the night, even the wee hours of morning, restaurants, food stores, and other shops were still open in Maadi, even though this was a sleepy little residential area compared to downtown.

I wondered if this division of the day derived from the demands of the intense summer heat that dominated several months out of the year. Basima had described for us her memories of growing up, when on hot summer nights, the streets of Cairo would be so full of people just walking, looking for an escape from their stifling apartments, that it was sometimes impossible for cars to pass. Even today, she said, the hot weather still propelled people out of their homes and on to the streets at night. And whether or not one had air-conditioning at home, the late night hours were still a welcome alternative to the mid-day sun for shopping in the markets. It made perfect sense that the intensity of the summer heat had such a determinative effect on people's habits and that these habits persisted into the other months of the year as well.

59

Each time she came, Mahabbah and I went over practical things, like asking for the time of day and giving directions. Mahabbah was patient and happy to review these conversational phrases with me. She spoke slowly and clearly and encouraged me to repeat the phrases after her, so I could get the pronunciation right. A natural teacher, she started asking me questions that would enable me to use the new words in sentences. It was fun and great practice, but I mostly enjoyed having the opportunity to just talk with her. The fact that Mahabbah spoke no English meant that there was no temptation for me to slip into my own native tongue. This forced me to find ways to express myself in Arabic and I was surprised at how well we did with my very limited language skills. I was already learning about Mahabbah's family and daily life, all in Arabic, even though I had been studying the language for less than a month.

One evening I suggested to Reuven that we speak Arabic at dinner and get the boys going on the kinds of conversational questions I was learning with Mahabbah. Reuven agreed and we spent most of dinner that night playing games, asking each other basic conversational questions like, What is your name? How old are you? Do you have any brothers or sisters? This was exactly the kind of language experience that was missing from the boys' classes at school. I felt that making conversation like this sometimes over dinner would help Noam and Amir, and me too.

Speaking Arabic at the table brought back memories of my parents trying to teach me and my younger brother German at the dinner table when we were ten and eight. *Kann ich bitte fleisch haben*? ("Could I have some meat, please?") is the first sentence that comes to my lips in German. The fact that I am a vegetarian only underscores the failure of this exercise to impart to me any truly useful German skills. But my parents, deeply ambivalent about teaching us German in the first place, and concerned that we might end up speaking English with a German accent, had waited too long. My brother and I had no interest and no patience. We wanted to relax and talk at dinner without having to work at expressing ourselves in a foreign language. My parents soon gave it up.

For us, speaking German at the dinner table was a hollow act. Was I encouraged to learn the language so I would be able to excel at school? Read Goethe and Schiller in the original? It was never said, and it never occurred to me that German literature was my heritage. We were not about to go to Germany; we did not even buy German products. Why learn German, except to speak it with older relatives, with whom I already spoke English? Language opens doors, but this door, which was in some ways the closest to me, had been slammed shut and I felt no desire to open it.

Instead, the heritage I had fully embraced was my Jewish heritage— and language was a significant piece of it. I had learned the Hebrew alphabet as a child but it was only in the first year of my rabbinical studies in Israel that I began to study Hebrew in earnest— modern Hebrew, Biblical Hebrew, rabbinic and medieval Hebrew. (Hebrew Union College, the rabbinical school of the Reform Movement, required taking the first year in Israel for this reason.) Two months into my studies, I spent a week volunteering at the first Reform Kibbutz in Israel, Kibbutz Yahel, in the Arava desert just north of Eilat. I helped plant the first crops of green peppers and onions and I discovered for the first time, how speaking Hebrew could lead to new friendships and earn me a special welcome into this community. Over the course of that year, I returned to the kibbutz as often as I could and spent hours talking with Israelis my age who were among the founding members of the kibbutz.

When our children were little, Reuven and I decided to make Hebrew the primary spoken language in our home. We wanted to give our children something we had never had and now longed for, ourselves: fluency in speaking and understanding Hebrew, the language of the Jewish people. The Hebrew language was the key not only to Israeli culture, but to the vast literature of Jewish tradition and to Jewish communities all over the world. Even though I wanted to do this, it was still a little bit of a stretch to speak Hebrew with my two eldest children, Rachel and Noam, and it took some getting used to. But I also took pleasure in my own increasing ease speaking Hebrew and expanding my vocabulary with new words like "diaper" and "pacifier." From the start, I made myself a rule that whenever I found myself starting to feel frustrated because of my inability to express feelings or ideas more complex than my Hebrew skills could manage, I wouldn't struggle—I would simply switch to English. Even though Reuven and I knew this went against all the experts' advice—that each parent be consistent in speaking just one language with the children—we did it anyway. It proved the safety valve that allowed us to speak Hebrew with our children most of the time.

61

There was less dissonance than one might expect between our efforts to speak Hebrew at home and the outside world our children experienced when they were young in Boston and then Los Angeles. They attended Jewish day schools where Hebrew was the language of instruction for half the day and they attended traditional Shabbat services each week. We spent several summers and sabbaticals in Israel where our children attended school and summer programs with Israeli children from a very young age. They all made friends with Israelis with whom they only spoke Hebrew. As we hoped, all three of our children have all been able to experience traditional Jewish prayer, text study, and modern Israeli culture in a way that is impossible without strong Hebrew skills.

Where speaking German at the dinner table had failed for me as a child as an isolated act, speaking Hebrew with our children succeeded because it was reinforced by the day-to-day life our children lived both in and outside of our home. Now we were living in Cairo for six months. We carried the emotional baggage of Arabic being the language of the other, even of the enemy, but it was also the language of new friends we had already made and hoped still to make. For the months ahead of us in Egypt, there would be every incentive to learn as much Arabic as possible and many opportunities to speak Arabic, if we were ready to make the effort. Now, at the dinner table, we would practice phrases we hoped to use with other people the very next day.

We decided that Fridays, when the boys were off from school, would be a good time to explore different parts of Cairo. The Nilometer, we thought, would be a fun and interesting place to start. We set out with Noam and Amir for the small island of Rhoda, downtown, in the middle of the Nile, just across from Fustat or "Old Cairo." The Nilometer is an ancient structure designed to measure the waters of the Nile. The annual flooding of the Nile, from ancient times until the twentieth century when the first Aswan Dam was opened, exerted the single most powerful influence on life in all of Egypt. In good years, the Nile would flood the river valley, leaving behind rich deposits of alluvial soil that meant farmers could look forward to high crop yields. In bad years, however, low levels of the Nile signaled looming disaster, as without enough water and a new supply of enriched soil, farmers could expect only poor crop yields or perhaps no crops at all. Everything depended on the Nile.

The first Nilometers were built by the Pharaohs. The depth of the Nile was such a sure indicator of crop size and the general economy, that Egypt's rulers used the Nilometer's measurements to determine annual tax rates. Measuring the Nile waters became a yearly event marked by a special ceremony. When the level of the Nile measured high, celebratory festivals would follow; a low water level would be met by fervent prayers for rain.

The Rhoda Nilometer is built into the bedrock of the small island and is one of several still in existence along the Nile. It consists of a deep square-shaped pit underneath a wooden cone-shaped dome, with an octagonal column extending from the dome, all the way down into the ground. This intricately carved marble column is scored with lines to measure the water level and dates from the ninth century, making the Nilometer one of the oldest monuments of Egypt's Islamic era. Centuries ago, at the annual meter-reading ceremony, water was let into the pit from the Nile through tunnel openings at the bottom of the well. The crowds in attendance would wait anxiously until the water rose to the river's level and its measure could be read, forecasting prosperity or hardship. Inscriptions from the Quran in beautiful calligraphy, celebrating the importance of water, decorate the beams surrounding the column.

We had the Nilometer to ourselves that morning, and we talked the guard into letting us climb down the narrow stairs that wound their way around the column all the way to the bottom of the pit. The steep climb down was worth it, we all decided, when we looked up to discover intricate geometric designs painted on the domed ceiling in the Ottoman style, in gold and bright colors.

Leaving the Nilometer, we followed a short walkway that took us back to modern times — a museum dedicated to one of Egypt's greatest cultural icons of the twentieth century, the legendary singer Umm Kulthum. Over thirty years after her death, Egyptians still rave about Umm Kulthum's powerful voice and her electric performances. On display were some of her famous costumes, including the trademark scarf she always held when she performed and her signature diamond studded sunglasses. We sat and watched a short film of Umm Kulthum's life and heard some of her recordings. When Umm Kulthum's father, an imam, first discovered her talent, he trained her himself and started her off on her performing career, disguising her as a boy to avoid shocking the local religious authorities. Eventually, the whole country used to stop to listen to her concerts broadcast live on national radio on Thursday nights. For some it was nothing less than a spiritual experience. Even today, Egyptians can hear her performances on the radio the first Thursday of every month.

Umm Kulthum came to be known as "the Face and Voice of Egypt." She was best known for her expressive renderings of traditional Egyptian music and poems that she set to music. While Umm Kulthum also performed in films for a brief period, she quickly gave up film in favor of concerts where she and her audiences could enjoy the intensity of her music rising out of their direct relationship. When Umm Kulthum died in 1975, over three million Egyptians attended her funeral. We viewed some of the emotional footage that showed the millions grieving as though they had lost a family member or their beloved.

We were puzzled that the film about Umm Kulthum began and ended with footage of battle scenes from Egypt's wars against Israel. The inflammatory anti-Israel sentiment expressed seemed gratuitous. What did this have to do with Umm Kulthum? From the film we learned that she was a staunch supporter of Nasser and from the early 1950s on something of a political activist. Following Nasser's lead, she often linked her nationalist fervor with strong condemnation of Egypt's archenemy, Israel. In 1967, after Egypt's defeat in the war against Israel, Umm Kulthum gave a series of benefit concerts to support Egyptian troops and lift the nation's spirits. The filmmakers perhaps chose to frame Umm Kulthum's life with this war footage, depicting Egypt standing strong against Israel, as an expression of her pride in the Egyptian people.

While this war footage might be understood as a reflection of what had been the sentiment of Umm Kulthum and the Egyptian people at the end of her life in 1975, I saw the filmmakers' choice as sadly reflecting sentiments still very much alive among Egyptians today, even though Egypt and Israel were at peace by treaty since 1979. The film seemed to be saying that just as Umm Kulthum was a source of great nationalist pride in Egypt to this day, so was the image of Egypt "standing strong" against Israel. There were daily attacks on Israel in even the English language Egyptian newspapers I read and television news reports.

I had already learned to be prepared for the ever-present undercurrent of anti-Israel hatred in Egypt, but I was not expecting it here in a film that celebrated an Egyptian cultural icon. For me, it somewhat marred a pleasant day's outing as I wondered how open I could be to this culture that regularly expressed enmity and even hatred for my people. We had come so far to learn about and appreciate Egypt's cultural past and present, but I was not sure I could always compartmentalize my reactions.

Almost a month after arriving in Egypt, I finally met my Arabic teacher. At the Alexander School's director's suggestion, I decided to begin with a private teacher to avoid any further delays, with the possibility of shifting to a small class in the future. The Alexander School was located on a small residential street near the French School, just off of Canal Street. I liked the informality of the "house" setting and I could feel myself relax as I walked up the stairs. As I entered the building, I saw a young woman I assumed was Zayna, my teacher, sitting on an upholstered couch in the lobby, waiting for me.

"*Masa al khayr* (Good afternoon)," she said, rising and extending her hand.

"*Masa an-nur*," I responded. She smiled at me shyly. Zayna was wearing a long denim skirt and a long-sleeved white blouse, typical of religious women's dress, in neutral colors that would not draw overdue attention to her. Her hair, neck, and shoulders were modestly covered by her pale orange and white *higaab*. She was young—only twenty-three, as I would soon learn. She could be my daughter! I thought to myself. I had expected an older, more experienced teacher, and, I must admit, my first response was mild disappointment to have waited so long, only to be assigned a young teacher, perhaps lacking in experience. I realized I needed to relax and give Zayna a chance before jumping to conclusions.

"Let's sit in this room," she said, motioning to one of the empty classrooms. We went in and sat down. Zayna wanted to know how long I had been in Egypt and how long we planned to stay. I told her we intended to stay for six months.

"Only six months!" Zayna seemed surprised. "Why do you want to learn Arabic if you will be here such a short time?" I explained that I wanted to be able to communicate with people here and hoped to have the opportunity to come back in future years. I did not want to mention at this first meeting that I also hoped to speak Arabic in Israel, with Israeli Arabs and Palestinians.

Zayna seemed satisfied with my answer. She explained that while she knew I had been studying Arabic on my own, she thought it best to start at the beginning of the curriculum, moving quickly over what I already knew, and spending more time on the material that was new to me. This way, she explained, I would begin with a strong foundation and not be missing anything. I agreed and pulled my chair up to better see the book she was opening in front of me.

"*Masri-Masriyya-Masriyin*" said Zayna, pointing to somewhat old-fashioned drawings of a man and woman standing next to a picture of the Egyptian flag. These were, I gathered, the masculine, feminine, and plural forms for the word "Egyptian." I repeated the words after Zayna. I especially liked the sound of the word "*Masriyya*," lingering on the doubled "y" sound. I already knew the word "*Masri*" but the feminine and plural forms were new to me and I was excited to learn a pattern for forming nouns that would have wide application. The pattern was exactly as in Hebrew, I thought to myself, happily.

"*Agnabi, Agnabiyya-Agaynab*," she continued. These, I knew, were the words for "foreigner." Egyptians and foreigners, I thought to myself, that says it all. Are you one of us? Or are you a foreigner? Anywhere I walked in Maadi and Cairo, young children regularly said "Good morning" or "How are you?" to me in English as we approached each other. Sometimes they smiled. Sometimes they giggled. On occasion, they

65

mocked the accent of my Arabic reply. Given my uncovered short-cut hair and my modest but European-style dress, it was obvious that I was a foreigner.

But my being immediately pegged as a foreigner said more about Egyptian society than it did about me. The Egyptian population is so homogeneous today that anyone who looks non-Arab is assumed to be a foreigner. This was a new experience for me. Nowhere I had ever lived, in the United States, or Israel, or Europe, had the world been divided in quite this way between locals and foreigners. Our American ex-pat friends, who had been here for years, were still foreigners. Even Maureen, who was married to an Egyptian here and was bringing up her husband's two children from a previous marriage as Muslims was immediately seen as a foreigner when she walked the streets of Cairo. I too had already found myself labeling people this way as I walked the streets of Cairo: "Foreigner... Egyptian... Egyptian...." I had to admit that I felt a special kinship sometimes when I walked by someone I assumed was American or European, as long as they were not behaving in a way that embarrassed me, and I realized that unconsciously I assumed they were here only temporarily. I seemed to have absorbed the view that the only people who really belonged here were the non-Western Egyptians.

I repeated the words for "foreigners" and we went on to other basics. This is really fun, I thought to myself, pleased that I would be going home with a lot more words to work with even after just one class. I took notes in both English and Arabic, frustrated with how long it took, but Zayna encouraged me to write in Arabic and waited patiently.

"You learn quickly," Zayna observed with some surprise when later I repeated verb conjugations in the imperfect form with ease. Again, the forms corresponded exactly to the Hebrew imperfect tense. Certain nouns were also the same or very similar, such as *yom* for "day" and *beit* and *bayit*, which meant "house" in both Arabic and Hebrew. I wanted to tell Zayna that I spoke Hebrew and be able to share the many parallels between Hebrew and Arabic that I found so interesting, but I knew if I mentioned Hebrew, Zayna would probably realize I was Jewish.

Zayna followed the curriculum closely and introduced the suggested vocabulary step by step, going over the words on the page and writing related words on the board. After reviewing each set of words once, we moved on to the next one. I definitely would need to drill more on my own if I wanted to really learn any of these new words, but I decided not to say anything. I could practice at home and I preferred to take advantage of the opportunity to learn as many new words as I could during class time. I was not sure how experienced a teacher Zayna was, nor was I convinced the curriculum was a particularly good one, but it was clear that I could learn a lot from Zayna and I liked her. I left class an hour and a half later, my head swirling with new verb forms that I couldn't wait to try.

On the way home I decided to stop at Café Greco, a popular European style café in Maadi, to review and organize my notes over a cup of coffee. I ordered my coffee in Arabic, *bidoon kaffeine* (without caffeine) and the man behind the counter smiled at me, pleased that I was making an effort to speak Arabic. I told him I had just been to my first Arabic class and at his request, showed him what I was learning.

"Anytime you have a question, feel free to ask me," he offered.

"*Shukran.* I will," I answered. This was the kind of encouragement that propelled me forward, even when I wondered how much I could really learn in six months.

A few minutes later, I sat very contentedly rewriting my notes and repeating words and simple sentences over a steaming latte. I was almost deliriously happy.

There were times when I marveled at how comfortable I already was in Maadi, and I would have to remind myself that I had not always lived among people wearing *higaab* and *galabiyas*—in fact, it had only been a little over a month since we arrived in Cairo. Living in a part of town where we saw many of the same people every day helped us feel at home, as did the fact that people seemed so friendly.

"It's all about relationships, here in Egypt," Kathy had commented the first time we got together. "You either like it and have time for it and everything works for you, or you don't, period. That's just the way it is here." Luckily, we had the time and we enjoyed it. For me, going out and doing errands was a great way toward accomplishing one of my main goals, speaking Arabic. In another culture, this would have been more difficult.

There was even a culture around extending greetings to people. Anyone you passed on the street or saw in a shop, if you saw them on a semi-regular basis, you were expected to acknowledge with a greeting,

67

even if you did not know their name. This was a real greeting, not just a nod, or a smile, or a casual hello. Ideally, you would begin with "Good morning" or "Good afternoon" and then move on to "What's new?" or "How are you?" and respond to their similar questions. This was enough if one was just walking by, but if one had the time and inclination, conversation would generally continue. Muhammad, the stationery store owner, for example, regularly asked about each member of the family by name.

The greetings started as soon as I walked out the door of our apartment building. Across the street, one or more of the hotel employees were invariably standing outside, having a smoke. "*Sabah al khayr*, good morning!" one of us would begin. I would usually pause for a brief exchange, sometimes extended by interest in a particular subject. Then, as I made my way down the block toward Road Nine, I would pass three or four pairs of security guards whom I saw almost every day, and I would initiate or respond to the greeting sequence again. Only with a few people did I usually have real conversations, but the greetings alone, repeated day after day, established a human connection that made us more than anonymous strangers. When someone was away for a few days, I noticed and then said something, and they did as well. This was different than city life in the U.S., where we often see people on a regular basis but choose to remain anonymous and do not even exchange a word.

68

One might argue that this was just an example of Arab etiquette, a superficial expression of friendliness at best, but I experienced in it something more. It was a regular and expected way of acknowledging the other person as a person, not just someone fulfilling a role for you as cashier, taxi driver, or shopkeeper. Even though class and status are much more important in Egypt than in the U.S.—and are often acknowledged with titles of more or less respect, depending on the person's profession and class—on some level, the culture of greetings was a way of cutting through all that to acknowledge the humanity of the other person.

I decided that Americans had a lot to learn about the art of living in community from Egyptians. Take the culture of being helpful, for example. Between my unfamiliarity with the area and the circuitry of Maadi's little streets, I found myself asking for directions on numerous occasions. In almost every case, when I asked someone on the street for directions, the person would start to explain and then pause and say, "Come, I will show you" and walk with me to my destination. Each time I was surprised and touched that a stranger, without a moment's hesitation and no evidence of feeling put upon, was ready to go out of his or her way in order to be sure I made it to where I wanted to go. I could not remember anyone in the U.S. ever accompanying me when I asked directions, nor could I remember doing this for someone else.

I learned another lesson in Egyptian helpfulness from Muhammad at the Internet Café. I was interested in downloading Norton anti-virus updates on my laptop and found it impossible to do so because I was in Egypt and had an American account. I spoke with Muhammad about it one afternoon and he tried to help me, without success. When I came back to use the Internet the next day, to my surprise, he had done some research and learned I would need to purchase the Egyptian Norton anti-Virus software and install it on my laptop. He gave me a piece of paper with several names and addresses of dealers from whom I would be able to purchase the program. Delighted to have the information, I returned home, made some calls, and found one dealer who had what I needed in stock. His store was in a different part of Maadi, too far to walk, so I hailed a taxi on the street.

69

As I was soon to discover, the culture of helpfulness also had its downside. That is, the obligation to be helpful is so strong in Arab culture that one is expected to never respond to a request for help by saying no, or even "I don't know." It was considered far better to try to help, than not to try at all.

Since I had only a vague idea of where I needed to go, I asked the taxi driver before entering his taxi if he knew how to get to the address. He nodded yes. I got into the cab, looking forward to seeing a new part of Maadi. Ten minutes later, in the middle of a fairly crowded commercial area in the eastern section of Maadi, the taxi driver asked me where he should turn off the main road and it quickly became clear that he had no idea where the street in question was located. Several times, he slowed down and asked other drivers, each of whom waved him somewhere. Finally, after backtracking several times, more hand-waving advice led the driver to confidently make a left turn, then a right, which placed us in a residential neighborhood. Now he drove slowly and asked someone else about the address before making a few more turns and stopping in front of an apartment building with the right house number but on the wrong street. Part of the challenge, I could see, was the fact that the numbered streets did not always follow one another in sequence, and neither did the buildings on a given street. The driver shook his head sadly and we headed back to the main street and tried again. Thirty minutes later, but no closer to success, I wearily asked the driver to take me back to my apartment.

This time the culture of helpfulness had backfired. I would have much preferred a simple "No, I can't help you" from the beginning. But that, apparently, was not how things were done in Egypt. With all good intentions, the driver had tried to be helpful but he had failed me and I was annoyed at the time and expense. He was apologetic, but seemed to feel I should not have gotten into the taxi without knowing where I wanted to go. I was at fault? Another case of different expectations based on our two cultures? Or was he just trying to save face?

After talking to some of my ex-pat friends, I learned that on several counts my driver and I had been speaking a different language. His assumption that someone getting into a taxi should know how to get to the destination reflected a typical Egyptian attitude, according to my friends. At the same time, I was operating as an American, and even though I asked him if he knew how to get to the address before getting in the car, I also assumed that as a taxi driver, he would know how to get around in Maadi.

But even more basic, I did not understand at the time, that the obligation to be helpful in Arab culture is so strong, that a "no" or "I don't know" is often feared to be misunderstood as a personal rejection. Better to try and help—and fail—than refuse to try. While the taxi driver might simply have not wanted to give up the fare, as I assumed, he also was acting in accordance with a culture that discouraged saying "No" or "I don't know." I could not get out of my American point of view on this one—no matter how I looked at it, I preferred the honest approach. But when it came to helping someone asking directions by walking them to their destination—this was something I had learned from the Egyptians that I would try to take home with me.

There were other cases when we found ourselves caught in the net of wildly different expectations and rules of communication. One day, shortly after moving into our apartment, we were having problems with our television and satellite hook-up and Reuven arranged for someone from the electronics shop on Road Nine to come to our house and fix it.

The man came and spent about half an hour working on the television and at the end shook his head sadly, unsure of how to fix the problem. He got ready to leave and I asked him what I should pay him.

"*Mafeesh*—nothing," he answered. "I couldn't fix it."

"But you spent all this time," I protested," "I want to pay you for your time." He raised his hands and said, "You don't have to pay me anything." This did not seem fair and I wanted to pay him something, but I had no idea what was appropriate. I made a guess and handed him five Egyptian pounds. He thanked me, put the money in his wallet, and left. I told Reuven later what had transpired and he thought I had done the right thing, though he wasn't completely sure.

The next day, Reuven went to the same electronics shop for an electric extension cord and when he came home he had this news to share with me: "Guess what Ahmad said when I got to his shop today? 'Your wife did not pay me enough. Why didn't she pay me enough?'"

"You're kidding!" I was flabbergasted. How was I supposed to know if I had asked and he had answered "nothing"? Reuven did not know either, but it seemed that when Ahmad told me I should not pay him anything he was being polite. He apparently assumed I knew the rules of the game, and was also just being polite, and that in the end, I would pay him appropriately.

"So how much should I have paid him? What did you end up giving him?" I asked.

"Twenty pounds," Reuven answered.

A few weeks later, Reuven observed something that put my communication failure with Ahmad into even clearer focus. Two men on the street were talking, one with money in his hand, clearly offering to pay the other for something. The second man was shaking his head, "No you don't have to pay me, it was nothing." This back and forth went on for a while until the first man finally threw the money down on the ground in frustration, turned on his heels and walked away. The second man waited for a moment, then picked up the money with a smile and pocketed it before walking away himself.

When Reuven shared the story with me we both laughed, recognizing again how much the rules of social interactions are as much a foreign language as the spoken words, and realizing how much we still had to learn. It

71

was so easy for us to be doing the wrong thing, even when we were trying so hard to figure out what was expected. It felt a little bit like being actors on stage in a play for which we were the only ones who did not have the script.

Finally we had our first guests for Friday night Shabbat dinner, just a few weeks after settling in. This was something Reuven and I had been looking forward to as another step in making a home and a life for ourselves in Cairo, and we invited the two couples who had already made us feel welcome and had been helpful to us in more ways than we could count: Kathy and Paul, and Maureen and Hamdi. Maureen, a friend of a colleague of Reuven's, had first contacted us while we were still back in the States, with the offer to help us find housing. The American daughter of Christian missionaries, Maureen was a highly respected ethnomusicologist specializing in traditional Egyptian music. While she still occasionally lectured on the topic, she had shifted from academics to what might be called arts advocacy. She was currently involved in a variety to efforts to preserve and promote Egyptian folk arts. She had met Hamdi, her Egyptian husband, while studying at the university in Cairo. Hamdi was also involved in the arts as a professional actor, musician, and storyteller. Their two children, Yasmin and Zahir, were teenagers roughly the ages of our sons.

Over dinner the conversation quickly turned to the major news of the week – a ferry disaster in which over one thousand people had drowned. There had been many accusations thrown left and right immediately after the incident. Basima, our apartment owner, had expressed great sadness over this tragedy, noting that it was the poorest of the poor who were the victims, as was so often the case in Egypt. She explained that the company had been cited for the ship being unsafe, but because of the heavy traffic of the season, the company had kept using the ferry. Since our conversation with Basima, other details, even more disturbing, were revealed in the press: even after the fire was reported the captain refused to return to shore, reassuring people that the problem could be dealt with easily. People wearing life jackets were even told to take them off. Efforts by the crew to put out the fire resulted in the water flooding the deck and causing the ship to become unstable and eventually capsize. Remarkably, instead of evacuating passengers in the lifeboats when it became clear the ship was going to sink, it was the captain who was the first to leave, and the crew "jumped ship" in the lifeboats, leaving passengers to fend for themselves.

The company owner promised 15, 000 LE compensation for the family of each victim, saying this was the maximum payment allowed by Egyptian law. According to the papers, the company had been responsible for previous accidents as well but was never punished, since the owner enjoyed immunity from prosecution as a member of the Egyptian Parliament. While the government had promised to conduct an inquiry into the ferry disaster, such promises, according to Maureen, were rarely followed up with effective action.

"The problem here is there is so much corruption and *no* accountability," Maureen said. "Government negligence leads to these terrible tragedies and then there is a lot of talk. The government promises to pay compensation to the victims' families, like in this case, but the families are never paid. No inquiries are ever carried out, or if they are, the announced fines are never collected and no one is ever punished.

"Do you remember the movie theater fire?" she asked Kathy and Paul. They both nodded and Maureen explained: "A few years ago there was a terrible fire in one of the major downtown theaters. Lots of people were killed. The rescue response was so slow and many of the hospital workers were so indifferent that many deaths occurred that could have been avoided. But nothing was done about it."

This was hard for me to imagine, I said, in light of the warmth and helpfulness we experienced everyday from strangers.

"That's different," said Paul. "There is a difference between individuals and an institutional response." The others agreed.

The lack of accountability and the absence of the rule of law — suspended by state of emergency legislation since Mubarak assumed power in 1981 — were among the most disturbing aspects of Egyptian society for all of us sitting around the table. Ironically, given the suspension of the rule of law, individual efforts to respond to others in need could easily backfire. Hamdi told us about a friend who had seen a young woman pedestrian hit by a car and had accompanied her to the hospital. Hamdi's friend found himself sharply questioned by the police about his relationship to the young woman and ultimately arrested and thrown in jail. He had to spend the night trying to stay awake so he would not end up like another man in his cell, bleeding heavily from a razor blade attack by another inmate. This was a police state, we were reminded, and the arbitrary rule of force posed such a threat that people generally tried to blend in and not attract notice of any kind. It was not a system that rewarded individual initiative and civic responsibility.

Hearing such things, I marveled at the fact that people like Kathy and Paul could live here indefinitely. It was clear to me that our being here for only six months allowed us the luxury of focusing on the good, while making do with the seriously problematic aspects of Egyptian society, with the lack of the rule of law protecting basic freedoms being at the top of the list.

Shortly before nine, Hamdi got up and excused himself for having to leave early. As he explained to us earlier, he had promised to attend a small gathering of men in his family to meet a potential marriage partner for his niece. A relative's request must not be refused.

One particularly bright and sunny spring day after Arabic class, I decided to walk the whole way home along Canal Street. I usually walked only part of the way along this quiet and picturesque street, and then turned onto Road Nine to do some errands on my way home. This day, however, I decided to just enjoy the gardens. I walked slowly, taking in the bright purples, reds, and yellows of flowers planted in geometric patterns with water flowing in little canals between the small beds.

A group of gardeners was sitting in a circle, apparently on a break. One of the men was just pouring tea from a pot that had been heating over a small fire. I nodded and said hello and commented on how beautiful the garden was. They returned my greeting and seemed pleased with the compliment. I continued walking, almost exuberant in my enjoyment of the warm sunshine and the bright blue sky of a perfect spring day.

Up ahead, the gardens gave way to a less well-kept grassy stretch. There was a stand of eucalyptus trees, evenly spaced in a way that suggested these too had once been carefully planted. Only when I came right up next to the trees did I notice them: swastikas in red spray paint on the trunk of every tree.

I felt suddenly deflated, like a hot air balloon that had taken a sudden hit. This was not the first time I had seen a swastika in Cairo, but the timing and location made this particular incident more painful. A moment earlier I was still reveling in what I had learned that day in Arabic and the beauty of the Canal Street gardens; the swastikas felt like a betrayal. I wondered if the intent was primarily anti-Israel or anti-Jewish, and then I wondered if that distinction really mattered.

The swastikas appeared to have been painted some time ago. Day after day, for months if not years, people had been walking by and no one had been disturbed enough by the sight of the swastikas to paint over them. This was actually more troubling to me than the fact that someone had painted them on the trees in the first place.

I didn't know who I could ask about the swastikas, but I finally had a friend with whom I could discuss it. Debbie was an American Jew who worked for an NGO and had been living in Cairo for several years. A former college roommate of one of our friends, she had already proven to be a great resource for things to do in Cairo, as well as for understanding some of the experiences we had that left us puzzled. Though we had not yet met, Debbie and I had already had several long phone conversations. I told her about the swastikas and asked her whether or not she was open about being Jewish in Cairo.

"At work, everyone knows I am Jewish," she replied, "both the Egyptians and the Americans. For the most part, I haven't told people, but they all know. And I get questions and comments sometimes about Israel's latest political move, or a Jewish holiday—like I'm 'the resident Jew.'"

Outside of work, she explained, she generally did not share the fact that she was Jewish except with good friends. "It's not worth it," she said. "It's not that I am nervous really, just that there's really nothing to be gained from telling people." I mentioned that I wanted to have more discussions with people to learn how they felt about politics and Israel. "You are far more likely to learn what they really think about Israel if they *don't* know you are Jewish," Debbie quickly responded.

Like others we had talked to, Debbie explained Egyptians' animosity toward Judaism was more an issue of being anti-Israel than being anti-Jewish, but she added that most Egyptians did not distinguish easily between Jews and Israelis. And from her own experience she noted that many Egyptians, whatever their personal views on the subject, were very nervous about being seen talking to an Israeli. This was a police state, she reminded me, and whatever the actual risk was, people were afraid of being thrown in jail if the wrong person saw them talking to an Israeli. "I never invite my Egyptian friends over at the same time as my Israeli friends," she remarked. "They're just too uncomfortable."

Debbie's words made me think of something that had happened just a week ago, when we were returning home on the Metro. We saw Muhammad from the Internet Café standing near the train car door, not too far from where we were sitting. We smiled and raised our hands to wave, but we stopped when Muhammad only made a barely perceptible nod in our direction and then resumed his reading. There was no question that Muhammad had seen us, but he was deliberately acting as if he didn't know us. Was this the same Muhammad who greeted us so warmly and had been so friendly and helpful to us in his store? Perhaps he just wants to be left alone on his day off, I thought, but I was still confused and hurt by his behavior.

When we all got off in Maadi, Muhammad walked right by us and went on ahead, not even making eye contact. Maybe Debbie's comment explained it. We knew that Muhammad thought we might be Jewish or Israeli. Could this be enough to make him uncomfortable demonstrating in public that he knew us and was on friendly terms with us? This new explanation of his behavior could be way off base, I realized, but I did not have a better one.

We finally got together with Debbie for Shabbat lunch at her apartment, only a fifteen-minute walk from where we lived. Debbie, a tall woman in her late forties with shoulder-length brown hair, greeted us warmly when we arrived and immediately directed her attention to the boys, in a natural effort to make them feel at home. She lived on the second floor in a large and airy, very nicely furnished apartment. I was immediately drawn to Debbie's bookshelves. Her work had taken her to South Africa, Tanzania, and El Salvador, and her books reflected her wide-ranging interests. There were novels by South African, Israeli, and Egyptian authors as well as some of my favorite Jewish writers and women writers, books about international development and books about art, which all beckoned to me. I did not know what to pull off the shelf first. "If there's anything you'd like to borrow, feel free," she said, with a generosity of spirit that would prove to be second nature to her. I joined her in the kitchen to finish arranging salads and put them out on the dining room table.

Debbie had also invited a couple she thought we'd like to meet. Steve, one of her friends from work, was a Jew from the States. His wife, Musheera, was a Muslim woman who was born in Tunisia. They had met at college and married shortly after graduation. They were bringing up their two children as Jews, they said, although they celebrated the holidays of both religions at home.

Musheera explained how she had really looked forward to moving to Cairo, excited to live once again in a Muslim country, and expecting to find a cosmopolitan culture like the one she had experienced growing up in Tunisia, but she was deeply disappointed. "Egypt is a far cry from a cosmopolitan society," she said, shaking her head. "It may have been once, but it is the opposite today." "People here are very close-minded and inflexible, even though they are warm and friendly when you first meet them," she continued, very definite in her tone. "You don't know what they really think. They will say something warm and friendly— what they think you want to hear—but the fact is, that is often not what they are really thinking. I know because I really talk to people. I talk to everyone—shopkeepers in the markets downtown, and people we meet through Steve's work. And I also sometimes hear what they say when they don't know I understand Arabic."

Reuven and I asked her if her intermarriage contributed to her discomfort in this society. Musheera recalled a recent incident when someone actually stabbed a man and woman who were kissing in public. "I am really scared sometimes that as a Muslim woman married to a Jew, I could end up the victim of such an attack," she confided.

Over lunch, Debbie mentioned that there had been an interesting lecture at work on "what Egyptians wish Americans knew about Egyptian society before they came to Egypt." "You missed a really good talk," she said to Steve. "That is, until Israel came up and the Egyptians lashed out with the typical anti-Israel tirades." For most Egyptians, she and Steve explained, anti-Israel sentiments were not only based on the past wars and border issues with Israel, or even the Palestinians. Fed by these issues, but taking on a life of its own, were the Egyptians' views (not unlike other Arabs in the Middle East) that Israel was responsible for virtually every evil in the world today. "They believe the *Mossad* (Israeli security) is responsible for everything — the Iraq war, 9/11, even the suicide bombings last year in Cairo," Steve said, shaking his head sadly.

"Even Egyptians who work with you?" I asked. I knew some Egyptians and Arabs believed all these things, but I had assumed ignorance and lack of education contributed to the stereotypes. Egyptians working for an American NGO, I thought, would have a more nuanced view of the West and of Israel.

"Yes, even those working for an NGO," Debbie said. "They are just barraged by the media. You know the joke about the news in Egypt?" she asked. "The daily news is simple—just three items: first, you have a photo op with Mubarak and some foreign dignitary shaking hands. Then you move on to the terrible thing Israel is responsible for that day. Then you conclude with the weather. That's it."

Everyone laughed, but Steve and Debbie went on to banter about the degree to which people's views were shaped by the constant identification of Israel with the evils of the world and both real and imagined threats to Egyptian society. "The government tries to keep the public's eye on how great Mubarak is in maintaining Egypt's standing in the world and keeping Israel in its place," Steve concluded.

Then we turned to Egyptian attitudes toward Americans. Here Musheera used even stronger language. "They *hate* Americans," she said. "They *really hate* us. They may act warmly, but again, that is not what they are really thinking and feeling."

There had certainly been instances in which I too had encountered coldness and even hostility, such as the two men working in the membership office at the Naadi, the health club, but these experiences had been far outnumbered by positive instances of friendliness and warmth. Was it only a facade? Or could it be that the shopkeepers in Maadi were really more open because they interacted so much with foreigners? Was I trying so hard to like the people and the place in which I was living that I was denying the reality of anti-Western and anti-Jewish feeling around me? Or had my experiences just been different so far because we had not yet told people we were Jewish?

A few days later in class, Zayna went over with me the names for lots of different professions. Baker. Secretary. Policeman. Pharmacist.

We talked about Zayna's current work and career goals. Zayna was the first in her family to attend college. She graduated two years earlier from Ein Shams University, one of Cairo's most prestigious universities, with a degree as a Spanish-Arabic translator. She was not able to find work as a translator, so she was teaching Arabic and Spanish while studying for a more advanced degree in translation, hoping that this would increase her chances of finding work in her field.

Zayna did not complain, but listening to her, I recalled articles I had read lamenting the fact that while Egypt has made great advances in making university education available, there is a growing problem of university graduates unable to find work they have been trained for, and in many cases, unable to find any work at all. Even though Zayna had not found full-time work as a translator, she seemed to be doing quite well in pursuing her career. I was impressed with her seriousness and initiative.

79

Still speaking mostly in Arabic, we also talked about the occupations of Zayna's parents and siblings, which proved a great way to learn more about her and her family. Her parents both worked in administrative office jobs. Her sister was studying to be a doctor. It was an extremely demanding course of study, Zayna said, and she studied all the time. Her brother was studying to be a lawyer and was interested in human rights law. Zayna and her siblings were all taking pursuing careers that involved advanced academic work. I would have liked to know more about her brother's interests in human rights and I hoped this would be a topic we could return to, maybe when my Arabic had improved.

"*Inti bitishtaghalee ey*? What kind of work do you do?" she asked me. I struggled to find a way to say what it is I do professionally, without giving it away that I am Jewish. "I am a high school teacher. I teach literature, I said. "What kind of literature?" Zayna asked, "English literature?" At that moment I decided to tell Zayna the truth. I explained that I was Jewish, and a rabbi, and that I taught Jewish texts, like the Torah with early rabbinic commentaries and the Talmud. Zayna seemed to be fine with the fact that I was Jewish and she was interested that I could be a rabbi as a woman.

We talked for a while about the similarities between Arabic and Hebrew and I shared with Zayna some of the words that are similar in Arabic and Hebrew, like *shams* and *shemesh* for "sun" and *baraka* and *berakhah* for "blessing." I also explained that the basic structure of the language and the way of building verbs is very similar in the two languages. Zayna seemed very interested and asked a few questions. I was happy I would finally be able to share this kind of information when it came up in the future.

Returning to Zayna's question about my profession, I asked her for her advice in finding a way to answer people's questions about my work without saying that I was Jewish.

"You can say that you teach Hebrew literature," she said simply. "People will understand that and will not assume you are Jewish. I have a friend who is studying Hebrew literature right now at the university," she told me. That fact intrigued me too and I would have to ask her more about her friend's studies.

80 Then I brought up the whole subject of our having been advised to be quiet about being Jewish and asked for her opinion. She thought about it for a moment and seemed to hesitate. "For most people, I think it would not be a problem," she said, "but I think it is better not to tell everyone. For me, it is not a problem," she added, smiling shyly. I believed her.

Chapter 4
Meeting the Jews of Cairo

راح الخيط والعصفور

Both the line and the bird have gone.
~Arabic Proverb

ON ONE OF OUR SHABBAT AFTERNOON WALKS THROUGH THE
winding streets of Maadi, Reuven and I came across an unexpected sight
just blocks from our apartment.

"Look," Reuven said, pointing across the street. I was so intent on
the pink and white foxglove in the English-style garden in front of us
that I did not see it right away. When I looked up I saw an attractive,
square domed building. Only after a few moments did I notice the
Magen David, the six-pointed Jewish star in the stained glass window
above the front door. A synagogue! Right in our neighborhood! How
had we missed this on our earlier walks? The building itself seemed in
good condition. I wanted to look more closely at the synagogue but
three armed security guards were sitting in front of a wooden booth
to the left of the building. (As we would learn, most Jewish sites in
Cairo were guarded by the police or security.) We asked the guards if
we could walk up to the building and they shook their heads no. When
we inquired if the synagogue was ever open, they shrugged. We walked
around the building looking for any hints about its history or its current status. The single inscription was the name "Meyr Biton" chiseled
into the stone wall above the main door of the synagogue.

Inspired by the find of a synagogue in Maadi, I started reading and discovered that Jews not only had once lived in Maadi—they had been among
the key players responsible for establishing and developing Maadi as one of
Cairo's most beautiful garden communities. In 1888, Egypt's ruler, Khedive
Tewfik, granted a consortium of three Jewish bankers the right to build
and operate Cairo's first railway from downtown Cairo to Helwan, which
opened a year later. Members of these same three Jewish families joined
with a few others to form the Delta Land & Investment Company in 1904

and initiated plans to build the town of Maadi. The company's leadership was roughly half Jewish and half British, paving the way for the decidedly Anglo flavor of Maadi's English-style villas and gardens and the British character of the Naadi, the Maadi Sporting Club, which became the center of Maadi's social and cultural life in the 1920s and 30s.

Meyr Biton, the man whose name was chiseled above the entrance of the Maadi synagogue, was one of the Jews most involved with Maadi's early development — not as a financier, but as its principal landscaper. He was the main force behind the beautiful landscaping for which Maadi was famous. In addition to acquiring and overseeing the planting of the flowering trees along all the streets of Old Maadi, Biton was also responsible for developing the nurseries and orchards that would ensure an ample supply of trees, flowers, and vineyards for the growing garden community.

Far more than just a job, the beautification of Maadi grew to be Meyr Biton's life's passion. Known as "Mr. Mangos and Bananas"—a play on his initials and his passion for fruit trees—Meyr Biton was something of a legend in his own time. He could often be found walking or riding his donkey along the streets of Maadi, overseeing the work of the gardeners. Lucky for the gardeners, Biton could easily be sighted from a distance by his Australian bush hat, as he was a bit of a drill sergeant and had little patience for their resting or napping on the job.

Several of the main streets and squares in "Old Maadi" were named after the Jewish businessmen who had figured so prominently in Maadi's beginnings. All of these streets and squares now have different names. The traffic circle nearest our home proved an interesting case in point. The circle was originally called *Midan Suares*, in honor of the three Suares brothers who had played a leading role in Maadi's development. Cairo's first rail line, built and managed by the consortium, had already come to be known as the "Suares Line." Felix Suares and his two brothers, Joseph and Raphael, were known for their leadership in banking and financing, real estate, and the sugar industry, as well as for developing Egypt's national rail lines.

In recent decades, unaware of the historic role of the Suares brothers, Cairenes started pronouncing *Suares* as *Sawiris*, assuming that the circle was named for the prominent contemporary Egyptian family with that name. Ironically, the Muslim Sawiris family plays a role today that

82

is strikingly parallel to that of the Jewish Suares family almost a century earlier. In both cases, three brothers achieved prominence in finance, real estate, and business, making a major contribution to Egypt's economic development at the same time that they achieved wealth and influence for their families.

The other two members of the original Jewish consortium also had central squares in Maadi named after them. Today's *Midan Mustafa Kamel* in one of the most beautiful parts of Maadi, was originally known as *Midan Menashe*, in honor of Baron Jacques de Menashe. Menashe served on the board of directors of some of Egypt's most influential businesses, including the National Bank of Egypt, the Alexandria Water Company, and the National Insurance Company. Today's *Al Naadi* Avenue and the square bordering on the *Naadi* originally bore the name *Cattaui*, in tribute to Moise Yacoub Cattaui Bey, the third member of the original consortium, and a member of one of the oldest Jewish families in Egypt. Moise Cattaui Bey served as president of the Cairo Jewish Community as his father had done before him. Like the other Jewish men originally honored with popular streets and squares named after them, Cattaui was one of Egypt's best known and respected businessmen, serving in key roles of several companies and banks over the course of his lifetime.

83

Despite the heavy involvement of Jews in the planning, funding, and development of Maadi, few Jews actually lived in Maadi in its early years. Most of the Jewish investors in the Delta Land Company were part of Egypt's *haute Juiverie* and mixed freely with Egypt's highest social circles. Their homes were among the grand villas in the wealthiest parts of Garden City, Zamalek, and Giza, closer to downtown Cairo. Apparently they preferred not to relocate to Maadi, even as their carefully planned garden community started to develop.

It was only in the 1930s that significant numbers of Jews began moving into Maadi. These new Jewish residents were members of Cairo's growing and prosperous middle class. They included the managers and owners of Cairo's leading department stores (some like Hannaux, Cicurel, and Pontremoli, with their original Jewish names still on their facades), bank managers, and insurance brokers, lawyers, and publishers. They spoke fluent French and frequented the Maadi Sports Club. With the growth of this community, the Meyr Biton synagogue was built in 1934, and the area around the synagogue came to be informally known as the "Jewish Quarter of Maadi." By the start of World War II, Maadi's population was almost one-third Jewish.

What was the experience of the Jews of Egypt during World War II and in the years leading up to the creation of the state of Israel, I wondered, and when and under what conditions did Egypt's Jews leave? I realized I did not know the answer to any of these questions and started reading more.

During World War II, by most accounts, the Jews of Egypt fared relatively well. They were spared the government sponsored pogroms experienced by Jews living in Syria, Iraq, and French North Africa. In fact, Egypt proved a haven for thousands of European refugees during the war, including Jews, mostly from Yugoslavia, Czechoslovakia and Austria. Later they were joined by Jewish refugees from Libya, Iran, and Yemen.

There was one point during the war that the Jews of Cairo and the rest of Egypt did suddenly fear for their safety. In 1942, when the German Field Marshall, Edwin Rommel, was heading toward Egypt with his troops, many Jews desperately tried to leave the country. Before their plans could materialize, however, Rommel's troops began their retreat and most of the Jews stayed put. By May 13, 1943, the war in North Africa ended and a special service of thanksgiving was held at the Maadi synagogue, where the shofar was blown, as it was, according to some neighbors, at every service after that until Hitler's defeat.

Meanwhile, the Jews of Egypt faced a growing threat from a different direction. The Muslim Brotherhood, founded in Egypt in 1928 by Hasan al-Banna as one of the first modern Islamic fundamentalist movements, advocated rule by Islamic law in Muslim countries and an end to British involvement in the region. The movement began to rise in popularity in Egypt during the Arab Revolt against Jewish immigration that raged in British Mandate Palestine from 1936 to 1939. The Muslim Brotherhood rallied support for the Arabs of Palestine, framing the issue as both a Muslim and Arab concern.

Increasingly in this period the Muslim Brotherhood and other nationalist and pan-Arab groups in Egypt failed to distinguish between Zionists and Jews in their attacks in the Egyptian press and calls for the boycott of Egyptian Jewish merchants. In April and May of 1938, anti-Zionist demonstrations were held in Cairo and Alexandria in which young Muslims marched through the city centers shouting, "Throw the Jews out of Egypt and Palestine!" By the late 1930s, the leaders of the Muslim Brotherhood and the nationalist group, "Young Egypt," had adopted the antisemitic rhetoric of Hitler and his followers, claiming, for example, that the major political and social problems of the Muslim world were the result of a Jewish conspiracy.

Shortly after the war, on November 2-3, 1945, the Jews of Cairo experienced the first significant incidents of anti-Zionist and anti-Jewish violence. The Muslim Brotherhood, "Young Egypt," and Muslim university students had planned protests against the Balfour Declaration, the official British statement issued after World War I in support of the establishment of a Jewish homeland in Palestine. The demonstrators marched through the city to the central Al Azhar mosque where the leaders conducted the Friday prayers. Soon the crowds numbered in the thousands. The anti-British and anti-Zionist rhetoric of the speeches and slogans stirred up the demonstrators and the chanting marchers soon began throwing stones at stores with Jewish names. In the violent riots and looting that followed, Jewish department stores proved among the main targets; the downtown Ashkenazic synagogue was also looted and burned. The Egyptian government and the press roundly condemned the violence, but even this reassuring official response could not undo the memory of violence, or of the crowds in the streets yelling "Down with the Jews! No Jews from now on! Long Live Palestine!"

At the same time, attempts to organize on behalf of a Jewish homeland in Palestine in the 1940s met a mixed response from Egypt's Jews. In the face of the increasing nationalist and Islamic fundamentalist enthusiasm, even before the riots of November 1945, Jewish leaders were concerned that Zionist activity might put their communities at risk. Those who supported the Zionist efforts to recruit and organize for *aliyah* and train Egyptian Jewish youth in self-defense and Hebrew, wanted these activities to be discreet. As a result, the clandestine efforts to smuggle young Jews out of Egypt over land and sea were all on a small scale. From the end of World War II to 1947, only several hundred Egyptian Jews along with nearly one thousand Jewish refugees were transferred from Egypt to Palestine. Many of these Jewish refugees had been placed in special camps under U.N. auspices in Egypt.

The concerns of Egypt's Jewish leaders were borne out. In the days leading up to the establishment of the state of Israel, the Egyptian press began to question the loyalty of Egypt's Jews more vociferously and warned the Jews against any involvement in support of the Zionist "colonization" of Palestine. After arrests of Jews, police raids and searches of fifty homes and hotels in Cairo, subsequent concern and rumors prompted King Farouq to publicly declare in early May that the majority of Egypt's Jews were loyal to the country. Farouq insisted that measures were only being taken against Zionist activists.

On May 14, 1948, David Ben Gurion, Israel's first prime minister, formally declared the establishment of Israel as a Jewish state, based on the Jews' national rights to a homeland and the U.N. resolution of November 29, 1947, which had partitioned Palestine into Arab and Jewish states. Immediately, five of the seven member nations of the Arab League, including Egypt, invaded Israel. Over the next several weeks, about one thousand Jews were arrested and detained for association with Zionist activities, or because they were suspected of being communists; some were never clearly linked with either movement. Many of those arrested were placed (along with communists and members of the Muslim Brotherhood) in internment camps near Cairo, Alexandria, or in the Sinai, where the sanitation and living conditions were extremely poor. By the end of 1949, most of the interned Jews had been freed, but on the condition that they leave the country and never return.

From late May until early 1949, while Egypt and Israel were at war and martial law was in effect in Egypt, the assets of about seventy Jewish individuals and firms in Cairo and Alexandria were seized by the government. Included were high profile businesses such as Jewish-owned department stores in both cities. Most of the businessmen targeted had been active Zionists, but others had no prior involvement in Zionist efforts. The largest Jewish banks and firms were not sequestered, presumably because of the efforts of most of Egypt's wealthiest Jewish families to distance themselves from Zionist activities. While this measure proved temporary, it added to the economic insecurity of the Jews. Many Jews had already been affected by the Company Law of 1947, which required all companies to employ a minimum of 75 per cent Egyptian nationals. Even though most of Egypt's Jews in 1948 had been born in Egypt and many had been there for generations, only about 10,000 of them were actually Egyptian citizens. Roughly 30,000 had kept or obtained foreign nationality, and 40,000 lacked any citizenship at all. While the Company Law did not target Jews specifically, many Jews suddenly found themselves ousted from their jobs as a result of the new quotas.

Following Israel's declaration of statehood and the ensuing war between Egypt and Israel, there were several outbreaks of violence against Jews in Cairo. In June 1948, a bombing in the Karaite section of the Jewish quarter destroyed a dozen homes, killing twenty-two Jews and wounding forty-one. On July 15, Israeli planes bombed a residential neighborhood in Cairo, resulting in many casualties and the destruction of many homes. The fact that this attack came during Ramadan, while people were gathered to break the fast, undoubtedly contributed to the anger of local residents who marched through the Jewish quarter, looting several stores and homes. Four days later, after the incorrect reporting of a second Israeli attack in Cairo, the famous Jewish-owned Cicurel and Orteco department stores downtown suffered severe damage in a large explosion. The blast was so strong that about five hundred other stores in the area were also damaged and several people were killed.

While some attribute the government's failure to respond vigorously to the violence to its own anti-Zionist or anti-Jewish sentiments, others point to the government's fear of the Muslim Brotherhood's growing power as the true cause of their inaction. The Muslim Brotherhood had moved to the forefront of the Arab nationalist movement that was then gaining momentum throughout the Arab World. While its leadership espoused non-violence, certain factions were turning to an ideology of violence and the movement as a whole was perceived as a growing threat to the monarchy. It is worth noting that the Egyptian government itself did not actively foment anti-Jewish sentiment or violence, as was the case in some other Arab countries. Organized Zionist activity became illegal but most Jewish communal institutions such as schools and hospitals were allowed to function, though some were required to share the names and addresses of their members with government officials.

While about 22,000 largely lower middle-class Jews left Egypt between 1948-51, most of Maadi's Jews chose to stay. The next several years saw enormous political changes in Egypt. The 1952 Revolution brought down the monarchy and raised up Abdel Nasser, who, over the next two years, secured his power base and eventually became Egypt's president, a position he held until his death in 1970. During the republic's first two years, however, Muhammad Naguib served as president. Naguib made several overtures to the Jewish population, occasionally visiting synagogues and speaking warmly to the gathered crowds. Many Jews who had considered emigrating were reassured by Naguib's words and actions and decided to stay in Egypt.

Nevertheless, from 1952 to 1956, approximately 10,000 Jews left Egypt, with half heading for Israel and half for other locations. Several factors rather than a single one probably influenced the decision to emigrate. In 1954, several young Egyptian Jews, working on a mission directed by Israeli agents that came to be known as "Operation Susannah," were arrested in Cairo and Alexandria and charged with espionage and sabotage. In this covert operation, the young Zionists set bombs at several foreign-owned sites (there were no injuries or deaths) in order to cast doubt on the stability of the Egyptian government and forestall British withdrawal. The trial received a great deal of international attention and concluded with two men condemned to execution, two acquitted, and the rest sentenced to long prison terms; (prior to the trial, one man was tortured to death in prison and another committed suicide). "Operation Susannah" and the subsequent trial contributed to Jews being increasingly viewed as potential subversives in Egypt, and to the Jews' increasing uncertainty about their long-term security in Egypt. At the same time, the nationalization of businesses under Nasser resulted in some of Egypt's most prosperous Jews losing their businesses and others losing their jobs. For many of the Jews who left during these years, financial loss seems to have been a primary factor.

By far the largest wave of Jewish emigration from Egypt followed the Sinai War of 1956. In 1957, citing the "Triple Aggression" of Israel, Britain, and France in the Sinai, Egypt expelled all French and British nationals, including Jews with passports from either of these countries. While these expulsions did not target Jews per se, economic measures issued during this same time period did. In the first months after the outbreak of war, over 500 Jewish-owned businesses were sequestered and their bank accounts were frozen; over 800 additional businesses managed by Jews were blacklisted and had their assets frozen. In addition, legislation was passed in 1956 that enabled the government to deny Egyptian citizenship to people classified as Zionists; by 1958, the language of the new laws and speeches of government officials no longer distinguished between "Zionist" and "Jew." While there was no violence directed against the Jews, as had been the case in 1948, these economic and political measures made staying in Egypt less tenable for Egyptian Jews of all classes.

Within a few months, 14,000 Jews left Egypt and a large percentage of Maadi's Jews were among them. Meyr Biton's widow, Regina Chamma Levi, who had been responsible for the synagogue, was deported as a French national. Over just a few weeks, the synagogue went from being open several times a week for services to suddenly needing visitors to form a *minyan*, the traditional ten-men quorum required for prayer. Many of the Jews who left in the wake of the Sinai War had to leave behind their assets; they arrived in Israel and other countries totally impoverished and were never allowed to reclaim their property or its value.

Another 19,000 to 22,000 Jews left Egypt over the next several years as both official and unofficial economic harassment of Jews continued, making it increasingly difficult for Jews to practice as doctors, lawyers, or engineers, or earn a living in business. Like those expelled and pressured to leave before them, they were issued exit documents stamped "one way—no return." By the early 1960s Maadi's Jews had virtually all left and the synagogue ceased to be open on a regular basis.

Only about 7,000 Jews were still in Egypt in 1967 when once again, war broke out with Israel. The Egyptian authorities responded to the renewed conflict by arresting and imprisoning most of the Jewish men, spurring a final wave of emigration after which only about 700 Jews remained in Egypt. When the last of the Jewish men were released in 1970, they and their remaining family members were forced to leave the country, renouncing their right to return. The number of Jews living in Egypt continued to dwindle until at present, most estimates put the number at under 100. But the Maadi synagogue, closed officially in 1967, did not remain closed indefinitely.

In 1981, two years after the conclusion of a peace treaty between Egypt and Israel and the opening of the Israeli Embassy in Cairo, the first bar mitzvah in almost thirty years was conducted in the Maadi synagogue for the son of an Israeli diplomat, Zvi Mazel. Over the next few years, Maadi continued to attract Israelis working in their Cairo embassy and soon, the Meyr Biton Synagogue once again was open for Yom Kippur services. I assumed this was still the case and wondered if the syna-

89

gogue was ever open on Shabbat, hoping that we would have the chance to attend services there while we were in Egypt.

A few days after our discovery, I called the Israeli Embassy to see if they knew if the synagogue in Maadi was ever open for services. The secretary connected me with Elie Antebi, the Israeli Consul General to Alexandria, and we had a very pleasant conversation in Hebrew. Elie was interested in our backgrounds and why we were in Cairo and he seemed pleased that we would be there for another four months. He explained that he worked in Alexandria only two or three days a week and the rest of the time at the embassy in Cairo. Like us, he lived in Maadi. Elie informed me that because of the number of embassy employees living in Maadi who were interested in attending services, the synagogue had been open for Shabbat services the year before on a regular basis, but it was once again closed. Elie was an Orthodox Jew and the synagogue in Maadi was the only one close enough for him to walk to. He was not sure of the reasons for the synagogue's recent closure. This, he said, had been the decision of Carmen Weinstein, the president of Cairo's Jewish Community Council. Elie seemed to be making an effort to speak carefully and not to cast blame. He noted that there were various constituencies that wanted different things. "What constituencies?" I asked.

"The main synagogue in Cairo is the Adly Street synagogue downtown, *Sha'ar Hashamayim*, ("The Gates of Heaven"). It's a beautiful synagogue, open for most of the holidays, and sometimes for Shabbat." This was the synagogue, Elie explained, where the few elderly Egyptian Jewish women who were still alive attended services on the holidays. These women were the only real remnant of the Jewish community that had thrived here in Cairo before the massive exodus in the late 1950s. Elie thought that Carmen had some concern about fewer people coming to the Adly Street synagogue when the Maadi synagogue was open. On the other hand, Elie explained, most of the Jews who wanted to attend services in Maadi like himself, did not travel on Shabbat, and were not able to get to the Adly Street synagogue. "So, there are people here who would like the Maadi synagogue to be open every week. But I don't know the whole story," he concluded diplomatically.

Before hanging up, Elie invited us to join him on Friday night for Shabbat dinner. I accepted, pleased that we would be able to meet him so soon and thinking how nice it would be to celebrate Shabbat with other Jews. I was eager to hear more about his experience as an Israeli living in Cairo.

Two days later, as the sun was setting, Reuven, the boys, and I walked over to Elie's apartment in Maadi for Shabbat dinner.

"I'm really looking forward to speaking Hebrew," Noam said, as we walked at a fairly good clip. He noted with some surprise that trying to learn Arabic had made him appreciate how well he spoke Hebrew. Amir agreed.

When we arrived at the apartment building, I looked around, expecting to see security guards. The Israeli Ambassador lived a few blocks from us in Maadi and the streets around his home were cordoned off to create a security zone of several square blocks, with road barriers and three or four security police at every intersection. There had to be security here too, but I didn't see any sign of it.

We walked upstairs and were greeted by Elie at the door.

"*Berukhim haba'im, tikansu*, welcome and come on in," he said warmly, shaking our hands and motioning us to come in at the same time. Elie was a slightly built man in his early fifties, unassuming, and a bit shy.

"I would like you to meet my good friend, Yoram, one of the Embassy's press attaches. He will be joining us tonight." Yoram, a tall man with a slightly graying hair, greeted us with a firm handshake. Even as we were standing, exchanging pleasantries, one of Yoram's several pagers went off. He quietly excused himself and returned a few minutes later. The evening would be punctuated by Yoram frequently having to excuse himself to take a call. I was curious about the kinds of issues he might be dealing with, but did not want to be intrusive, so I didn't ask.

While Yoram was on the phone, Elie showed us pictures of his family. After years of living abroad as a diplomatic family, Elie's wife and children had decided to pass on Cairo and were now living in Jerusalem. Elie tried to return home every two weeks for Shabbat and every few months, his wife came to Egypt.

Elie, it turned out, loved to cook, and he and his housekeeper, Mary, had prepared a sumptuous feast, Middle Eastern style, with lots of colorful salads and hot dishes. Over dinner, we kept returning to Elie and Yoram's experiences living as Israelis in Egypt. They both spoke Arabic fluently. Elie, born and raised in Beirut, had moved to Israel when he was fifteen. Yoram, whose family was originally from Iraq, was born in Israel

91

but heard Arabic spoken around him all through his youth. Both men were enthusiastic about their experiences living in Egypt and like us, had found the people to be very warm.

We wondered out loud what Elie and Yoram thought about how public we should be about being Jewish.

"I don't think it's anything to worry about. I am totally open about being Jewish and Israeli, and I have never had a problem," said Elie.

"Is it possible that people are just being polite, or that they're intimidated by the fact that you're a diplomat?" I asked.

"Could be," he admitted.

"Do you normally walk around with a *kippah* (yarmulke)?"

"No, that's a good point. I guess it's probably best for you to not make it obvious that you are Jewish. But if it comes up, I don't think you need to hide it."

Yoram disagreed and thought we could be completely open about being Jewish.

"I was once in a museum speaking Hebrew with Israeli visitors and an Egyptian stood next to me for a minute, listening, obviously curious.

"'You're Israeli?' he asked finally. I nodded.

"'Hmph,' he grunted with disdain. 'Ariel Sharon.'

"I looked him straight in the eye. 'Egyptian? Hmph… Mubarak.'

"The man looked at me in surprise and then burst out laughing. He clapped me on the shoulder and before we parted, we had a real conversation and exchanged numbers. We're still friends today."

Conversation turned to the Jewish community of almost 80,000 that had once prospered in Egypt, and the radical changes that had swept Egyptian society during the 1950s. Yoram and Elie lamented that Cairo had once been an open, international, and cosmopolitan society and in that environment Jews had thrived individually and as a community, contributing enormously to Egyptian society culturally and economically. It was after Nasser came to power, nationalizing industry and introducing more state control in the 1950s, that most foreign nationals, such as the British and French emigrated, leaving behind an increasingly homogeneous and closed society. Most of the Jews of Egypt left as part of this exodus, Elie and Yoram claimed, not because of the creation of the state of Israel, as many people today assume. Even without the Arab-Israeli conflict, they suggested, these Jews still would have left Egypt.

Yoram pointed out that one particular event in Israel's history had dire consequences for the Jews of Egypt. During the Six Day War in 1967, Egypt's military police had rounded up and jailed most of the Jewish men who were still living in Cairo, keeping them in prison for three years. During this time, most of the Jews still in Egypt left. When they were eventually released, these Jewish men and any remaining family they had were also forced to leave Egypt.

As Yoram and Elie noted themselves, not everyone agrees with this narrative. The classic "Zionist" narrative popularized within Israel and assumed by many Jews today is that Jews suffered centuries of second-class citizenship and persecution in Egypt as in the rest of the Arab world, from the time of Muhammad on, parallel in ways to the persecution they suffered in the Christian world. According to this view, the Arab countries were alike in expelling their Jewish populations after the creation of the Jewish state in 1948, and this was but the climax of a long period of persecution. This narrative supported the Zionist view that Jews can never enjoy full security and safety anywhere in the world without a Jewish homeland to which they can look for refuge when necessary. At the same time, there was irony in the fact that in the Arab world, the very establishment of the Jewish homeland prompted the greatest persecution.

Egyptians often voice a markedly different narrative, arguing that Jews thrived in Egypt over the centuries without the persecution they encountered in Christian Europe, and in fact sought out refuge in Egypt and other parts of the more tolerant Muslim Arab world to escape the worst periods of persecution by Christians, including the Holocaust. It was only with the creation of the state of Israel and the ensuing wars between Egypt and Israel, they argue, that Jews suspected of Zionist loyalty were targeted as enemies of the state. Even then, this narrative claims, most Jews continued to prosper and chose to remain in Egypt until they lost their jobs and businesses as a result of Nasser's policies of nationalization in 1952. The Jews who left Egypt, according to this narrative, did so by their own choice, not because they were forced out, and they often chose to settle in Paris and New York rather than Israel.

Both these narratives have their shortcomings with the truth lying somewhere in between. Jews generally fared far better under Islam than

Christianity, but they still were second-class citizens and sometimes suffered greater persecution including occasional violence. The creation of the Jewish state led to a "Second Exodus" of Jews from Egypt and the other Arab countries, but the particulars differed significantly from one country to another. While most of the Jews of Iraq left between 1948 and 1951, the majority of the Jews in Egypt and Morocco only left later, after the 1956 and 1967 wars. In some cases Jews were expelled; in others they chose to leave for a whole variety of reasons, including, but not limited to, increased persecution. At times, the pressure on Jews became so intense that the line between expulsion and choice was indeed very thin.

For example, while most of the Jews who left Egypt technically "chose" to do so, increasingly this choice was the result of extreme economic hardship and in the face of arrests and imprisonment, all the result of their being Jews.

I found it interesting that Elie and Yoram, representatives of Israel, had articulated a nuanced point of view that differed from the classic "Zionist" narrative, and I was curious to know how Carmen Weinstein viewed the recent history of Jews in Egypt that she herself had lived through. I was already planning on trying to meet with Carmen, and this conversation further piqued my interest in the recent history of Egypt's Jews.

Our conversation with Elie and Yoram turned to relations between Israel and Egypt today. "I would like to see more *interaction* between Israelis and Egyptians. That's why we are here, of course," Elie said, motioning to Yoram and himself. "Egyptians and Israelis today are separated by their stereotypes and their fear—from both sides. We're trying to bring more Israelis here so they can experience Egyptian society themselves, and meet Egyptians face to face, not just in their heads. And we need to bring more Egyptians to Israel. When people meet each other and get to know each other, even a little bit—it changes everything."

Yoram responded with a nod and mentioned that he had attended the African Cup Finals together with some other Israelis.

"It was really an experience," he said. "We were standing in the bleachers, cheering the Egyptian team on, along with everyone else. The open pride and excitement that was erupting all around us was contagious. It was an important moment for us as Israelis, to see this kind of Egyptian nationalism. And they seemed to welcome our being there, and to have us join in. It was something special for all of us."

Yoram was pleased that at least one major Egyptian magazine had reported on the presence of Israelis at the game and that many Egyptians had read about it.

"We need more things like this," he remarked. "Egyptian society is at a critical juncture. In another twenty years or so, I think, we will all look back and see this time we're living in now as the turning point—in a positive sense. There is change in the air... questioning.... We—and the Egyptians—cannot really see where they are heading with any clarity, because everything is in flux. But I am optimistic," he concluded with a smile. Hearing him speak with such conviction made us feel hopeful too.

Right after Shabbat, I called Carmen Weinstein, introduced myself, and asked if I could meet with her to learn more about Cairo's Jewish community. Carmen perked up when she heard I was a rabbi, and at her suggestion, we arranged to meet two days later at the Maadi synagogue. I wondered if I would have the chance to see the inside of the synagogue.

It was pleasantly warm the afternoon we met and Carmen suggested we sit outside for tea. Carmen is a confident and energetic woman in her seventies and speaks excellent English. Trailed by her little white dog, she led the way to a white plastic table and chairs in the shade, and in Arabic, asked a man whom I assumed was a personal assistant, to bring us some tea and cookies. He nodded and disappeared into the cottage that was next to us, on the synagogue grounds. Carmen is often referred to as the "gatekeeper" of the Jewish community here, and she gave the impression of being used to being in charge.

After only a minimum of small talk, Carmen asked whether I could read the *Megillah* (the Biblical book of Esther that is written by a scribe on a parchment scroll) for the Jewish community's Purim celebration at *Sha'ar Hashamayim*, the synagogue downtown. Purim is a festive Jewish spring holiday with a Mardi Gras flavor, built around the black humor tale recalling the deliverance of the Jews of the Persian Empire from an evil plot to destroy them. It would be an honor, I told her, and Reuven would probably be happy to read as well. Carmen seemed pleased.

The tea and cookies arrived and Carmen shooed her dog away. Over the next hour, she proved very willing to talk about the history of the Jewish community and even more interested in sharing her thoughts about its present character and needs. She was more reticent when it came to talking about herself. But I was curious about Carmen's own experience, as she had come of age in the 1940s and early 50s, arguably the most turbulent period of modern Jewish history in Cairo. Born and raised in Cairo, Carmen was part of the small minority of Jews who chose, even after most other Jews had left, to stay in Egypt. I hoped to learn more about her experiences and would try to return to them later in the conversation.

Carmen is only the second woman to serve as president of Cairo's Jewish community. She succeeded her mother, Esther Weinstein, who served as the first female president for eight years until she passed away in 2004. As president, Carmen divides her time between responding to the needs of the thirty or so elderly women who make up the core of the Cairo Jewish community, and fulfilling her responsibilities as the main spokesperson and representative of the Jewish community. She also manages the community's website and newsletter, "Bassatine News," which is a major source of information about Cairo's Jewish community and responds to a regular stream of inquiries about the community and individuals' efforts to locate their family records. She welcomes visitors like myself and arranges for people to visit the synagogues and Jewish cemetery. But perhaps her greatest passion is her work advocating and raising funds to preserve and maintain the physical heritage of the Jewish community in Cairo—the synagogues, the Jewish cemetery, and the libraries in two synagogues. To this end, Carmen is in regular negotiations with Egypt's Supreme Antiquities Department while also trying to raise funds from abroad.

As we started talking, Carmen was quick to note that throughout our long history, Jews have always lived in Egypt. According to the Hebrew Bible, even our earliest ancestors, Abraham and Sarah, lived in Egypt temporarily when Canaan suffered a famine. Three generations later, in the face of an even greater famine, Joseph brought his entire family to Egypt and it was there that the Hebrews soon developed into a nation forged by the experience of oppression and slavery. When, several hundred years later, Moses led the Israelites to liberation and the long journey back to Canaan, some Israelites stayed behind, and many believe that Jewish life continued in Egypt virtually uninterrupted to this day.

Carmen pointed out that, in addition to Biblical writings, the earliest archaeological evidence of a Jewish community outside of Israel was found in Egypt, on Elephantine Island off the coast of Aswan, dating back to the eclipse of Pharaonic Egypt. Legal documents and letters in Aramaic found there suggest that Jewish soldiers were serving in a military installation during the Persian occupation of Egypt in the fifth and early fourth century B.C.E., probably guarding the Nubian border. We were planning to visit Luxor and Aswan with the boys during their spring break and I made a mental note to go to Elephantine.

I asked Carmen what she thought was the richest period of Jewish history in Egypt, and after only a moment's thought she answered, "I would have to say, the time of Maimonides." Maimonides, one of the greatest Jewish scholars of all time, was the *nagid*, or leader of the Jewish community in Cairo in the twelfth century. There were over seven thousand Jews in Egypt at that time. Then, as now, most Jews lived in Cairo. The Maimonides synagogue, including the *beit midrash*, ("house of study"), where Maimonides used to teach, still stands and is open to visitors in *Harat al-Yahud*, the old Jewish Quarter.

The Cairo Geniza, a repository discovered by the Cambridge scholar Solomon Schechter in 1896 contained documents dating back to Maimonides' time and earlier. A virtual treasure trove for historians, the Geniza opened a unique window onto Jewish life in the Middle Ages. The Geniza was first uncovered in the Ben Ezra synagogue in what is now the Cairo's Coptic quarter. Later, other parts of the Geniza were found discovered in the Jewish cemetery. A *geniza* (Hebrew for "hiding place") is a storage place for any old documents or books that according to Jewish law could not be thrown away or destroyed because they contained the name of God. Even ordinary letters and official papers that contained God's name simply in a formal greeting or expression, would have been saved in a *geniza*, which would have been stored typically in a synagogue attic or basement, or buried in a cemetery.

The *Cairo Geniza* stands out as a unique find because it contains such a wide range of documents, both religious and secular, primarily from the tenth to thirteenth centuries. Mixed in with marriage contracts and leases, rabbinical court records and personal letters, shopping lists, and even children's written homework assignments have been discovered. These documents offer us glimpses into the daily life of Egypt's Jews during the Middle Ages. They attest to the important role Jews played in the economic and cultural life of Egypt and to the good relations that existed between Arabs and Jews in that period.

The twentieth century, Carmen noted, achieved another kind of "Golden Age" for the Jews of Egypt -- a time of great prosperity, when many Jews were not only comfortable, but actively contributing to the economic, cultural, and intellectual life of Egypt. This was the "cosmopolitan" era of Egypt with a decidedly European flavor, a world many of the Jews who left Egypt never stopped missing with wistful nostalgia.

"What was Jewish life like in Cairo when you were a child?' I asked Carmen. "The Jewish community here in Egypt was not very religious," she responded. "We kept the holidays, the traditions, but people didn't keep kosher with all the details." There were several Jewish schools where Hebrew was taught in addition to a "regular" curriculum, she noted, and non-Jews attended as well as Jews. Typical of Jews of her class and background, Carmen grew up speaking French at home and attending an English-speaking school. It was only later in life that she learned Arabic.

On the question of the choices made by Egyptian Jews from the late 1940s through the 1960s, whether to stay or to go, Carmen said that most Jews who left did so after the 1952 Revolution and mostly because they could not find work. Her family was fortunate to have owned a printing press and stationery business that was quite successful and therefore they had no need to leave. She believes that were it not for economic reasons, namely, the post-revolution reorganization of the economy, many more Egyptian Jews would have elected to stay in Egypt.

We soon found our conversation moving from some of the peak moments of Jewish history in Cairo to the present reality of the surviving Egyptian Jewish community. Just how many Jews still live in Cairo and do they constitute a "community" are in fact questions of controversy today that prompt different answers, depending on whom you ask. Carmen maintains that there are about one hundred Jews in Cairo, and that this population certainly constitutes a community. She notes that among this number there are those who are quite assimilated and do not actively affiliate with the Jewish community. The core, she estimates, is made up of about thirty elderly women, many of whom are physically ailing and not well off financially. Most of these women, having stayed in Egypt because they were married to non-Jews, are now widowed and living alone. Carmen sees to it that their basic needs are met and also raises funds for

the women to escape Cairo's stifling heat for a week or two in the summer and vacation in Alexandria's cooler breezes by the sea.

In sharp contrast to Carmen, some of the Jews who left Egypt during
the "Second Exodus" and now live in the U.S., France, and Israel, when
asked about the Jewish community in Egypt, ask "What community?"
They point to the dwindling numbers of Jews still living in Cairo and Alexandria and claim that the local Egyptian Jewish community will soon
cease to exist at all, and even now, is not a viable community.

At the heart of this debate is the question of what should be done
with the valuable artifacts of Jewish life that remain in Cairo. Carmen
noted that this dispute goes back to at least 1997, when she received
a letter from the Historical Society of Jews (H.S.J.E.) from Egypt, informing her that a delegation would soon be arriving in Egypt to take
the Torah scrolls and holy books to their rightful place in New York.
The H.S.J.E. staked its claim to the artifacts on the fact that with only
a few elderly Jews who cannot even make a minyan without outside
visitors, no true Jewish community can be said to exist in Egypt any
longer. They argued that the Torah scrolls and other artifacts of the
Egyptian Jewish community rightfully belong to and should be used
by the Egyptian Jews now living in Paris and New York and Israel.
Alternatively, they argued, these sacred objects should be placed in a
museum in New York, Paris, or Israel, devoted to the history of the
Egyptian Jewish community, but not in Cairo, where almost no Jews
would ever see them.

This written request of March 1997 catapulted Carmen, her mother,
and others in the Jewish community into action. Carmen had long been
involved in efforts to preserve the physical heritage of the community,
beginning with her activism on behalf of the Jewish Bassatine Cemetery. In fact, in the previous year, a heated debate had erupted among
Cairo's Jewish communal leadership over the issue of preserving Cairo's synagogues and their artifacts. Emile Russo, then president of the
community, had apparently viewed the sale of synagogue properties
and their artifacts as a useful mechanism to raise income for the Jewish
community. Growing frustration and anger over Russo's moves, allegedly
made without consultation with the board, led to an impromptu board
meeting in 1996 at the Adly Street synagogue while Russo was away on
a cruise. (A newspaper article at the time described it as a "coup" in the

Jewish Community Council.) The members present at the meeting voted unanimously to overturn the Council's statutes and for the first time in recorded history, allow women to serve on the board of directors. Next, they elected Carmen's mother, Esther, to serve as the Council's president, and Carmen to serve as Vice President. Now, the preservation of the remaining twelve of the original thirty-nine synagogues and their artifacts, together with the Bassatine Cemetery, moved to the center of the Jewish Community Council's agenda.

100

When Carmen received the letter informing her of the intentions of the H.S.J.E., her response was immediate and brief. She informed the senders that unless they had the signatures of the Egyptian authorities, they would not be able to take any of the Torah scrolls or *sefarim* ("religious books") out of the country because they had been registered with the Antiquities Department and Ministry of Culture.

Since then, the debate has continued to rage in public and private between the organizations representing Egyptian Jews living in the U.S., France, and Israel on one hand, and the communal leadership of the Jews still residing in Egypt, on the other, over whether the shrinking remnant of elderly Jews still living in Egypt constitutes a community, and where the artifacts truly belong. On both questions, Carmen's position is clear.

"Jews have always and *will* always live in Egypt," she confidently maintains. Carmen believes that the dwindling number of Jews that we see in Cairo at present is but a low point in the constant swing of the pendulum of history and that at some point in the future we will see a new upswing in Jewish numbers. She wants Cairo's twelve remaining synagogues maintained, not only as a testament to the Jews who lived there in the past, but in the hopes that they will one day be used again by Jews. In addition, she would very much like to see a museum in Cairo dedicated to telling the story of the history of the Jewish community in Egypt and the history of Egyptian tolerance.

"It is very important for people here to know and remember that there used to be a large Jewish community here that made important contributions to every aspect of Egyptian life—the arts, the economy, politics—everything," she argues. "People also need to learn about past periods of tolerance and respect for different national and religious groups. It is an important part of our heritage as Egyptian Jews."

I asked Carmen if she had ever experienced antisemitism directly. "Not really," she answered. "Antisemitism here is directed against Israel, not the Jewish religion. And let's face it — Israel has done some terrible things." After a moment's pause, she added, "The problem is that Egyptians don't always distinguish between Israel and Judaism. And whenever things are bad in Israel, they are bad for us here."

Her confident air returned immediately as Carmen summed up her view of Egyptian-Jewish relations. "The problem really is one of ignorance. It is like the opera," she declared. Carmen smiled at my quizzical look and proceeded to explain her comment with a story.

"One day I was talking with a young Egyptian woman who worked for me and I made some reference to the opera.

"'Opera? What is opera?' she asked, 'Is that when people yell and scream while they are singing?' This generation doesn't know anything about opera. And they don't know anything about Jews. Most of them have never met a Jew. If you haven't experienced something yourself, you don't really know what it is. You only know what you read in the newspapers and see on television, and that's a problem. Most Egyptians' entire knowledge about Judaism is based on what they have seen and heard about Israel and the Jews on television and in the newspapers. I think if they suspended the media for ten years, then we would see peace in the world!"

As our conversation began to wind down, I asked Carmen if it was possible for us to go inside the Maadi synagogue for a quick look.

"It's not possible," she said. "It is not safe to go inside—we need to make some repairs." Did she think the repairs would be made in the next few months, I asked. "Perhaps, but I do not think so."

I mentioned that Reuven and I wanted to see Maimonides' synagogue and the Kapucci synagogue in the old Jewish quarter, and the Karaite synagogue as well.

"Just call me a few days before you want to go and I will arrange for someone to meet you at the Karaite synagogue," Carmen generously offered. "And in the case of the other two, I will have someone take you to the Jewish quarter and inside the synagogues."

We made our way back to the gate and said our good-byes.

"Let me know soon about Purim," Carmen reminded me. I assured her that I would.

A few days later, I called Carmen to say that we would read the *Megillah* on Purim and also to arrange for us to see the Karaite synagogue. Reuven and I weren't sure how interesting this would be for the boys so we had decided to go on our own.

The Karaites still exist today as a little known community of Jews who maintain their roots date back to the Second Temple period, when what would eventually become "Rabbinic Judaism" was beginning to develop through the efforts of the Pharisees. According to the Karaites, rabbinic interpretation, or the "Oral Torah," veered too far from the content as well as the binding authority of the written Torah. They rejected the authority of the Talmud and the entire rabbinic enterprise that had become the central guiding force of normative Jewish life. While the Karaites developed their own interpretations of the Torah in their attempt to follow its laws over the centuries, any practices later determined to be in violation of the written Torah, would be rejected. For example, the early Karaites prohibited the kindling of lights on Friday evening to be used on Shabbat because of their understanding of the Torah's prohibition against the kindling of fire on Shabbat; rabbinic authorities ruled that the kindling of such lights in advance of Shabbat was permitted because light was necessary for the joy of Shabbat. (Later Karaite authorities reversed their earlier prohibition for the same reason; to this day, Karaites remain divided on the issue.)

The term *Kara'im* was first applied to the followers of 'Anan ben David in Jerusalem in the eighth century. By the ninth century, Cairo had become a major Karaite center, even though a number of important rabbis had declared Karaite doctrines to be heresy. Despite this official censure, over the next several hundred years, the Karaites continued to thrive, at times even outnumbering the Rabbanite Jews in Cairo. By the modern period however, the numbers of Karaites had declined and in 1948, only 5,000 of the 80,000 Jews in Egypt considered themselves Karaites. Despite tensions between Karaite and Rabbanite approaches to Jewish law and practice, Karaites have always been recognized as Jews by both the Jews and non-Jews of Egypt.

The Karaites of Egypt were among the Jews who had most assimilated into Arab culture in Cairo. Some of the Karaites' distinctive practices seemed to flow as much from their integration into the culture and norms of Arab society as from their understanding of the Torah. For example, the

Karaites believed Jews should remove their shoes when they prayed. While they cited the example of Moses removing his sandals before approaching the Burning Bush, undoubtedly they were also influenced by the parallel Muslim practice. Similarly, Karaite synagogues, like mosques, consisted of a large room with rugs instead of chairs for people to sit on. In fact, Egyptians sometimes referred to Karaites as "Muslim Jews."

The Karaite community of Cairo was centered in *Harat al-Yahud*, the Jewish Quarter, the one place in Cairo where most Jews spoke Arabic in their homes and schools. Many members of the community worked as goldsmiths and jewelers, and by the twentieth century, those who had become most prosperous moved into the more middle-class and cosmopolitan neighborhoods of Heliopolis and Abbasiyya. We wondered if any of this historic community still remained in Cairo.

103

Following Carmen's directions, Reuven and I took a taxi from the nearest Metro stop to the synagogue. We were looking for a military hospital next to which, Carmen said, we would find the synagogue. While we were still looking for the hospital, I suddenly found myself looking up at a huge *Magen David* ("Jewish star"). The synagogue standing in front of us was much larger than what I had expected, and it was boldly decorated with several Jewish stars. When this synagogue had been built in the early 1940s, clearly Jews had felt no need to hide.

We were greeted and graciously welcomed by two men, the synagogue caretaker and the librarian, both of whom introduced themselves as "Ibrahim." First they proudly showed us the library housed in a rectangular room about the size of a dining room. The library included books about the Karaite community in both Hebrew and Arabic and, most interesting to us, a number of handwritten manuscripts of Karaite prayer books. Ibraham the librarian told us he had studied Hebrew and Judaism for four of his five years at Al Azhar University. He spoke about the respect and appreciation for other religions that he was taught from the beginning of his university studies.

"*This* is true Islam, not the extremist views publicized today in the media, he said. "One cannot be a true Muslim without an understanding of the Torah, and that is why I became interested in learning Hebrew." Ibrahim explained that he also managed the library at the main synagogue downtown, Sha'ar Hashamayim, where we would be reading the Megillah for the Purim celebration in another week.

Talking with Ibrahim reminded me of our visit to the Ben Ezra Synagogue on our first trip to Cairo. Ben Ezra is in the heart of today's Coptic quarter of Cairo and was originally a Coptic church that in the late ninth century was sold to the Jewish community and turned into a synagogue. Famous because of the Cairo Geniza that was discovered there in 1896, the Ben Ezra synagogue was restored in the 1980s and is a popular tourist site today. Ibrahim reminded me of the Egyptian guide, Amjad, who had shown us around the Ben Ezra Synagogue. If Amjad had not had the tell-tale darkened spot on his forehead indicating the Muslim prayer practice of touching his forehead to the floor, I would have assumed he was Jewish. He had spoken fluent Hebrew and shared detailed knowledge about Judaism beyond the details of the synagogue. In response to our questions about his background, Amjad had told us that his original decision to study Hebrew at the university level had been with the goal of "learning the language of my enemy." However, to his own surprise, his early studies of Hebrew Scripture and Judaism had led him to a deep appreciation of the Jewish religion and religious texts and he had pursued advanced studies in both. I wondered how exceptional Ibrahim and Amjad were; how many Egyptians today who had studied about Judaism at the university level had come to a similar appreciation of Judaism? And how many continued to view Jews as their enemy and wrote about Jews, Jewish history, and texts in that mode?

Walking through the Karaite synagogue, it was easy to imagine how it must have looked when it was first built in the early 1940s, with Oriental rugs on the floor and flickering elegant candelabras. Small wooden lockers still lined the walls where people had once put their shoes before entering the sanctuary, identical to Muslim practice in a mosque.

Upon entering the sanctuary, our eyes were immediately drawn to the *aron kodesh* ("Holy Ark," where the Torah scrolls are kept) in the front of the room. Oil lamps, such as one would typically find in a mosque, still decorate the front of the sanctuary; dangling, empty chains in other locations bear testimony to other lamps that once adorned the sides and back of the sanctuary. A large chandelier still hangs in the middle of the room. A women's balcony in the rear of the synagogue looked out over the main floor.

Several Hebrew inscriptions were carved into the *aron kodesh* similar to what one might find in any synagogue. These included the words of the *Sh'ma*, considered by many to be the single most important Jewish declaration of faith: "Hear O Israel, the Lord our God, the Lord is One."

Did any Karaites still live in Cairo, we asked the two Ibrahims. "Only two women," one of them answered.

The synagogue was abandoned in the 1950s, a mere ten years after it opened and it had not been used since. Here and there around the room, a few decorated Sephardic-style containers used to hold Torah scrolls remained, standing ajar and empty, the Torah scrolls they once protected long gone. With bird feathers and excrement scattered over the floor, and a thick layer of Cairo dust everywhere, the synagogue was clearly not frequently visited, but the structure of the building still looked strong as a fortress. A window in the women's section was swinging open and closed, like a mindless drunk, swinging his arm aimlessly in the breeze. The derelict state of this synagogue was stark evidence that a Jewish community that once flourished simply is no more — and because this synagogue once housed a vibrant Karaite community, something so rare today, this empty shell of a synagogue represented a special loss.

105

Inspired by our visit to the Karaite synagogue, we decided to go with the boys to see the Maimonides and Kapucci synagogues in what used to be Cairo's Jewish Quarter. Again I called Carmen to make the arrangements, and on Friday, when the boys were off from school, we set out.

We went first to Adly Street synagogue and introduced the boys to Ibrahim, the librarian whom we had just met at the Karaite synagogue. He was happy to show us some of the rare books in the library, such as a 300-year-old volume of the Mishnah, the collection of Jewish Law first redacted in 200 C.E. We asked Ibraham if people came to the synagogue for Shabbat services. If people came on Friday evening before six when the synagogue closed, they could pray, he said, but he could not recall anyone coming for Shabbat services for months.

Ibrahim spoke warmly with the boys in Hebrew, telling them why he had learned Hebrew and how valuable it was for them to learn Arabic. "We must speak each other's languages so we can talk to each other, learn about each other's traditions, and understand each other better," he said, with his arm around Amir's shoulders.

We stood talking to Ibraham at the entrance of the Adly Street synagogue, waiting for the caretaker of the Maimonides and Kapucci synagogues to meet us. When he arrived, he hustled us into a taxi to the outskirts of *Harat al-Yahud*, the old Jewish quarter, where we got out and walked. Today the quarter is a working class neighborhood, colorful with the bustle of daily life and laundry hanging from balconies above. We did our best to keep up with our guide on the narrow, winding streets. I was excited to be finally on the way to Maimonides' synagogue. I thought about the awe-inspiring churches of antiquity I had visited in Europe and the many beautiful and historically significant mosques I had admired here in Egypt and in Turkey. Now I was looking forward to stepping inside the synagogue and *beit midrash* where one of our most famous rabbis had prayed and taught.

106

Maimonides is best known for his *Mishneh Torah* (1180), a code of Jewish law still influential today, and his magnum philosophical work, *The Guide for the Perplexed*. Among his many intellectual contributions, Maimonides introduced the Jewish world to Aristotelian thought, which he discovered in the great philosophical works of Al-Farabi, Avempace, and other Muslim Arab thinkers. The fact that Jewish scholars encountered classical Greek philosophy through Arabic translations and the works of Arab thinkers stands as only one example of the rich cultural interchange that characterized the Egypt of Maimonides' day.

As we wound our way through narrow alleyways, we glanced around, hoping to find at least a *mezuzah* in a doorway, some sign of Jewish life that had been left behind. When we saw tablets of the Ten Commandments over a small door, we knew we had arrived at the synagogue. The caretaker unlocked the padlock and let us in.

We stepped inside the crumbling shell of a sanctuary, completely open to the sky, with no single wall fully intact. Rising above the decaying mud brick walls from behind stood a new mosque, its walls brightly reflecting the sunlight, striking against the blue sky. The contrast was painful.

The caretaker pointed to the right and motioned for us to follow. He showed us the room that had served as the *beit midrash* where Maimonides once taught. There were several inches of water on the ground. Carmen had spoken about the chronic water seepage in the neighborhood and the major damage it was doing to both synagogues. She was trying to raise $1.5 million to repair the drainage problem in the immediate vicinity of the Maimonides synagogue, after which the Supreme Council of Antiquities had agreed to proceed with restoration work.

Maimonides was not only a renowned rabbinic scholar but an accomplished physician as well, tending to Jews and non-Jews alike. He served as Sultan Salah ad-Din's personal physician. On a number of different occasions, I had heard that people seeking healing used to come to the Maimonides synagogue from all over Egypt. They would sometimes even sleep here in the hopes that Maimonides would visit them in their dreams and advise them how to cure their ills.

I tried to imagine people sleeping on the floor of the synagogue and *beit midrash*, and wondered what the *beit midrash* might have looked like in Maimonides' day. Where would Maimonides have stood? Would he have circulated around the room as most of my favorite teachers over the years had done? Or would he have maintained a more formal distance from those who came to learn? I suddenly wanted to say the *Kaddish d'Rabbanan*, a prayer that expresses gratitude for past generations of teachers of Torah, but its recitation requires a minyan of ten Jews. In that moment, the full sense of what had been lost swept over me. Jewish life centered around the devotion to study and prayer had thrived here for centuries. In the space of a few decades, this life and its legacy had been reduced to a distant memory in the abandoned and decaying synagogue and *beit midrash* of Maimonides. I was overcome with a sense of sadness. Reuven and the boys seemed to be similarly affected and subdued. We spent a few minutes in respectful silence and then we quietly filed out of the *beit midrash* and what had been a small courtyard, through the entrance back to the street. Our guide padlocked the gate and motioned to us to follow him up the street to our next stop, the Chaim Kapucci synagogue.

This time, the doorway was similarly padlocked, but no external sign even indicated the presence of a synagogue. We stepped over garbage piled in the doorway, and I wondered apprehensively, what would we find behind the gate this time? But once inside, we were relieved to find this sanctuary in somewhat better shape. Here, a beautiful dome framed by a square shape typical of a Byzantine church defined the space, and while little adornment survives, one could imagine that this had once been a most beautiful synagogue. The wooden doors of the *aron kodesh* were intact and decorated with carvings of tall palm trees. The word "Zion" was decoratively painted in Hebrew on the women's balcony, indicating the direction of the Temple in Jerusalem toward which the men below should be praying.

The caretaker accompanying us seemed to think we had already spent enough time in the synagogue and was clearly ready to move on. We walked around the room and looked more closely at the carved wooden doors of the *aron* and then we left. I was glad we had come, but saddened once again at the recognition that a Jewish community that stretched back centuries, with one of the richest legacies of any in the world, had in the last fifty years been virtually reduced to the crumbling shells of a few synagogues.

We retraced our steps, at one point needing to step carefully over the prostrate forms of Muslim men and boys on the sidewalk outside the local mosque, which was packed for Friday prayers. We declined the guide's offer to accompany us back to *Sha'ar Hashamayim* on Adly Street and we decided to look for a place to eat lunch instead. Twenty minutes later, after forcing our way across fast-moving multi-lane traffic, we found a restaurant and stopped for *ta'amia* and *fuul*. Noam commented on my much-improved ability to cross streets and we all laughed. Everyone enjoyed the spicy homemade pickles and salads.

Later in the day I called Carmen to thank her for making the arrangements and tell her how much we had enjoyed our visit to the synagogues. She was pleased and asked if I would be able to go with her to the Jewish cemetery the following week. "I have *yahrzeit* (the anniversary of someone's death) for my mother and I would like it if you could say a prayer at the grave," she said. "It would also be a good chance for you to see the Bassatine cemetery." I told her I would be happy to go with her and say a prayer at the grave. I asked if Reuven and our sons could come too. She thought it was a fine idea and we arranged to meet not far from our apartment.

The next Friday morning, Reuven, Noam, and I walked over to meet Carmen in front of the Metro market (Amir had been invited to go to a friend's house for the day). Carmen turned out to be a fearless driver, on par with the most daring of any taxi drivers we had experienced in Cairo.

As we were nearing the cemetery, Carmen pointed to a boxy looking stone structure with a large dome to the left of us. It was a Karaite mausoleum she said, one of only two or three remaining in Cairo. Squatters were living in the mausoleum, Carmen told us, adding that constant vigilance was necessary to prevent poor families from similarly taking residence inside the Bassatine Cemetery.

When we arrived at the cemetery a few minutes later, a guard welcomed us and unlocked the iron gates. The only markings identifying this as a Jewish cemetery was the simple *Magen David* on the gates. Once inside, the guard's dog happily trailed after us as we followed Carmen down a path through rows of above ground rectangular cement sarcophagi where people's remains were buried. The marble decorative covers were long gone, and I was surprised to see that many of the sarcophagi were labeled in ink. Carmen explained that what we saw was the result of years of work restoring the cemetery. Cataloging the names and dates of the graves was still an ongoing effort. Ironically, where families were unable to afford marble coverings and had made do with simple stone slabs set into the cement, the original etchings of names and dates had survived. Carmen proudly pointed out the flowering pink bougainvillea and small palm trees at the cemetery entrance and along several of the paths. These were also the result of her efforts of the last decades.

We soon arrived at a small well-maintained area where the more recent graves were located. Carmen stopped in front of her parents' graves and placed the gladiolas she had brought with her across the two marble gravestones. The names of her parents were carved in Hebrew and English letters. I offered a short prayer and we stood in respect for a few minutes, then Carmen encouraged us to walk around and explore.

As we walked slowly through the cemetery, I was taken aback by the sheer expanse of it. I gazed around me at the rows of rectangular sarcophagi stretching endlessly in every direction. It was huge. I suddenly understood as I had not before, how large Cairo's Jewish community had actually once been.

The Bassatine Cemetery, I later discovered, was the second oldest Jewish cemetery still in existence in the world. Only Jerusalem's Mount of Olives cemetery is older. The Bassatine Cemetery was first established in the ninth century when Sultan Ahmed Ibn Touloun donated 120 *feddans* (over 504,000 square meters) of land to the Jewish community for a new cemetery. Saadiah Gaon (882-942 C.E.), the most important rabbinic authority of his day and one of the most important rabbinic figures in all of Jewish history, served as the head of Cairo's Jewish community at this time.

I also found it fascinating that fully *half* of Cairo's Jewish cemetery was originally designated for Karaites. What a lesson on how history is written by the victors! How many Jews today have even heard of the Karaites? Yet clearly, they constituted a major part of the Jewish community of Cairo through the Middle Ages, and were an active presence until the 1950s and 60s. And now, their half of the sprawling cemetery was completely gone, taken over by squatters, and their history all but forgotten.

Over the centuries, the Bassatine Cemetery had proved to be the resting place not only for Cairo's Jews, but ironically, for thousands of Jews fleeing persecution in Europe and seeking refuge in the more tolerant Egypt. In addition, a second Cairo Geniza, buried in the cemetery during the Middle Ages, was discovered in 1988, one hundred years after the main Cairo Geniza was discovered in the Ben Ezra Synagogue.

From the 1950s on, as most of Cairo's Jews left Egypt, the Bassatine Cemetery suffered increasing neglect and decline. Vandalism became a serious problem in the late 1960s, when local marble production could no longer meet the growing demand and the marble gravestones in all of Cairo's cemeteries became a target for theft and the black market. In 1978, Carmen Weinstein intervened to save the cemetery from being completely overrun, and tried, with only limited success, to raise awareness and funds locally and abroad. For ten years, Carmen paid for a cemetery guard out of her own funds.

The fate of the Bassatine Cemetery suddenly became international news in 1988 when city plans for a "Ring Road" around Cairo routed a portion of the road through the middle of the cemetery, threatening 300 graves. Rabbis and reporters from abroad suddenly raised a cry and delegations of Jewish leaders from Israel and other countries met with Egyptian officials. From the start, the Egyptian authorities expressed interest in finding a solution to the problem and in the end they agreed to build a bridge over the cemetery to avoid damage to the graves. The authorities also urged Carmen, as the Jewish community's representative, to build a wall around the cemetery to keep out squatters, already a serious threat to the cemetery. This was not only a problem for the Jewish cemetery, Carmen was quick to point out; Cairo's population boom was pushing increasing numbers of poor people to make their homes among the graves of all the city's cemeteries.

Carmen scrambled to raise the funds and the wall was finally built with the generous help of both Jews and non-Jews interested in preserving this historic site. Government officials and lawyers also helped the Jewish community succeed in removing the large numbers of poor people who had already made their homes among the graves of the cemetery. Years of accumulated garbage were removed and slowly, the work of restoration moved forward. Thinking about our visit to the cemetery and its effect on us, I could see why Carmen regarded her work to preserve and maintain the Bassatine Cemetery as one of her most important contributions to Cairo's Jewish community.

Just two days later, Amir and I made *hamentashen*, the triangular cookies stuffed with apricot and prune fillings that are traditional for Purim. We filled a few plates with *hamentashen* and other edible treats for *mishloach manot*, "gifts of food," meant to be shared with friends. We would deliver them on Purim, to the homes of friends who knew we were Jewish — Debbie, Elie Antebi, and Kathy and Steve. I would also bring a bag to Zayna. And no question—the four of us would enjoy the *hamentashen* too, as part of our first Jewish holiday celebration in Cairo.

The next night was the eve of Purim and we headed downtown to *Sha'ar Hashamayim*. We took the Metro and then walked to Adly Street, passing several large brick and stone movie theaters with old-fashioned neon signs still flashing. This had once been an elegant downtown and a wave of nostalgia for something I had not even experienced but could sense in the air washed over me.

We turned the corner and saw a cluster of military police and armored police vans with lights flashing up ahead. Israeli security officers were standing by barricades at the foot of the stairs in front of the synagogue. The officers asked us questions in Hebrew and had us sign in before waving us on to go inside. I found their presence strangely reassuring. We were with Israelis and other Jews, about to celebrate Purim, and all necessary measures had been taken to assure that we would be safe. I was not worried, but rather pleased that our presence as Jews had been acknowledged and a place had been made for us. After weeks of feeling like "closet Jews," it felt like a complete turnaround. But at the same time, I wondered if we should be more apprehensive. After all, this was a lot of security set up around the synagogue to make sure we would be safe. Without it, would we not be safe? I pushed away the thought as we climbed the stairs.

Inside, we were happily surprised to see about fifty people—older Egyptian women sitting on the side, Israelis with young children in costume up in front, and American college students, who I assumed were studying in Cairo, sitting on the other side of the room.

After we said hello to Carmen, Reuven went up to the *bimah*, the slightly raised platform from which the reading would take place, to look at the *Megillah*. I was still helping the boys find a place to sit when Reuven came down from the *bimah* to tell me that an Israeli man had just informed him that *he* would be reading the *Megillah*. How did I want to handle it?

Carmen, the president of the community, had asked us to read, I said, and we had spent time preparing. I was willing to share the reading with the other person, but I did not want to forgo reading altogether. Reuven agreed and returned to the *bimah* to try and work things out. A few moments later he motioned for me to join him. The Israeli man, already unhappy about sharing the reading with Reuven, was apparently even more unhappy that a woman had also been asked to read.

"It goes against *halakhah* (Jewish law)," he protested. Reuven and I politely noted that according to *halakhah*, men and women share the same obligation to hear the Megillah and therefore both are permitted to read it publicly for the community.

"Well, that is not our custom," he said impatiently.

"Custom is not law. And whose custom are you referring to?" asked Reuven. "Carmen, the head of the Jewish community, asked my wife to read. Did she ask you to read?"

"Fine, you read," he said, shrugging as he stepped down from the *bimah*.

After trying with only limited success to achieve quiet, Reuven welcomed people and asked them to sit down. He paused, and then started to read the *Megillah*. There was no microphone, and Reuven was straining to be heard over the talking. I suddenly realized that the Israeli who had been on the *bimah* with us was now standing off to the side, reading aloud his own personal copy of the *Megillah* to a small group of Israelis gathered around him. I wasn't sure if I should be angry or sad. Almost no Jews in Cairo, and still we could not get along well enough to celebrate the holiday together as one community.

It was increasingly difficult to hear either reading, since no attempt was being made by the Israeli parents to quiet down their young children.

Most of the Israeli adults were gathered on the side of the room, talking among themselves and not listening to the *Megillah* in any case. When Carmen's lawyer, whom I knew to be a Muslim, stood up and called for quiet so the *Megillah* could be heard, I felt embarrassed by the behavior of my fellow Jews.

The call for quiet was simply ignored. But some of the Israelis apparently could hear well enough that when their reader reached the point in the story that Haman's name is mentioned, they suddenly began stamping on the floor to enact the popular tradition of "drowning out" Haman's name. Naturally, this meant that they also drowned out Reuven's voice, even though he was at a different point in the story. The second time this happened, Reuven interrupted his reading and stepped down from the *bimah*. He walked over to the Israeli corner and calmly asked the people there to either join in the community reading, or if they wished to have their own reading, to move elsewhere, perhaps to another room in the synagogue. At first some of the Israelis argued with Reuven, but almost immediately, one person said, "Look, he's right," and the group agreed to be quiet.

Reuven returned to the *bimah* and resumed his reading. A few minutes later, most of the Israelis quietly left. While I was sad to see we could not celebrate as one community, I was more relieved to finally be able to hear without straining. When it was my turn to step up to the *bimah* and read from the *Megillah*, several cameras flashed, leading me to wonder if any women had read *Megillah* here in the past.

Immediately after the reading, an Israeli man came up to us and apologized for the rude behavior of so many of his "compatriots." He was most gracious and when we asked him his name, we were happily surprised to discover that we were speaking with Sariel Shalev, the director of Cairo's Israeli Academic Center, someone whom we had been hoping to meet. The Israeli Academic Center, we had heard, hosted biweekly public lectures by visiting Israeli academics and we were planning to attend. Meanwhile Carmen started gathering everyone for a light supper downstairs and for the next hour we enjoyed meeting and talking with people over salads and *bourekas*. The mood was festive and relaxed. When it came time for everyone to say goodbye we felt like our Purim in Cairo, despite its inauspicious start, had provided us with a little Jewish oasis.

114

Reuven reading the Megillah on Purim in Cairo synagogue

Chapter 5
Passover Break

كل يوم في حياتك هو بمثابة صفحة في تاريخك

Every day of your life is a page of your history.
~Arabic Proverb

"DIDN'T *WE* WIN THE YOM KIPPUR WAR?" NOAM ASKED
when he came home from school, referring to the October 1973 war between Egypt and Israel. It is known as the "Yom Kippur War" to Israelis and most Jews because Egypt and Syria had launched a surprise attack against Israel on Yom Kippur, the holiest day of the year for Jews, a day of fasting and religious services. Noam's question emerged from a discussion he had at school with his friend, Muhammad, a popular and well-respected senior who was president of the student body.

Muhammad sat next to Noam in their Egyptian history class. Earlier he had told Noam that he knew he was Jewish because he had been one of the student leaders the Head of School had first consulted with about the possibility of two Jewish boys attending AIS. Noam was very happy to discover that he finally had a friend at school with whom he could talk openly. And since Muhammad was an avid reader of history and politics, Noam had been especially looking forward to discussing the Middle East situation with him.

Noam explained to us that, according to Muhammad, the 1973 war between Israel and Egypt had been a victory for Egypt. "He said everyone sees it that way," Noam continued. "They even have a national holiday—called the 'October Victory Day.'"

"But if Israel won the Yom Kippur War, how can that be?" asked Amir, clearly puzzled.

Noam repeated Muhammad's account: the Egyptian army's attack on Israeli soldiers stationed in the Sinai had caught the Israelis by surprise. Since it was Yom Kippur, only the bare minimum of soldiers had stayed behind with their units in the Sinai instead of returning home to join their families. In the first few days of fighting, Israel had suffered heavy losses.

"I don't get it. Then how can the Israelis say *they* won?" Amir asked.

As we settled around the kitchen table for a snack and a longer discussion, Reuven and I affirmed what the boys already knew – that Israel and the West in general viewed the war as a victory for Israel. Reuven explained that after the initial two-pronged surprise attack by Egypt in the Sinai Peninsula and by Syria in the Golan Heights, Israel had regained within a few days all the lost ground on both fronts. In the Sinai, Israeli forces pushed forward, encircling the Egyptian Third Army on the road between Suez and Cairo. With Israeli tanks just twenty miles outside of Damascus and fifty miles from Cairo, the war ended when Israel, Egypt and Syria accepted a U.N. cease-fire under pressure from the United States and the Soviet Union. Had Israel pressed its advantage and moved into the Arab capitals, Egypt and Syria would have suffered the humiliation of total defeat. From this vantage point, the war seemed a clear victory for Israel, despite its initial disadvantage due to the surprise attack.

"But you know, for every event—especially a war—there are different points of view when it comes to explaining what happened, why it happened, and why it was important," Reuven said. "It is not unusual after a war for the two sides to view what happened differently. But I think this is a more extreme case than usual, with each of two countries presenting themselves as victorious in the same war."

I suddenly remembered that on the main road between Cairo and the airport we often passed a museum built to commemorate the October War. The taxi drivers would always point it out to us with pride. "We've been talking about going to the October War Museum ever since we arrived," I said, turning to Reuven. "Maybe now would be a good time." We decided to go the following Friday.

A week and a half later, the taxi dropped us off in front of the October War Panorama museum. The museum was a modern cylinder-shaped building set back from the road. Walking up to it, we pointed out to Noam and Amir that this was a government-run "showcase museum" where visiting foreign dignitaries were usually brought. The museum offered a perfect opportunity to hear the official Egyptian narrative of its relationship to the State of Israel. While it was dedicated to the 1973 war specifically, we expected the war to be presented in the context of a more sweeping narrative of Egypt's relationship with Israel, and we wanted the boys to be on the lookout for it.

Hoping to avoid large crowds, we had gotten an early start on the day, but already families with young children, and adults of all ages, were lining up. We joined the line and quietly waited our turn to buy tickets. Once inside, we were immediately ushered into an auditorium with comfortable stadium seating. We took seats in the front row. "What language do you speak?" a museum employee asked us politely and upon our reply, he handed us headphones marked "English." We sat back in the comfortable chairs, waiting for the presentation to begin.

Suddenly the room darkened and the military music began. Soon a narrator's voice, accompanied by the sound of missiles flying overhead and bombs exploding all around us, announced that on October 6, 1973, the Egyptian army had attacked Israeli enemy forces in the occupied Sinai Peninsula. The goal, we were informed, was to recover the territories Israel had seized in 1967. The spotlight moved over the diorama in front of us, highlighting miniature tank battles and plastic figures of unsuspecting Israeli soldiers, stopped in their tracks by the sudden attack. The narrator continued his account of the battle that was being re-enacted in front of us, proudly declaring the battle a victory for Egypt and a total defeat for Israel.

And then it was over. The lights went on, our headphones were collected, and we were ushered out of the auditorium, into a large room with uniforms and models of cannons, tanks, and weaponry from different wars on display.

"That's it? What about the rest of the war?" asked Amir. We were all a bit uncertain, but a few minutes later, when we exited the display room, another museum employee pointed us upstairs where a second multi-media presentation was about to begin. Apparently, the presentation was divided into two parts. Relieved, we sat down with the rest of the audience in the middle of the auditorium, this time with life-size models arranged in 360 degrees all around us. Again, we were handed English language headsets, and this time, the platform on which we were sitting began to move, carrying us through a "living diorama" that accompanied the narration. To our surprise, we were back at the opening battle of the war. The difference was that this time we saw depictions of hand-to-hand combat and the bloodied corpses of Israeli soldiers strewn across each other in the sand in the contorted positions of death. From all around us we heard bombs exploding and the staccato drill of gunfire. War is hell, I told myself, but I had to admit—it was seeing these depictions of dead Israeli soldiers that was most disturbing to me.

The second presentation ended just as suddenly as the first, with the narrator joyfully proclaiming the end of this battle a "lightning victory" for the Egyptians. There was no mention of the Israeli army's subsequent encirclement of the Egyptian Third Army in the Sinai. No mention of Israel retaking the Sinai Peninsula or of the resulting cease-fire. In fact, this "victory" was celebrated as a sounding defeat of Israeli air supremacy "once and for all." The lights went on, our headphones were collected with a smile, and we were directed back downstairs to the rotunda area.

Now we were really confused. We had certainly expected to hear a narrative of the war different from our own, but we were unprepared for the seventeen-day war being presented as a single two-day battle ending in total victory for the Egyptians. The fact that this was the official version of the war taught in public schools was even more disturbing.

"Well, I guess now we know why the Egyptians see this war as a victory for Egypt," said Noam, glum in his sarcasm. He, like the rest of us, would have preferred a presentation that was more substantive, offering us something serious with which to wrestle. Blatant misrepresentation and propaganda were too easy to dismiss.

We went outside and found a quiet corner where we could debrief. We were all troubled by the museum's seamless presentation that left no room to even imagine there was more to the war than a single battle that had ended in victory for Egypt. The boys wondered how a narrative like this could go virtually unchallenged in Egypt.

"Do we do the same thing in America?" asked Amir.

"Every country has its own national myths and biases, and as Americans and Jews, we do too," I answered. "But in a democracy, people usually hear different points of view. Any message put out there by the government is sure to be challenged by other voices in the media. It happens here too, but much less often." As an example, I reminded them of the Op-Ed piece we had been happy to see a few days earlier in Egypt's major newspaper, *Al Ahram*, questioning the Egyptian tendency to blame all its problems on Israel.

We talked about how the portrait of the October War we had just witnessed contributed to a sense of Egyptian national pride. In 1967, Egypt had suffered a humiliating defeat when Israel responded to intelligence of a surprise attack with a pre-emptive strike of its own against the Egyptian air force on the ground. Moreover, the Six Day War ended with the emotional loss of the Sinai Peninsula to Israel. Egypt's successful launching of a surprise attack against Israel in 1973 seemed to partially reverse the humiliation of the 1967 defeat for the Egyptian people.

"Muhammad said that without the Egyptian 'victory' in 1973, Sadat couldn't have gone ahead to make peace with Israel a few years later," said Noam. "They needed this victory for Sadat to be able to negotiate from a position of strength and for the people to be able to even begin to accept the idea of peace with Israel."

"That's probably true," agreed Reuven, recalling Egyptian President Anwar El Sadat's visit to Jerusalem in 1977 and his negotiations with Israeli Prime Minister Menachem Begin, which led to the Camp David Accords a year later. The Accords resulted in a peace treaty between Egypt and Israel and the return of the historic Sinai desert and peninsula to Egypt, a tangible gain for the Egyptian people. Without the prior restoration of Egyptian pride—with the perception of military victory in 1973—it would have been unlikely that Sadat could have pursued his peacemaking initiatives.

But the celebration of this victory also had a bellicose side, despite the Israel-Egypt Peace Treaty signed in 1979. Even today, Reuven noted, Mubarak continually conveyed the message that as long as *his* regime remained in power, the Egyptian people could rest assured that this legacy would be protected and the Israeli enemy—always looming as a potential threat unless the Egyptians were strong—would be kept in its place.

Our experience in the museum also made us question *our* version of "the Israeli victory" in the Yom Kippur War. Was it possible that we were also leaving out some of the story, or unfairly playing up the parts that contributed to our view of the war as a victory for Israel? The initial surprise attacks in the Sinai and in the Golan Heights had dealt a traumatic blow to Israelis that led to much soul-searching and ultimately, to Golda Meir's resignation as prime minister. While it was undeniable that Israel had regained its footing and stood, by the war's end, as the greater military force, it was also true that Israel would no longer be protected by her image of invincibility that since 1967 had served as a major deterrent to the Arab countries. Israel had won the war, but at the same time, it had lost more than just a battle.

While we were still disturbed by the museum's silence about Israel's comeback after the initial battle, the exhibit had helped us understand why Egypt felt it had achieved certain successes in the war. The fact that both countries could point to true achievements as well as serious failures may have helped convince both Sadat and Begin to take the historic risks they did and begin the process of peace-making. Still we came away troubled by what we could only view as the Egyptians' deliberate misrepresentation of the October 1973 War. But we all agreed that the October War Panorama museum had been a learning experience for us.

120

With Purim behind us, Passover was fast approaching and we turned our attention to solidify plans for a short trip to Israel to celebrate the Seder and the first part of the eight-day holiday with friends in Jerusalem. I told Zayna I would be away for a week and a half and that we were going to Israel as a family. I watched her face for a reaction. There was none, but an awkward silence. I decided on the spot to tell her about something to which she could respond. I would be visiting a couple of Arab-Jewish co-existence projects while in Israel, I told her, explaining that I was involved in a small family foundation that supports such efforts and describing some of its projects—a new Arabic language program being introduced into Jewish schools, a project in which Jewish and Arab mayors were working together to develop Industrial Zones that would benefit both their communities. Zayna listened with interest.

"So, you think Jews and Arabs can live together in Israel?" Zayna asked me.

"Yes, I do," I responded, "*Insha'Allah* (with God's help)."

She smiled slightly, but was again silent. I was not sure she agreed with me. We moved on to other subjects.

The next day in class, when I learned the word for "opinion," I decided to follow up on our conversation and asked Zayna what she thought about Israel, what was her "opinion"? She thought for a moment and continued slowly in Arabic, at times translating into English when I did not understand.

"I first want to say that I see a difference between Israel and Jewish people. I do not have a problem with Jewish people." Zayna looked me intently in the eye to make sure I understood. "The problem I have is with Israel's policies. I think that the Arab peoples and the Jewish people can live together, but only with equality for everyone." I could feel my body relax. On this point, at least, we agreed. Maybe there would be more points of agreement than I had assumed.

"But I have a question," she said, this time not hesitating to take the lead in the conversation. "Why do Jews need a *Jewish* state? Jews lived very happily in Egypt for many years, until the state of Israel was established."

I was a bit surprised that the conversation had moved so quickly to the question of Israel's existence as a Jewish state. Perhaps my hopes for wide areas of agreement had been premature. I answered Zayna in English, explaining that the history of the Jews over the centuries had convinced us of the need for a Jewish state where our safety and security would be guaranteed and not dependent on the will of others. She nodded and said "Hitler," to show me she had heard this argument. I was glad to see that she knew about the Holocaust, since this was not a subject generally taught in Egypt's public high schools, but I wanted her to know that it wasn't just the Holocaust that made Jews aware of the need for a Jewish state. I explained that Jews had been the victims of violent persecution and forced to leave different countries at numerous points in history.

"But *why*?" Zayna asked, giving me a penetrating look. In her intent expression, I saw a challenge. She seemed to be asking, what had the Jews done to provoke such attacks? Objectively speaking, it was not unreasonable, I told myself, to ask such a question. Even Jews sometimes wondered if it was partly Jewish behavior that prompted antisemitism.

"Usually it has little to do with what Jews do. Outbreaks of violence against Jews have more to do with what's going on in the society. In times of economic or social unrest, for example, leaders often look for a scapegoat that can be blamed as the source of all the people's problems." Zayna did not know the English word "scapegoat," so I tried to explain with examples. "Hitler rose to power during a severe depression, which he blamed on the Jews," I said. "And Germany had lost the First World War, which he also blamed on the Jews, although many Jews fought in it for Germany. Since Jews are a religious minority in every country, they have

121

often been used as a scapegoat in Christian and Muslim states. Jews need a Jewish state, a place where we can go to if we find ourselves once again the victims of antisemitism.

"Since Israel was created, Jews have come there from all over the world," I noted. "And not all the Jews in Israel came from Europe. Recently, large numbers of Jews have come to Israel from the Soviet Union and Ethiopia." I also pointed out that a large number of Jews living in Israel today—over one third—were the children and grandchildren of refugees from Arab countries who came to Israel in the late 1940s and 50s.

"But there is nothing in Islam against Jews living in Arab countries," Zayna protested. "I think if Jews were treated badly, this only came about in response to the creation of the state of Israel."

The establishment of the state of Israel had certainly been an issue, I agreed, and Jews had generally fared better under Muslim rule than Christian rule over the centuries. But I also pointed out that for centuries Jews had been second-class citizens in Arab countries, and had been the victims of violent attacks in these countries as well.

"Does that give them the right to take someone else's land?" Zayna said intently, the conversation heating up.

"But it's our land too," I responded. "Jews had their own state there two thousand years ago, until the Romans forced them to leave. The idea of returning to the land of Israel did not begin during or after the Holocaust. It goes back almost two thousand years, and it started as a religious idea, not a political one. For almost two thousand years we have prayed to return to the land of Israel, the land of our origins."

"You have had that prayer for almost two thousand years?" Zayna was clearly surprised. I was stunned for a moment when I realized she never heard the Jewish story of connection to this land. "Yes, since the destruction of the Second Temple in Jerusalem, in the year 70," I explained. Zayna seemed so skeptical of this idea that I decided that I would bring in a prayer book to show her some of these prayers. I wanted to be careful though. I was not sure how much political discussion our relationship could hold.

"I want to add just one more thing, Zayna," I said before leaving that afternoon. "I love Israel and am totally committed to the existence of Israel, but I do not always agree with all of Israeli policies. I believe there were serious mistakes made in how Israel was established as a country in relation to the Palestinians who were living there. It is a complicated situation and mistakes were made by all sides." We did not come to agreement, but we listened carefully to each other and heard what each other had to say. It was a hard conversation in some ways, but one I was very grateful for.

I came away from the class realizing that while I was eager to hear what people here had to say about Israel and gain a better understanding of their views, it was going to be harder to just listen than I had anticipated. I knew that most Egyptians were strongly opposed to Israel's policies and at times, her very existence. I had already encountered this point of view almost daily in the Egyptian press. But it felt very different to hear it rather than to read it, and to hear it from Zayna, someone I felt close to and respected. In a naive way, I was disappointed and hurt by Zayna's questioning Israel's existence as a Jewish state. If *she*, a young, university-educated Egyptian, questioned Israel's right to exist, how many other Egyptians had the same fundamental question? And if Egyptians were still asking this question, after almost thirty years of peace with Israel, what about the rest of the Arab world?

This was, I hoped, the first of many conversations I would have with Egyptians about Israel. While I knew that the greatest opportunity I had while living here was to come to a better understanding of Egyptians' points of view (and remembering the school director's advice to our sons, "When others discuss Israel, listen, don't argue..."), I had to be honest— I didn't just want to listen, I wanted to *engage*. I wanted the people who talked with me to also understand my point of view. I knew I was just one person, just one voice, and could not have much of an impact. But if I did not say anything, was that really better? Wasn't it important for Egyptians to also hear different points of view, for them to also realize there was more than one narrative? If they did not have the opportunity to hear from people like me, who are committed to Israel's survival as a Jewish state, how could we expect them to even question their point of view? I knew that it would be more difficult to pursue these conversations than I had anticipated, but I felt even more strongly that I wanted to find opportunities to do so.

Although we could have taken a one-hour flight, we decided to travel to Israel by way of the Sinai desert, where we planned to climb Mount

Sinai. We were in fact following part of the journey our ancestors began with the Exodus that we celebrate at Passover. According to the Hebrew Bible, the Israelites arrived at Sinai three months after leaving Egypt, and then continued on their long trek to the Promised Land. The journey that took our ancestors forty years would take us just a few days, and where they had trudged slowly over hot desert sands, we would make the trip in an air-conditioned bus.

Still, the first leg of our trip turned out to be a longer journey than we anticipated. What we were told would be a seven-hour trip stretched into almost eleven because there were so many stops to pick up passengers and for the driver to take breaks along the way. In fact, two stops and two hours after our departure, we were still trying to get out of Cairo!

124

But the frequent breaks in the trip proved an opportunity to talk with the other people on the bus, some of whom we quickly came to view as traveling companions. Across the aisle sat Izhar, an American-born Muslim of Indian descent in his early twenties who was working toward a Master's degree in Islam and Middle Eastern Studies. Izhar was spending the year in Qatar to improve his Arabic, and seemed to be on something of a spiritual search as well. Having gone on *Hajj*, the Muslim pilgrimage to Mecca earlier in the year, he now wanted to climb Mount Sinai.

Behind us sat Elene, a young woman from Australia in her thirties with a strong "Down Under" accent. Elene was on a different kind of spiritual journey. A deeply believing Greek Orthodox Christian, Elene was from a family that had been forced to flee Cyprus in the mid-1970s, at the time of the Turkish invasion; she grew up in Sydney, where she currently worked as a social worker. She described her trip as a personal pre-Easter pilgrimage; she planned to climb Mount Sinai and visit the monastery of St. Catherine at the foot of the mountain, and then head north to a Greek Orthodox monastery in Jerusalem for Easter. She intended to spend several weeks at the Jerusalem monastery, she confided to me, praying over an important life decision.

While I was musing about how Mt. Sinai like a powerful magnet still seemed to draw so many people on such different spiritual journeys to its peak, Reuven started talking with the man sitting in front of us, a dark-skinned Arab man with bright blue eyes, wearing jeans and a long-sleeved jersey. Rahim was not a tourist, but a Bedouin heading home to the town of St. Catherine. He explained to us that he was part of the Bedouin tribe of Jabaliya whose roots went back to the sixth century, when the Byzantine Emperor Justinian I ordered the building of a monastery at the foot of Mt. Sinai, and later sent a hundred Romanian guards from Macedonia to serve and protect it. Many of these men married local women. Over generations, they continued to serve the monks and came to form a separate tribe. Later they converted to Islam. Rahim noted that all the Bedouin living today in this part of the Sinai were descendants of this same tribe. Even now, he noted with a grin, their blue eyes pointed back to their Romanian origins.

We asked Rahim if he could suggest a Bedouin camping facility where we could stay near St. Catherine's Monastery and the next thing we knew he was on his cell phone arranging for someone he knew to meet us at the bus stop when we arrived. It was already dark when the bus pulled into the area, and we were grateful for Rahim's help when we stepped down from the bus and a man immediately stepped forward, shook hands with Reuven, and took our bags. Izhar and Elene decided to join us and we all made our way to a nearby camping hostel.

We arrived to find a crackling campfire around which other people were sitting on cushions, eating and happily engaged in a lively conversation. The laughter and mélange of languages and accents was inviting. Handing us small cups of strong, sweet tea, the host urged us to find a place to sit among the guests. We all found room to squeeze into here and there. Soon, bowls of delicious vegetable soup and plates of rice and beans appeared for dinner. I introduced myself to the man next to me, who told me his name was Dietrich and that he was on vacation with his wife and two young daughters from Frankfurt. They had been coming to this same spot for ten years, drawn to the quiet and the magnificent desert mountain hikes. He and his wife, Gisela, were Lutheran ministers, and Dietrich was also an artist. Almost immediately, we slipped into an engaging conversation about the spirituality of art and the challenges of interfaith work between Muslims, Christians, and Jews in Germany.

When Gisela joined our conversation, we found we had much to talk about, from my experience as a rabbi and hers as a minister. Within minutes we were comparing notes about how we related to traditional (male) God language in prayer, and how difficult it was at times to balance our own spiritual needs with those of the congregation when we led prayer services. I was almost dizzy with the intensity of our conversation over the intimate questions of belief and prayer. The fact that we practiced different religions but were engaged in the same struggles made the conversation even more interesting. With great reluctance, I finally pulled myself away to join Reuven and the boys and find out where we would be sleeping for the night.

The accommodations at Fox's Bedouin Campground were simple: the four of us were sharing one small room taken up almost entirely by a single platform bed on which six flat, skinny mattresses were lined up tight against each other. But what did we really need to do in the room except sleep? We brought in our bags and rummaged around for our toothbrushes, suddenly in a hurry to go to bed when we realized we had only a few hours to sleep if we wanted to hike up to the top of Mount Sinai before sunrise.

We turned out the lights in record time, and the next thing I knew, Reuven was whispering to us all that it was two o'clock in the morning and time to get up. We quietly wiggled out of our sleeping bags and got dressed, and traipsed outside to an outdoor sink to brush our teeth and splash icy water on our faces. The night air was cool and clear. We walked over to the campfire area, where Elene and Izhar were already sipping the hot tea our host would shortly offer to us.

The night sky was breathtaking. The stars strewn across the sea of black jumped out as dazzling points of light and looked almost close enough to touch. For the next two hours, we made our way up the gradual but steady incline. Men and boys of all ages in long white *galabiyas* stepped forward out of the darkness every few minutes, offering politely to take us up on their camels. Each time we declined with a shake of our heads. As we passed other hikers, we tried to guess what languages they were speaking from the brief snatches of conversation we heard. The smorgasbord of languages included French, German, Italian, Spanish, Greek, Russian, and several different Slavic and African tongues.

As we neared the top of Mount Sinai, we found it harder and harder to keep moving forward because the path was growing increasingly crowded with other hikers. To our dismay, it was already starting to get light. I feared that we would not make it to see the sunrise from the summit—and then suddenly, the space opened up and there we were, looking out at a sea of mountains, layer after layer, blues fading into grays into the distant horizon. In the next moment, *oohs* and *aahs* rose around us, as just a hint of glowing red peeked out from above the top of one of the most distant mountains. In moments, the scene before us was transformed, as the sun slowly floated up into full view. The expansive mountain ranges that spread before us in every direction were suddenly bathed in luminous pinks and oranges and golden tones. I had been here as a rabbinical student in 1978, but I had forgotten just how magnificent it was from the top of the mountain. The flow of molten rock eons ago had captured twists and turns in ribbons of color that seemed to still pulse with life. I thought of the beautiful words of Psalm 97:5: "Mountains melt like wax before the Lord, before the Lord of all the earth."

Next to us, a group of Africans started singing another prayerful and joyous psalm, their voices strong and clear. It was moving to see people of so many different faiths and ethnic backgrounds standing together, similarly struck by the natural beauty and the spiritual depth of this special place that Jews and Christians from the West call Mount Sinai, and Muslim and Christian Arabs call *Jebel Musa* ("Mount Moses"). To my mind, the second half of the verse from Psalm 97 also fit the moment: "The heavens proclaim God's righteousness and *all* peoples see God's glory."

We walked around, quietly taking in the spectacular views from every angle. Within an hour, the sun was high enough in the sky that it was already getting hot. On the climb up, we had gotten separated from Elene, but Izhar was still with us as we started to make our way back down. This time, we decided to take a different route, marked by a sign that warned us that we were embarking on a descent of over three thousand steps! Fossils and more dramatic rock formations greeted us at every turn; we took our time, but sooner than we expected, we found ourselves back at St. Catherine's monastery at the base of the mountain. We wanted to go inside but almost turned back when we saw how crowded it was. Then we noticed Elene just ahead of us, and we decided to explore the monastery with her. Afterwards, we walked back to our Bedouin campsite for a hearty breakfast, followed by a long nap.

It was late afternoon, and still very warm, when we woke up. Feeling a little groggy, Reuven and I decided to take a walk and explore the area behind the hostel, where there were some fruit trees and a dirt road. Some young Bedouin girls who lived nearby were also walking on the road. They were on their way to a friend's house for a birthday party, they told us, and seemed happy to talk with us, offering to share with us some fresh apricots and almonds from their garden that they were snacking on. The fruit was deliciously tart.

When their mother joined us, and heard that we were Jewish and on our way to Israel, her response was simply: "We all believe in the same God." She said she felt it was important to learn about each other's practices and beliefs so that we could better understand and get along with each other, and we agreed. The woman mentioned that when the area had been under Israeli rule from 1967 to 1979, the Bedouin had been well treated by the Israelis, which was a view we had heard before. The Bedouin are traditionally nomadic, desert-dwelling Arab peoples. Because of their nomadic life-style, the Bedouin have frequently found themselves in economic and political conflict with more settled populations, whether Israeli or Arab. Here in the Sinai, though, the Bedouin had apparently gotten along well with the Israeli authorities.

Soon the woman and girls arrived at their destination. As the late afternoon sun was beginning its descent, we returned to the hostel, where we spent a relaxing evening with Izhar, Elene, and the couple from Germany.

Early the next morning we exchanged email addresses and phone numbers and said our goodbyes to our fellow Sinai climbers. We took a taxi up to the border crossing between Egypt's little resort town of Taba and Israel's small resort city, Eilat, both located on the northern tip of the Red Sea, on the Gulf of Aqaba. From Eilat, the Jordanian port city of Aqaba is also visible to the East, nestled on the shoreline below the towering mountains that provide a stunning view.

At the border crossing, we made our way from one official to another, answering questions and having our luggage inspected before moving on to the next stop in the labyrinthine process of crossing the border. I took great pleasure in being able to speak Arabic with the Egyptian officials and then switching to Hebrew on the Israeli side.

Finally, we stepped out into the "Israeli" sunshine. We were home. It always felt like coming home when we arrived in Israel. But this time was even more emotional. Not only would we be able to let down our guard for the first time in months and wear our *kippot* openly on the street—Israel is the only country in the world where the main spoken language is Hebrew and even the calendar is Jewish. This Friday night, instead of having to hide our Shabbat candles behind closed curtains, we would hear the siren informing everyone in Jerusalem that it was time for Jews to light their candles and usher in the Sabbath.

Reuven hailed a taxi and asked the driver to take us to Eilat's nearby central bus station where we would catch a bus to Jerusalem. The driver wore a white *kippah*, and with his dark skin and accent, he appeared to be a Mizrachi Jew. I wondered from which Arab country his parents or grandparents might have come. He asked if we had been vacationing in Taba, a popular Egyptian tourist spot with a beautiful luxury hotel literally a few steps from the border crossing. When Reuven answered that we were traveling from Cairo, where we were living for half a year, the driver declared with authority, "There is no such thing as a good Arab." Reuven shot a quick look of disappointment my way, a look that probably matched my own. After two months of defending Israel, to be so quickly greeted by the mirror image of hate and categorical dismissal of the other was painful. We didn't even respond. We were too surprised and there was too little time. When we arrived at the bus station, Reuven paid the fare and we got out of the taxi.

I looked around for a bathroom at the bus station and finally asked a security officer who was sitting, reading a newspaper. Without lifting his head, he pointed down and to the left, indicating the restrooms were downstairs. I had to laugh. What a contrast to the way Egyptians regularly walked me to my destination whenever I asked directions. Israelis made jokes about this kind of rudeness; but at the same time, they took pride in the fact that when someone is truly in need—say, an elderly person who stumbles getting to his seat on a bus— Israelis are immediately on their feet, trying to help.

Twenty minutes later, we had settled into comfortable seats on the air-conditioned bus that would take us north to Jerusalem. From the window, we saw several kibbutzim, most of which were familiar to us. Over the years, we had spent several summers as a family on Kibbutz Lotan, a kibbutz established by the Reform movement in the 1980s, located forty minutes up the road from Eilat. Kibbutz Lotan had made its mark in recent years for its alternative building projects, models for self-sustaining communities, and groundbreaking environmental work in the region generally. As we drove north through miles and miles of desolate sandy and rocky desert, mountain ranges to both the east and west framed our view, and virtually the only signs of life were the occasional kibbutz and irrigated orchard of date palms. I loved the quiet open spaces of the Arava desert, and relished the four and a half hour drive ahead.

By the late afternoon, the bus finally started its climb up the desolate and hauntingly beautiful Judean hills, which signaled we would soon be arriving in Jerusalem. I eagerly took in the landscape, my eyes tracing the zigzags of sheep and goat pathways up and down the hills, searching for the occasional camels and Bedouin shepherds leading their flocks. With our final ascent I could feel my excitement bubbling almost like a child's.

Sooner than I expected, we were entering downtown Jerusalem. Reuven commented on the scene and how different it looked from downtown Cairo. In Cairo, once elegant European buildings stand as grimy testament to better days long gone, as congested throngs of pedestrians, many in traditional Muslim dress, compete with the horn-blowing traffic of trucks and taxis pushing forward with difficulty through the streets. Now, as we turned a corner, the vitality of Israeli society burst into view all around us. In every direction we could see new buildings going up and roads under construction. Colorful billboards advertised new films, concerts, and museum openings. Smaller signs announced classes and lectures with well-known rabbis.

Almost immediately upon entering the city, we were engulfed by impatient drivers honking their horns (maybe Jerusalem is not so different from Cairo after all, I thought) and trying to push their way through the congested traffic. Their efforts were frustrated by throngs of pre-holiday shoppers and visitors pulling suitcases after them as they tried to dart between the cars and cross the street. Hasidic men and boys, with black hats and side curls, and women and girls, in long skirts and sleeves, made their way among secular Israelis, sporting more colorful and somewhat less modest clothing.

Jerusalem stands unique in Israel as a city of contrasts—ancient and modern, religious and secular, Jewish-Christian-Muslim, Israeli and Palestinian, rich and poor. In fact, every tension experienced in Israel is heightened in the densely populated Jerusalem, where every religious and ethnic community scrambles and clamors for its foothold in the sacred city's identity. Even with all of its problems and challenges, I felt again, as I had on every visit, that Israel at its very core is an open, dynamic society. Culturally, intellectually, politically and economically, it pulses with the energy born of its diversity and its thirst for life. It is this openness and vitality that continues to inspire hope for its future.

Once we started walking around the city, I found myself noticing different things than on past visits. Instead of being struck by the Middle Eastern flavor conveyed in the mix of people, languages, music, and foods, for the first time I was struck with how European certain parts of Jerusalem felt. The proportion of cars and buses to pedestrians, people's dress, and the number of cafés and trendy restaurants, boutique shops and wine stores—mixed in among falafel stands and stalls selling nuts, seeds, and spices—stood in sharp contrast to most of Cairo.

But at the same time, this was hardly Europe. Middle Eastern culture is deeply integrated into the architecture and the flavors and sounds of the city. The foods that are considered to be quintessentially Israeli—falafel, pita and hummus, and "Israeli salad"—are also staples of Arab cuisine. Elegant old Arab homes set the tone of some of Jerusalem's most beautiful streets, and the street signs everywhere are in Hebrew, Arabic, and English. While I could not recall having noticed the street signs in Arabic before, repeatedly this was where my eyes were now drawn. And when I took a taxi, I found myself hoping for an opportunity to speak Arabic with the driver.

Our first day in Jerusalem, we walked over from our hotel to the Old City. As we meandered through the Muslim and Christian quarters, instead of seeing the atmosphere as exotic and different as I always had in the past, I immediately warmed to the familiarity of the colorful scene and scents, so much like the markets in Cairo. I realized that it was more than language we were learning in Egypt. I was starting to feel more at home in Arab culture. My reaction probably shouldn't have come as a surprise—we had just spent almost three months in Egypt—but I was surprised. Our experiences in Egypt were deepening our appreciation of Israel as a Jewish country, and at the same time, as a country that is part of the Middle East. We stopped at several shops to buy some olives and labne, a creamy and delicious soft cheese made from yogurt that goes especially well with fresh pita bread. Then we walked over to the children's clothing store of our old friends, Najeeb and Masoud, two Muslim Palestinian cousins whom Reuven had first met when he was eighteen and traveling in Israel. Reuven had been walking through the market in the Old City, when Najeeb and Masoud invited him into their shop for a cup of coffee. One cup of coffee led to another, and Reuven and the two cousins found themselves drawn to each other's sincerity and openness. They made plans to meet again in a few days. Soon Reuven had developed a close friendship with the two cousins, which continued to grow over the years as they married and started their families.

132

It was this friendship that had awakened Reuven's interest in learning Arabic and learning more about Islam. I also came to know and love Najeeb and Masoud and their wives, Bahiyaa and Ameena. We always visited them when we were in Jerusalem and enjoyed delicious meals and their expansive hospitality in their beautiful old home in the Muslim quarter of the Old City. In the earlier years of friendship, their families regularly joined us for dinners in our Jerusalem apartments as well, but for periods during the two Intifadas (the Palestinian uprisings beginning in 1988 and 2000) Najeeb and Masoud had been too nervous to come into western Jerusalem with their families and we were equally uncomfortable about visiting them in the Old City.

I hoped we would be able to visit Najeeb and his family at their home on this visit even though we were only in Jerusalem for a short time. I was very fond of Najeeb's wife, Bahiyaa, but had always been frustrated that we could not speak to each other without the help of someone translating. Now I was eager to see if she would understand my rudimentary Egyptian Arabic and if we would be able to speak to each other without an intermediary.

As always, it was a warm reunion with Najeeb and Masoud, and soon we were exchanging family news over small cups of thick Turkish coffee. Najeeb called home and while still on the phone, invited us to join his family for dinner the following evening. Not only would we see the family, but we would also be able to see the new home they had built in a village east of the Old City.

The next afternoon, we met Najeeb at his shop and drove home with him in his old Peugeot. We had to pass through a checkpoint but it was only a short wait going through to the Palestinian side. We could see that the line of cars going into Israel was much longer. Once inside Najeeb's village, he pointed out the concrete security wall separating his village on the southeastern slopes of the Mount of Olives from his shop in Jerusalem, making what had once been a 10-minute drive to work into a 30-minute trip. He shook his head, more in sadness and frustration than anger. The wall was made of gray concrete slabs and stood over 15 feet high. It was an eyesore. I thought about how such an imposition of concrete would be experienced by people who lived in the village even if they weren't particularly inconvenienced by it.

The Israeli government had begun the construction of the Security Barrier in 2002, at the height of the Intifada, to prevent suicide bombers from entering Israel. It consisted of stretches of security fencing combined with deep trenches and sections of concrete wall. Opponents of the Security Barrier argued that it moved beyond security needs to unilaterally establish the future border between Israel and an eventual Palestinian state in several locations setting the Security Barrier well within the Palestinian side of the "Green Line," the pre-1967 borders. While the Israeli Supreme Court had ruled in several instances that Israel had to move the Security Barrier to mitigate the negative impact on Palestinians, it had not disputed the legality of the wall itself. While many aspects of the Security Barrier continued to provoke controversy, it was hard to argue with its proven effectiveness in halting the suicide bombings in Israel. At the same time, it was undeniable that the Barrier was a hardship for thousands of Palestinians who worked in Israel, and had an impact on Palestinians like our friends who had nothing to do with the violence against Israelis.

Soon we arrived at Najeeb and Bahiyaa's home on the other side of the village. The new house had more rooms and bigger rooms than their house in the Old City and a kitchen filled with modern appliances. Outside there was a small garden already blossoming with young fruit trees and the view from their living room windows extended out over the hillside where sheep were grazing. Two upstairs floors still under construction would eventually be home to two of their sons and their families. After years of struggling to make a living, Najeeb and Bahiyaa were clearly enjoying the fruits of their labor. Their previous house in the Old City had only one bedroom; their six children had slept on futons spread out on the living room floor each night.

Embracing Bahiyaa and greeting her in Arabic was a thrill. When I continued in Arabic and asked how she was doing, her face lit up and her eyes widened. We hugged again and to our mutual delight, quickly moved into our first real conversation. I followed Bahiyaa into the kitchen where we continued talking, bringing each other up to date about our children, as I helped her with the final preparations for dinner. I was happy to hear that their daughters as well as their sons had gone on to college or university after high school.

When we sat down to dinner with the others, the conversation grew more complex and we had to include more English and translation. Najeeb told us that one of their sons had recently been arrested. Ironically, he had been working for an Israeli construction company building homes in Kiryat Arba, a settlement near Hebron. On his way to work, he was stopped at a checkpoint and mistakenly identified as a Palestinian who had been seen throwing rocks at Israeli soldiers. He was released from prison the same day only because his Israeli employer had intervened. Without this intervention, Najeeb said, "Who knows how long he would have waited for a trial and what the verdict would have been?"

For the first time in our experience, Najeeb and Bahiyaa sounded bitter. They were angry about their son's experience and that of many of their friends. While they were doing well economically, they were aware that their children had limited opportunities that they could look forward to. They had nothing good to say about the Palestinian Authority either. It was very sad to hear their discouragement and we could only express our sadness and concern.

Still we had much to share and after dinner, we all sat huddled around a new computer, admiring pictures of their now grown children, their daughters' weddings, and their beautiful grandchildren. Not so long ago, our children had played together in each other's living rooms, and now they were starting families of their own.

When we got into Najeeb's Peugeot for the drive back to Jerusalem, Reuven asked Najeeb to let us off near the Damascus Gate of the Old City, saying we could walk to the hotel from there. It was such a nice night, he said, he wanted the chance to walk a little bit in the night air. Later I asked Reuven why he had told Najeeb to drop us off there instead of driving us to our hotel. "I didn't want him to feel uncomfortable driving in the Jewish part of Jerusalem," Reuven responded. Even though he felt it was safe for Najeeb to be there as a Palestinian, he knew that Najeeb preferred not to risk the humiliation of being stopped and questioned by Israeli authorities, as had been the experience of other Palestinians he knew.

As we walked, I asked Reuven what he thought the chances were today for a Jew and a Palestinian in living in the Old City to meet and strike up a friendship like he did with Najeeb and Masoud in the early 1970s. He shook his head sadly. In the first few years after 1967, he recalled, some Jews and Arabs lived in mixed neighborhoods, like Abu Tor in Jerusalem, and frequently formed friendships, but by the late 70s that was already changing. Today, he thought, spontaneous friendships like this were probably a rare occurrence.

135

Even before we left the States for Cairo, we had decided to spend the first days of Passover in Jerusalem. Celebrating Passover in Egypt without any Jewish friends or Jewish community was just not an option. We made plans to join some of our Jerusalem friends at their Seder.

Twice before, Reuven and I had celebrated Passover in Jerusalem with our children. Passover, along with Shavuot and Sukkot, are the three major pilgrimage festivals in Judaism. Even though Jews no longer make the pilgrimage to Jerusalem as they did from Biblical times to the destruction of the Temple in 70 C.E., Jerusalem is still a place that feels like the center of the Jewish world, especially during these festivals. In the days before Passover, I took special pleasure in being surrounded by an entire city preparing to celebrate the holiday with a variety of different accents, melodies, and old recipes to share with family and friends.

The Passover Seder we had come so far to attend was at the home of Etty and Daniel, old friends from my year as a rabbinical student in Jerusalem. They were already married at that time, an American couple a few years older than me, who decided to make their home in Israel. Modern Orthodox in practice, they lived in a Jerusalem neighborhood popular with English-speaking immigrants and known for its mix of religious and secular Jews.

Just walking into their apartment felt like a homecoming to me. My eyes were instinctively drawn to Anna Ticho's haunting charcoal sketches of the Judean Hills on the walls. I found comfort in the warm colors of their living room and velvet cushions adorning the overstuffed chairs and couches.

Etty and Daniel had a daughter Noam's age, Nili, who gave us all big hugs and introduced us to the other guests, an Israeli family with two other teen-aged children, and another Orthodox couple originally from England. Eager to get started, Etty invited us all to take our seats at the long table they had set up for the Seder. Daniel led the Seder in his strong baritone voice and we all took turns reading from the *Haggadah*, the ritual retelling of the story of how we were once slaves in Egypt and how God delivered us from the oppression of slavery. From Seders past with Etty and Daniel, I knew this Seder would last till midnight with spirited songs and lively discussions.

Our friends and their guests were curious about our sojourn in Egypt and we were happy to answer their questions over the multi-course dinner. We told them about some of the challenges we experienced living as Jews in Cairo, which they could readily understand. We also told them how much we were enjoying the warmth and friendliness of the Egyptian people we were meeting. Noam and Amir had a lot of stories they wanted to share about the people they had come to know.

Prompted by the themes of the Seder, I found myself sharing how problematic it felt to me to be thanking God every day in the morning prayers for taking us out of Egypt when I was there, living in Egypt by choice, hearing the sounds of Egyptian children at play in the school-yard behind our building. What did it mean to be saying these words of prayer now? I knew my questions would draw a response from my religious friends, but I pushed on. Didn't these prayers perpetuate our view of Egyptians as the enemy, ignoring the many centuries when Jews had flourished again in Egypt—and even the current situation, complex as it was? Wouldn't it be better to thank God for having taken us out of slavery, rather than for taking us out of a particular place? Wasn't the essence of our Seder celebration the fact that God had redeemed us *from slavery*, not from Egypt per se? As anticipated, a lively discussion ensued, moving from history, prayer, and ritual to the current political situation and back again.

As the conversation continued over dinner, we turned to a subject closer to home for most of the people sitting at the table—the continuing tensions between the Israelis and Palestinians. The Israelis were unanimous in their approval of the Security Barrier. Nothing else, they said, had been able to halt the steady stream of suicide bombers entering Israel. I understood and sympathized totally with their point of view, remembering the year we had spent in Israel from 2000 to 2001, the first year of the Intifada. We were all afraid to let our kids use public buses. Only now, Etty commented, were "people beginning to feel like they could breathe again." At the same time, I couldn't help thinking of Najeeb and the hardship and humiliation that the Security Barrier was causing him and thousands of other Palestinians every day.

Etty and Daniel and their friends were grim about the political reality that their children would soon face when they entered the army. None of them had ever imagined when they came to Israel in the 60s and 70s that their children would grow up to face even greater hatred and violence in a still unresolved and festering conflict between Israelis and Palestinians. They all admitted that they were less certain than ever that peace was possible. The disillusionment around the table was palpable.

"I hate to say it, but the Right was proved right. Who is there, really, to talk to on the other side?" said Daniel, once a staunch supporter of the peace talks. "How can there ever be peace when Palestinian children are being raised to hate us?" he asked, referring to disturbing images of Jews and Israelis routinely used in Palestinian textbooks. Yet everyone gathered here realized that most Palestinians were not suicide bombers and wanted the same things for their children that the Israelis wanted for theirs. Wasn't there any way the cycle of hatred and violence could be stopped? No one had an answer. Here, it seemed, was our enslavement.

I felt like there was almost no space to stand between the conversations with our Palestinian friends and our Israeli friends on these two successive nights. How fitting, I thought, that the theme of the evening is *Mitzrayim*, which is the Hebrew word for Egypt, but literally means "narrow straits," or the confining space from which we seek liberation.

But with the words we read and sang to conclude the Seder after the meal, the *Haggadah* reminded us that even in the deepest darkness there is always a glimmer of light and always reason for hope. Like Jews everywhere, we opened the door to the prophet Eliejah, who, it is said, will herald the coming of the Messiah or the messianic future of peace. The words of the *Haggadah* called us to move from slavery to freedom, from despair to hope, and from sadness to joy. Together our voices wove harmonies around the traditional Hebrew words.

As expected, it was after midnight when we walked back to our hotel, our Seder concluded and our long-anticipated reunion with our Israeli friends completed. We felt it had been a full and stimulating evening and we all agreed that it had been a good idea to come to Israel to celebrate Passover.

Our trip to Israel also allowed me the opportunity to meet with representatives of several projects supported by a family foundation with which I had been actively involved for over twenty years. The foundation was established in the 1930s by the parents of one of my aunts by marriage to 138 support Israel's development as a thriving modern state. My aunt's parents were strong Zionists and good friends of David Ben Gurion (whom my aunt refers to simply as David), and the largest grants over the years were to support desert agriculture research and scholarship programs at Ben Gurion University of the Negev. I had served as a board member, along with my aunt, uncle, and cousin, since the early 1980s, identifying new projects to consider and participating in decision-making about the allocation of funds. For several years now, we had been concentrating our efforts on organizations working to improve relations between Jews and Arabs in Israel through education and economic development. My cousin, Howard, had arrived from the States for several days of meetings and he scheduled them so that I could join him for the first two days.

Our first meeting, over breakfast at our hotel, was with the administrators of an Arabic language program currently being introduced into fifteen public schools in Haifa and Carmiel. This program is unique in that it introduces spoken Arabic instead of the literary Classical Arabic usually taught in Israeli Jewish schools. We were impressed to learn that after only a few months, the program was already proving so successful that other school districts in Tel Aviv and Jerusalem were asking how they could participate. In several of the schools, parents had requested similar classes for themselves to be offered at night. Since I was immersed in learning a spoken dialect of Arabic myself, I took a special interest in what the administrators of this program were telling me and immediately saw its potential for helping Israeli Jews and Arabs to get to know each other.

Right after the meeting, Howard and I drove north to Furadeis, an Arab town on the Carmel coast, to meet with the Jewish and Arab co-executive directors of an organization called Sikkuy, the Association for the Advancement of Civic Equality in Israel. One of Sikkuy's projects that we were supporting was the Jewish-Arab Mayors Forum, a project in which mayors of Arab and Jewish communities were teaming up in pairs to develop Joint Industrial Zones to provide jobs and tax revenue for both their communities. Sikkuy hoped to develop a model that could be replicated around the country. In the past, most of the established Industrial Zones exclusively benefited Jewish communities.

We met with the mayor of Furadeis and a few other municipal leaders of both Arab and Jewish towns, as well as Shuli and Ali, the Jewish and Arab co-executive directors of Sikkuy. When we first arrived, I tried out my Arabic with Ali, and he responded with some surprise and warm enthusiasm. Someone overhearing us asked where I learned Egyptian Arabic and I explained. Even though we went right back into English so as not to leave anyone out, I could see that my efforts to learn and speak Arabic were much appreciated.

139

The mayor shared with us the outline of their particular plans for an Industrial Zone, and spoke positively about the progress that had already been made, as well as his hopes for this and future joint projects. After the meeting, we drove around the village and saw first-hand the crowded living conditions and the lack of separation between the residential, commercial, and industrial areas. Reducing the residents' daily exposure to toxic chemicals in the air and water was one of the eagerly anticipated benefits of the new Industrial Zone. After the tour, Howard and I headed back to Jerusalem in time to join Reuven and the boys for a late dinner.

Early the next morning, Howard and I met with the Arab and Jewish co-principals of the "Hand in Hand" school in Jerusalem where Jewish and Arab children, both Christian and Muslim, study together, learning both Hebrew and Arabic, with Arab and Jewish teachers working in pairs in every classroom. Except for these "Hand in Hand" schools in Jerusalem and the Galilee, and a handful of others around the country, most elementary and secondary schools in Israel were either Jewish or Arab. The school we were visiting was closed for Passover, but we were able to see the classrooms and hear about both daily routines and some of the special cultural programs in which families of students participated. I was pleased to hear that friendships frequently moved out of the classroom and brought children and their parents to each other's homes.

Even after the second Intifada, the principal informed us, the school had a waiting list of families hoping to enroll their children.

Later in the day, we met with several people from the Citizens Accord Forum, an organization started at the height of the Intifada by a Knesset member, Rabbi Michael Melchior, to create opportunities for greater communication and understanding between Jews and Arabs in Israel. We were particularly interested in hearing about one program, a media initiative called DUET, in which Jewish and Arab journalists had started writing for each others' newspapers on issues of controversy, in the hopes of exposing readers to points of view they normally did not have the opportunity to read in their own language. The articles appeared quarterly in an attractive 8-page insert in some of Israel's most popular Hebrew and Arabic language newspapers. The organizers spread out before us sample pages of the last several inserts, some in Hebrew and some in Arabic, which included interviews, articles, and photo essays taking the reader into Jewish towns and Arab communities around the country. The inserts had met with a positive response from both Arab and Jewish readers. Howard and I came away from the meeting enthusiastic about recommending that the foundation provide funding for the project.

While our friends on both sides of the Security Barrier reflected the deep disillusionment that so many Israelis and Palestinians feel, at these meetings I saw a different side of Israel in these grassroots efforts that our foundation was trying to support. I was impressed by the high quality of these programs and the people involved in them. Each organization was headed by Arab and Jewish co-directors. These were not newcomers to the challenges of co-existence, but some of the most experienced and well-respected professionals in the field. It was clear that at least some people were experiencing changing facts on the ground and there were reasons for hope in improved opportunities for Israeli Arabs and improved relations between Israeli Arabs and Jews. I came away from my meetings with a renewed sense of the urgency of this work.

The next day, Reuven, the boys and I headed back down to Eilat on the bus, crossed the border into Taba, and returned to Cairo in a shared private taxi. It was hard for us to leave Israel and return to a society in which we would once again be "the Other" on a daily basis. Because it was still Passover, we would have the added challenges of observing the last few days of the holiday without attracting attention to ourselves.

Both Reuven and I felt the weight of the effort of this reverse Exodus as we drove toward Cairo. But once we reentered the city and the lights ahead beckoned, we felt renewed excitement to be back in this rich and intriguing culture so different from our own, and to have the chance to get to know it even better.

Back in Cairo, our first Passover challenge was what the boys would bring to school for lunch for the next two days, since we did not eat bread or pasta products during the holiday. We did not want them to bring sandwiches made with *matzah,* the flat, unleavened bread Jews eat during Passover, which would be likely to prompt questions, but they agreed that boiled potatoes would work and would even be a nice change. I also made several trays of *matzah kugel,* a Passover adaptation of Eastern European noodle pudding that the boys could bring to school without attracting the special notice that *matzah* would.

141

When I walked into the Alexander School later that afternoon, Zayna and I greeted each other with warm hugs and kisses on both cheeks. It was so good to see her. Zayna asked me if I would like some tea, something she had never done before, and without thinking, I said yes. She went into the kitchen and I realized that unless the tea was served in glass or a paper cup, I was about to compromise my normal Passover practice of only eating on dishes that were kosher for Passover (glass was always kosher) but I did not want to make an issue of it. This was one of those moments that food could bring us together or separate us and the correct choice seemed clear. After a few minutes in the kitchen, Zayna returned with glass cups of tea for us both. When she sat down I gave her a plate of matzah kugel wrapped in plastic. I explained what matzah and kugel are, and that this was one of our family's favorite Passover dishes. Then, with a smile, Zayna reached into her cloth shoulder bag and pulled out a plastic bag full of colorfully wrapped candies.

"This is for you and your family, from our holiday celebration that took place while you were gone—Muhammad's Birthday!" she said. We laughed over the fact that we had each brought sweet treats to share from our respective holidays.

The first week back in Egypt, perhaps emboldened by our time in Israel, we started telling more of the Egyptians we knew that we were

Jewish. Noam took the lead, starting with his friend who worked at the hotel across the street, whom we referred to as Hotel Muhammad (as opposed to Internet Café Muhammad and Stationery Store Muhammad).

"Guess what!" Noam asked, when he returned from a long talk with Muhammad. "Did you know Bush and Condoleesa Rice are Jewish?" While the very idea struck us as hilarious and we all laughed, such a wildly exaggerated view of Jewish power was also deeply disturbing. How could a university-educated, intelligent young man like Muhammad not question something like this when he heard it, we wondered. It seemed incredible.

When I told Seif and Umar, the two men at the hotel across the street, that we were Jewish, they responded by saying that they had already figured it out, and that it really did not make any difference to them.

"You know Imad's Christian, and we're all best friends," they pointed out. This surprised us. We had always assumed Imad, our doorman, was Muslim. Seif and Umar's point was clear. They were religious Muslims but the fact that Imad was a Coptic Christian—and that we were Jews—posed no problems for them. We talked about the recent stabbings of Coptic Christians in Alexandria, and Seif shared his frustration that it was the extreme cases like this that got into the newspapers and had such a pervasive impact on people's views, when in reality the vast majority of Christians and Muslims in Egypt got along well. He had a point about the sensationalist nature of the news here, like everywhere, but I questioned how positive most Coptic Christians' experience was in Egypt. I had met Egyptian Christians who were quick to speak of the prejudice against them in Egypt.

But the person I was most concerned about telling we were Jewish was Mahabbah. I did not want to do anything that might damage a relationship that felt so precious. Mahabbah came to work two days after we returned from our trip, and when we were in the kitchen, she asked me where we had traveled. Had we gone down to Upper Egypt to see the Pharaonic temples? No, I answered, suddenly realizing I did not want to lie. Taking a breath, I turned to her and answered, "We went to Israel."

Mahabbah gave an involuntary start and took a small step back. "Israel?" she said with an emotion somewhere between distrust and distaste. "Why would you want to go to Israel?"

"We are Jewish." There, I said it. No going back now. I explained to Mahabbah that we had gone to Israel to celebrate the Jewish holiday of Passover.

To my surprise, Mahabbah did not blink an eye at the news that we were Jewish. She said something about Jews not eating bread on Passover. How did she know, I wondered, and asked if she had ever worked for a Jewish family before. No, but she knew about Judaism, she assured me with a confident smile, from television and movies. I realized that Mahabbah had probably seen the popular television series based on *The Protocols of the Elders of Zion*, one of the most famous and flagrantly antisemitic tracts in history, which had aired the year before during Ramadan. This wasn't necessarily good news.

I showed Mahabbah the boxes of matzah and some other foods special for Passover that we had brought back with us from Israel. She was particularly interested in the matzah and asked how it was made. I tried not to think about the blood libel stories she might have heard.

143

When Mahabbah walked into our house the next day, she was carrying two large bags stuffed full with large sheets of a crispy, thin bread. "*Egyptian matzah!*" she said proudly. "I made it for you." She explained that this was a popular bread in the Arab world called *ruqaq* or *ro'a'* in Egypt. Though it was eaten year-round, it was considered a special food to eat when Muslims celebrated the *Hajj*, the annual pilgrimage to Mecca, Mahabbah said. The end of the *Hajj* was marked by a major holiday, *Eid al-Adha*, "The Festival of Sacrifice." On this holiday, Egyptians eat *ro'a'* with a special meat dish commemorating the near sacrifice of Abraham's son, Ishmael. (In the Quran, the son who is almost sacrificed is not named, but later Muslim tradition identifies him as Ishmael, Hagar's son; in the Torah, it is Isaac, Sarah's son). Because it was flat, unleavened bread, Mahabbah thought it could also serve as matzah. She clearly liked the idea that this same flat bread could play a role for us both in our respective religious traditions.

I was really touched. Instead of seeing it as a barrier, Mahabbah had absorbed the fact that we were Jewish and turned it into an opportunity to share something from her tradition, in a way that she hoped would add to our celebration of the Jewish holiday. After all my worries, I was deeply relieved to see that my special friendship with Mahabbah was not only intact, but that it could expand its boundaries to include this kind of sharing.

144

Cairo Cityscape

Chapter 6
The World of the Pharaohs

أكتب على الرمال الأشياء السيئة التي فُعِلَت لك، ولكن أكتب على قطعة
رخام الأمور الحسنة التي حدثت لك

Write the bad things that are done to you in sand, but write the good
things that happen to you on a piece of marble.
~Arabic Proverb

145

EVEN BEFORE OUR ARRIVAL IN EGYPT, WE HAD BEEN PLAN-
ning to spend the boys' spring break in Upper Egypt, famous for the
larger than life temples and tombs of the Pharaohs. The terms "Upper"
and "Lower Egypt" date all the way back to the two kingdoms of Ancient Egypt. Even after these kingdoms were united in 3100 B.C.E., the
Pharaohs continued to be known as the "Rulers of the Two Kingdoms."
That these names have persisted to this day, points to the incredible hold
of Ancient Egypt on the imaginations of Egyptians and foreigners alike.

Sometimes confusing to visitors, "Upper Egypt" is actually the south-
ernmost part of the country, while "Lower Egypt" refers to the northern
region. The reason is that these names originated with the dominance of
the north-flowing Nile River, the lifeline of Egypt from antiquity to the
present day. The Nile River enters Egypt from Sudan to the south, and
flows north through the entire length of the country up to Cairo, where
it branches out into spindly fingers of rivulets reaching out to the Mediterranean Sea. Virtually all of Egypt's 80 million people live in proximity
to the Nile, either in Cairo and the fertile Nile Delta area further to the
north, or points further south along the banks of the Nile.

On our first visit to Egypt, we had spent several days in Luxor exploring the temples and underground world of royal tombs. Portraits of
the gods and goddesses, which were carved into stone in striking poses
recalling well-known mythic tales, extended over every inch of the towering temple walls and columns. Bright colored images of the gods and
goddesses similarly adorned the tombs' walls and ceilings. There was so
much to see, we barely scratched the surface, and we left with the hope

that we would be able to return some day. This time we would spend a full week, beginning in Aswan and Abu Simbel, and concluding with three days in Luxor. We were all looking forward to seeing more Pharaonic temples and art—even Amir who had already spent a few days in Luxor on his class trip.

What is it about these temples and tombs that so captivates and inspires people? Is it simply the beauty of the art itself? Or the fact that these paintings, sculptures and buildings are over three thousand years old? Perhaps it is the particular mix of the foreign and the familiar, with glimpses of how different life was thousands of years ago in a world of Pharaohs 146 and sphinxes, and at the same time, offering scenes of everyday life with which we can identify. All of these answers seemed to offer something, but none of them fully satisfied me. I wondered if on this trip I would gain any insight into the question that had tugged at me since our first visit. I also wondered if in this high-density tourist area, we would find the opportunity to actually connect with any people who lived here. Would we be able to get a taste of life in this unique region of Egypt if we weren't living here, but just spending a week, like thousands of other tourists?

Getting off the beaten path and meeting locals while staying in hotels in Aswan and Luxor would be a challenge, but we would try to stay open to the unplanned encounter. That, I decided, really was key. Five years earlier, while Reuven and I were exploring one of the temples in Luxor with all three of our children, our teenage daughter Rachel had gotten into a conversation in Arabic—her first without Reuven by her side—with a group of young women her age, and a few minutes later, one of the girls came back to us with her mother and invited us all to come for tea later in the afternoon at their home. The visit had been lively and fun for all of us.

We took the night train from Cairo and awakened with the already hot sun, still several hours from Aswan. We passed through miles of Egyptian farmland that offered a glimpse into centuries gone by, with farmers slowly guiding water buffalo pulling their plows and young boys working hand-crank pumps to fill their buckets with water from the well. Small fields of sugar cane and golden wheat rippled in the sun, punctuated by top-heavy palm trees with their fronds waving gently in the wind, adding a distinctive Egyptian flavor, just as tall and skinny cypress trees add their unique dark green accent to farmers' fields on the European side of the Mediterranean.

We arrived in Aswan and after a brief search, found a small hotel to our liking, with rooms overlooking the Nile. In an open-air market near the hotel, Reuven and I bought vegetables and bread and cheese for what would be our Shabbat lunch the next day. Walking back to the hotel, we exchanged a few words in passing with a young man who complimented our Arabic and asked where we were from. When he heard we were from the United States, he asked what our real background was. We knew by now what that meant and Reuven answered that we were Jewish. The young man expressed surprise that we lived in the States if we were Jews.

"Many Jews live in the States and many Jews used to live in Egypt too," Reuven answered.

"I know," the man said, "but they've all left, thank God!" Reuven asked the young man why he had said that, and he answered, "Israelis kill women and children, and Jews are bad (literally 'dirty') people—that's why!" Reuven stayed calm.

"There are Arabs who are terrorists and kill innocent people. Does that make all Arabs bad people?"

"No," the young man answered warily.

"What's really bad is making hateful, sweeping generalizations about other groups of people," Reuven continued and with that, we walked away.

I was slightly shaken by the young man's outburst. If we wanted to experiment with being more open about being Jewish, I needed to be prepared for reactions like this. I thought Reuven had responded well. There was even a small chance the young man would think about what he had said.

Since we had already faced similar situations and surely would again, I wondered out loud if we could come up with any additional response that might, even in a brief conversation, effectively challenge Egyptians' assumptions about Israelis. Something like, "Should I believe everything I read and see in America that is said about Arabs? If not, should you believe everything you hear and read about Israel and Jews?" While this didn't deal with all the issues, it recognized and built on the prevalent Arab sentiment that Arabs and Muslims are generally portrayed in a negative light in the West, and that Americans are too quick to accept negative stereotypes of them. It was not clear to either of us how many Egyptians would be willing to concede the parallel in their own percep-

147

tions of Israel. But Reuven and I agreed that this approach stood a better chance of being heard than any actual defense of Israel, which would in all likelihood fall on deaf ears.

As we often did when we traveled, we planned ahead for Shabbat and made arrangements with a boatman to take us out the next morning for a sail on the Nile in a *felucca* the sleek wooden sailboat that has been sailed on the Nile since antiquity. We paid him in advance, just as we paid for our Friday night dinner in a restaurant in advance, so that we would not be spending money on Shabbat. In both cases, we explained that for religious reasons we did not spend money on the Sabbath, and in both cases, the other person responded respectfully and made it clear that they understood. Reuven shook hands with them and we were confident that in this culture, where personal honor and respect is so important, the agreements would be honored.

We set out early the next morning. All of us were looking forward to our sail on the Nile, having admired the *feluccas* gliding smoothly through the water with the wind in their sails the day before. But the wind seemed to be elsewhere that morning. This was something we had not even considered. We took turns rowing alongside "Captain Nur," our *felucca* captain, hoping the lull in the wind was only temporary.

Our first destination was Kitchener's Island, known for its lush botanical gardens, after which we planned to make a longer stop at the larger and much more famous Elephantine Island. The two islands sit side by side in the middle of the Nile, so close to the shore that they were visible to us even before we set out in the boat, and we took our time, enjoying the quiet.

Two little boys, who looked to be about seven or eight years old, paddled up to us in wooden boats so tiny they could paddle them with thin slats of wood held in each hand. The boys cheerfully launched into a string of well known folk songs representing every language and nationality under the sun, in the hopes that one would be ours and we would be moved enough to pay them for their efforts. Because it was Shabbat, we had brought no money with us, but that wasn't something we could explain to the boys. We tried to express our genuine appreciation for their sweet young voices with our smiles and "bravo's" but their disappointment was clear. Captain Nur gave them a few coins and they moved on in search of better prospects.

The boys and Captain Nur were Nubian, as is true of much of Aswan's population. Originally from the area of Sudan and Upper Egypt, the Nubians are darker skinned than other Egyptians, and have more typically African features. They still identify as a distinctive people, with their own language, history, and traditions. When the British-built Aswan Dam proved inadequate to control the flooding of the Nile, Nasser ordered the building of a much larger High Dam that was constructed through the 1960s. This building project included the creation of Lake Nasser, which put hundreds of Nubian villages under water. The dam project led to more than physical relocation for the bulk of the Nubian population of Aswan. It meant the destruction of the Nubians' ability to live as a coherent community. They were forced to relocate to many different villages and cities spread throughout Egypt. While most Nubians today still speak Nubian at home, their children do not have the opportunity any more to speak, read, and write in their own language at school. There are also no "afternoon schools" for the transmission of Nubian language and culture. As if sensing the dangers of total assimilation, Aswan boasts a new and quite magnificent Nubian Museum, with beautiful and informative displays on the long and rich history of the Nubians in Egypt. We could not help wondering what efforts, if any, were being made to help preserve *living* Nubian culture and traditions.

Captain Nur was happy to teach us a few Nubian phrases like "Hello, how are you?" and "I am fine, thank you. How are you?" and we had fun practicing them with him. When we landed on Kitchener's Island, we discovered to our delight that the entire island was covered with beautifully landscaped and elaborately designed botanical gardens. Ambling through sweet smelling gardens of flowering trees and plants, we greeted three middle-aged men who were taking a break from their gardening work with *menebu*, ("hello") and they responded warmly. We ended up trying out our newly acquired phrases with them, to their amusement. With little language in common to carry us forward, the men improvised with a few simple magic tricks and games, mostly for the boys' amusement. We all tried them and had a few laughs before continuing on our walk. Simple as it was, our exchange with the men had been fun, and it would not have happened if we had not learned those few Nubian phrases.

From Kitchener's Island we continued to Elephantine Island. I was looking forward to this, because for years I had read about the Jews who had lived here in the fifth and fourth centuries B.C.E.—the first Jewish community outside of Israel for which there is archaeological evidence. As Carmen had mentioned, the legal documents and letters in Aramaic that had been found here suggested that the Jews living here had been soldiers serving in a military installation on the Nubian border during the Persian occupation of Egypt.

High expectations are not always a good thing when traveling and sure enough, Elephantine proved disappointing. There were no ancient ruins to be explored, and no sign of the rich historical significance of the place. But there was a village that was easy to identify as Nubian, with mud brick houses painted in striking blues, pinks and yellows, some decorated with geometric patterns typical of Nubian homes. It was already quite hot, but we enjoyed walking around the village until some of the village children discovered us and insisted on following us, trying to sell us cokes and souvenirs.

We never found much wind but enjoyed our rowing expedition in any case and once back on the mainland we had a lazy day that included a dip in the small hotel rooftop pool and a beautiful sunset over the Nile.

The next day we got up at 3:30 in the morning and traveled on a tourist bus further up—south, that is—to the Great Temple of Abu Simbel. The twin temple structures were originally carved right out of the cliffs during the reign of Ramses II in the 13th century B.C.E., as a lasting tribute to him and his queen, Nefertari. In the 1960s, the entire structure was painstakingly cut into blocks and relocated to the shores of Lake Nasser, (the largest lake of human construction in the world) when the High Dam project in Aswan threatened to submerge this most famous and beautiful of the Pharaohs' temples under water.

Abu Simbel was originally built as Egypt's "Gateway to the South." It was designed to impress the nations to the South with the immense power of the Pharaohs, and a silent warning to any would-be attackers. The enormous and striking reliefs on the temple walls and columns, portraying Ramses on his life journey from king to deity, the sheer size of the towering columns and temple, and the fact that they are still standing today, over three thousand years after being carved into stone, combine to make the temple a truly awe-inspiring sight. Looking down the length of the temple from the entrance, the viewer can see the final destination of Ramses' life among the gods, several of whom sit next to Ramses and face the viewer from the far end of the temple. They are dramatically framed by the architecture of the temple, as the series of columns forming the main colonnade seem to recede into time and space. And outside the temple, the photographs I had seen did not prepare me for the actual experience of looking up, squinting into the sunlight at the massive, towering figures of the Pharaoh and his queen, sitting regal and silent, seeming to defy the passage of time.

On our way back to Aswan, we stopped to see the Temple of Philae, dedicated to one of the most important and beloved of Egyptian goddesses, Isis. This temple had also required relocation when the High Dam was built, and it was now situated on an island of the Nile outside of Aswan. Egyptians worshiped Isis at this temple, complete with animal sacrifices, well into the sixth century C.E. According to our guide, it took a special emphasis on the cult of Mary for those Egyptians who converted to Christianity to make the full transition away from the worship of Isis. The main temple structure and colonnades were built in the Ptolemaic and early Roman periods, mostly in the ancient Egyptian architectural style. We spent most of our time walking up and down the main colonnade, looking up at the capitals crowning the elegant columns, each one a unique display of artistry around lotus, papyrus and date palm motifs.

We struck up a conversation with the boatman who took us to and from the Temple of Philae. Muhammad seemed the name of choice here too in Aswan, and this Muhammad was a Nubian young man with a contagious grin and warmth, and a ready sense of humor. Later that same evening, we happened to see Muhammad when we were eating dinner in a popular "floating" restaurant on a barge along the bank of the Nile not far from our hotel. Muhammad came over to our table when he saw us waving to him and told us he was there to meet some friends with whom he gets together regularly to play Nubian music. They were not performers, but played for their own and others' enjoyment. Reuven asked Muhammad if he could direct us to a shop where we could find some good CDs of authentic Nubian music, and Muhammad asked us to wait a minute. He returned a few minutes later with a CD in hand. He insisted on it being a gift, saying it cost almost nothing.

Ten minutes later, Muhammad and eight of his friends returned to our table and pulled chairs into a circle that included us. With the ac-

151

companiment of two traditional hand drums that they passed around between songs, they proceeded to sing their hearts out. They sang their favorite Nubian folk songs, most of them love songs. We didn't understand the words of course, but it really didn't matter. With or without Muhammad's one line explanations, the African-sounding music completely won us over.

Feet tapping, bodies swaying, hands clapping... the rhythms and melodies were contagious and we joined in, sometimes even singing along. There was an older Nubian man on the barge restaurant next to ours, sitting at a table by himself, lazily smoking a cigarette. He gave the young men a big grin and thumbs up when they started singing and soon he too was tapping his feet and singing along.

Muhammad and his friends clearly loved these songs and their joy was irresistible, as we felt ourselves drawn into their circle of music and warmth. This was how folk music was meant to be sung and shared. We stayed well past our bedtime and when we finally pulled ourselves away it was with the sense that we had just experienced a rare and wonderful musical treat, offered in a personal way that would stay with us long beyond our months in Egypt.

The next day we traveled to Luxor on a minibus with just two other people and an excellent tour guide who did not tire of our questions. On the way, we stopped at the Temple of Edfu, the second largest and the best preserved temple of ancient Egypt, built by the ancient Greek Ptolemies. When Alexander the Great died in 323 B.C.E. leaving no heirs, his empire was divided among his key generals and Ptolemy was granted an area that included Egypt. He and his descendants ruled Egypt until the Roman conquest in 30 B.C.E.

The Ptolemies built this grand temple on a site that was already considered by the Egyptians to be holy, on the foundations of a temple dating back to the New Kingdom. Our guide explained that the Hellenistic rulers presented themselves as Pharaohs when they conquered Egypt and they built magnificent temples such as the ones we were visiting, fully in the style of ancient Egypt and dedicated to the Egyptian gods. These rulers took pains to establish their authority in a way that would be least offensive to the Egyptians, and they allowed the people they had conquered to continue practicing their ancient traditions instead of imposing foreign ways upon them, hoping to minimize the chance of rebellion. The Temple of Edfu was dedicated to the Egyptian falcon god Horus. While the Greeks could identify Horus with their own Apollo, for the Egyptians, he was clearly portrayed here as Horus, with all his mythic tales depicted on the temple walls and columns. Despite their efforts, the Ptolemaic rulers eventually faced local rebellions that over time weakened their empire and facilitated the Roman conquest in 30 B.C.E.

While Luxor is smaller than Aswan and we had been looking forward to having a few days there, the day we arrived turned out to be a holiday—the annual celebration of spring. For local residents this apparently meant spending the day outside, and the streets were bulging with people strolling and picnicking absolutely everywhere, with many people plunking themselves down for a picnic right in the middle of the sidewalk! We were quickly overwhelmed by it all, and once we had found a reasonable and clean hotel, once again overlooking the Nile, we tried to take refuge down below along the banks of the Nile. But even here we proved fair game for people peddling boat rides and cold drinks. In the end, we escaped to our hotel balcony, which, it turned out, was a perfect place to admire the purples and pinks of the sunset over the river.

One of the things we were most looking forward to in Luxor was visiting the tombs in the Valley of the Kings. Even though we had seen comparable tombs in the Valley of the Queens on our previous visit, we were bowled over by the colors and clarity of the painted figures of the gods and goddesses adorning the walls. Each tomb was different and we enjoyed trying to figure out who the various gods and goddesses portrayed were. Our favorite was Nut, goddess of the night, spread across the ceiling of one of the tombs, her arms outstretched over the day and night skies. Nut is a well-known figure portrayed in several tombs, as she swallows the sun each night and gives birth to it again at dawn. We had already bought a reproduction of one of the most famous of these portraits of Nut, from the tomb of Ramses VI, and we were also taken with this slightly different ceiling painting.

But contrary to what one might expect, we were even more impressed by the Tombs of the Nobles. In keeping with the lesser status of their sponsors, these tombs are smaller and less famous than the Tombs of the Kings and Queens, but their artwork is actually more spectacular and better preserved. Our favorite was Ramose's Tomb.

Ramose was the governor of Thebes during the reigns of two Pharaohs—Amenophis III, followed by the controversial Akhenaten, whom many people believe introduced monotheism to the Egyptians with the worship of the single Egyptian god, Aten. In his famous work, *Moses and Monotheism*, Sigmund Freud theorized that Akhenaten's monotheistic beliefs later became the basis for Judaism, and that Moses himself was an Atenist priest, forced to leave Egypt with his followers after Akhenaten's death. Most scholars however reject Freud's theory, pointing out that Akhenaten, who died in 1336 or 1334 B.C.E., lived almost two centuries before the first archaeological and written evidence of Israelite culture.

154

Ramose's tomb is one of the few monuments dating from Akhenaten's reign in the mid-1300s B.C.E., during the Eighteenth Dynasty. Elements of traditional Egyptian practice along with the worship of Aten appear in the low relief carvings on the wall. One of the panels features Ramose's anticipated funeral banquet. Groups of men carrying ducks, flowers, and grain offerings, alternate with groups of women, their arms raised in lament, reflecting typical Egyptian practice of the times. On another wall, people are bowing down to the sun, depicted with long rays extending down in what appears to be a representation of Aten.

The detailed portraits of couples attending the funeral banquet and burial of Ramose are unique in that they convey a tone of comfortable intimacy, in sharp contrast to the formality of most ancient Egyptian art. The women are portrayed with one arm affectionately around their husbands' shoulders, and their other hand clasping his arm. The artistry of all the scenes covering the four walls of the tomb is breathtakingly beautiful. The facial expressions, the braided hair and clothing all come to life in the fine detail.

The artwork of the tomb was left unfinished, a fact attributed to Ramose's departure from Thebes to follow Akhenaten to his new city at Tell al-Amarna. It was there that Akhenaten established his new form of religion in earnest, a change accompanied by a unique style of art reflecting far greater emotion and vulnerability. This radical innovation in both religion and art proved short-lived. When Akhenaten was succeeded briefly by a female Pharaoh and then by his son, Tutankhamun (or King Tut), the new Pharaoh gradually returned to the tried and true ways of previous Pharaohs.

The unfinished sections of the walls of Ramose's tomb still reveal the sketches that would have guided the hands of artisans carving into rock to create additional relief panels. There is no color here, only the striking black outline of the couples' eyes, highlighting their graceful beauty and their way of following the viewer with a haunting sense of life.

While I studied the wall carvings, Reuven and Noam decided to explore what looked like a passage to another room. We were the only people in the tomb and the guard said it would be all right though there was nothing much to see. Ten minutes later, they returned and Noam was almost beside himself in excitement.

"You have to see this!" he exclaimed to Amir without saying any more. Amir followed Noam and Reuven back through the passageway and they showed Amir the mummified human skull they had found lying on the ground. The boys together with Reuven examined the skull as best they could with the small flashlights they had with them. That cinched it. Albeit for entirely different reasons, Ramose's Tomb achieved unanimous status as our family favorite.

Also following Amir's lead, we went to Medinet Habu, one of the less visited temple sites, but one he had been talking about ever since his class trip to Luxor two months earlier. Amir acted as our guide and we all admired the deeply etched relief carvings that have survived the centuries, with more color preserved than at most of the other temples.

The high outer walls boast two towering mirror images of Ramses III, facing each other from the right and left sides of the entrance, with each figure of Ramses proudly clutching a cluster of his victims by their hair, his other arm raised high, ready to slay them with his sword. Ramses performs this act as the great gods, Amun-Re and Re-Horakhty, look on from each side and present him with the sword of victory.

Inside these high protective walls, the exterior walls of the temple portray dramatic scenes of the king defeating the Libyans and Sea Peoples--seafaring raiders whose identity (perhaps Philistine or Greek) is still debated by scholars. Several rooms inside portray scenes of family life, including the Pharaoh playing a board game with his daughters. We spent a couple of hours exploring the temple complex at leisure.

It was already getting quite hot, so we concluded our time at Medinet Habu with cold drinks at a café across the road, before heading up the

155

hill to the smaller village of Gurna. Gurna is known for its "Workmen's Tombs" made by the same artisans who created the incredible art inside the tombs of the Pharaohs. Some of these tombs were built and decorated over a period of thirty years because the artisans could only work on their own tombs on their days off, which apparently came only once every ten-day work week. The boys found it interesting to contemplate a ten-day week and the fact that there is nothing in the natural cycle of time that dictates a seven day week, something we take so for granted.

There were no other tourists, only guards sitting in front of the tombs, looking bored. Climbing down into the tombs, and then following a narrow passageway that opened into the burial chamber, empty of the usual tourists, we felt almost like we had discovered the art ourselves. To our amazement, the artisans' tombs were even more striking than the nobles' tombs we had seen the day before. Never having been restored, they nevertheless looked like they had just been painted. The scenes of everyday life, in strikingly bold "autumn" colors, revealed a wide range of subjects ranging from barbers cutting men's hair, to people harvesting crops in their fields. The animals, people, and plants were all painted with fine detail in a style that was more decorative than realistic. Dancing figures of Anubis, the popular god with the body of a man and the head of a jackal who is associated with mummification and the afterlife in ancient Egypt, also adorned the walls. It felt like a special privilege to see this kind of art, artwork that reflected the activities of daily life and the ideas and beliefs that held enduring value for the artists.

Later in the day, Reuven and I decided to go back to the Temple of Karnak, where we had visited on our first trip. This temple complex is arguably the most impressive of the Pharaonic sites, both in terms of its size and scope. The site is 1.5 kilometers by 800 meters—large enough to contain ten cathedrals. One section alone is dominated by 134 towering papyrus-shaped pillars of stone. Approximately thirty Pharaohs contributed to the building of different structures in Karnak over more than 1600 years, resulting in the wide range of structures and styles represented. The largest ancient obelisk still standing in the world today graces the entrance of the temple, built by Hatshepsut, the female Pharaoh who ruled from 1479-1458 B.C.E., during the Eighteenth Dynasty. But even more impressive than the tall obelisks and statues that adorn these temples is the fact that virtually every inch of the towering walls and columns is covered, floor to ceiling, in carved hieroglyphics and scenes of the Pharaohs and gods and goddesses in ever-changing combinations.

Seeing Hatshepsut's obelisk reminded me of the experience of visiting her temple on our previous visit. This female Pharaoh's temple is built into the most spectacular of locations, sheltered below the mountains that are home to the Valley of the Kings and Queens. The temple is striking in its simple lines and colonnades, and it stands as my favorite, even though much of the artwork was damaged by Hatshepsut's successors who wanted to wipe out any memory of her existence. My interest in the female Pharaoh had been piqued on our previous visit and had led me to read a biography of her life. I still found myself intrigued by this lonely female figure who had defied history in taking the throne to rule for twenty-two years as the fifth Pharaoh of the Eighteenth Dynasty, and overcame great odds to become one of the most capable and successful Pharaohs of Ancient Egypt.

Walking slowly through the temple, I was struck again by two themes that dominate Karnak and the other Pharaonic temples and tombs. The first is the unabashed celebration of the power of the Pharaohs and the gods. Even in their only semi-divine human form, the military power of the Pharaoh was celebrated so triumphantly, with larger-than-like Pharaohs engaged in battle poses that dramatically pointed to their military prowess and power. These depictions also put the Pharaohs' military victories into a larger context of significance, celebrating their success in fulfilling their responsibility, with powers granted them by the gods, to preserve order against the ever-threatening forces of chaos and evil. I could imagine that these images of power and might would have awakened strong feelings of allegiance, inspiration, and awe in their followers.

But the power of the Pharaohs was nothing compared to the power of the gods and goddesses. They were immortal and their will could determine the fate of humans. The Pharaohs played a vital intermediary role between the people and their gods. The temples were dominated by scenes of the Pharaohs bringing offerings to the gods and goddesses, and one or another god conferring on the Pharaoh the power to rule.

The second theme—the power of the gods and the Pharaoh's quest for immortality—was even more pronounced, and it cast the celebrated military power of the Pharaoh in an interesting light. However powerful he might be, no Pharaoh could control his own fate.

Pharaohs, like everyone else, faced the normal threats of disease and aging, compounded by the constant dangers of war, internal rebellion, intrigue, and betrayal. Even the greatest of the Pharaohs were haunted by the examples of those whose hard-won accomplishments had been quickly and quietly undone by succeeding Pharaohs. Each Pharaoh, in his temples and portraits of monumental size, pushed the theme of overpowering his enemies as far as it would go. But none stopped there. The images in every temple portrayed the Pharaoh in his journey from king to deity, first making offerings to the gods, then being judged by the gods, being accompanied into the afterlife, and finally, joining the gods as a deity.

158

Only eternal life with the gods and goddesses provided a lasting destiny that no conquest or riches, however great, could ensure.

Even with the advances of modern medicine and longer life spans, human beings today still struggle with the meaning of life in the face of death. We may disguise and deny the onset of aging and delay our movement toward death. We segregate the dying so we don't need to confront it on a daily basis, but it is still something with which we must contend.

In the art of Ancient Egypt, we see the Pharaohs playing out this age-old struggle in dramatic colorful form. The rawness of their strivings resonates with the strivings buried within ourselves, of which we may not even be conscious. Perhaps it is this striving for immortality that best explains our fascination with the Pharaohs' temples and tombs. Even the monumental size and expanse—"larger than life"—reflect this same desire: the Pharaohs wanted to be larger than life. They wanted to live forever. The mummies, the tombs, the pyramids, the obelisks—all speak to this same driving urge. Perhaps, even more than the beauty of the architecture and the art itself, this raw human striving behind the art is what really draws us. We see in the images a particularly dramatic way of playing out the universal human struggle against the ultimate defeat of mortality.

It was strangely ironic, I decided, walking around Karnak. Who knows what awaited the Pharaohs, or what awaits any of us after death? But here we are, thousands of years after the Pharaohs lived, ogling their tombs and temples, fascinated by their accomplishments, their gods, and their beliefs. It is not exactly the immortality they longed for, but the stunning preservation of the Pharaohs' temples and tombs and our fascination with them does seem to have accomplished for the Pharaohs at least a certain kind of immortality, the result of their longing itself.

That night, we decided to have dinner away from the crowds of tourists, on the other side of the Nile in the village of Medinet Habu. We took the public ferry across the river, instead of crossing in a private motor boat as most tourists do, but it turned out to be rush hour in Luxor, and we found ourselves standing on the ferry with several hundred local residents on their way home from work and shopping. It was only a five-minute ride, so we were surprised to see so many people buying soft drinks and snack foods on the boat, but this seemed to offer a welcome chance for many to relax a bit between work and home. We enjoyed actually being thrust into the normal daily life of ordinary people instead of being among tourists. Standing on the top level of the ferry, we took in the local scene around and below us, and the clear, starry sky above.

When we got off the ferry on the other side, we followed the crowds up a dirt road into town, and I noticed two men selling fabric from their wooden cart alongside the road. It looked like it could be fabric for *galabiyas*, the long robes men wear here, so I said something to Reuven and we stopped to take a look. Sure enough, the deal was, you picked out the fabric you liked and one of the men would take you to the tailor, who would make you a *galabiya* on the spot. The boys had been talking about getting *galabiyas* for months, and since these were very light weight summer cottons, Reuven decided to get one too. There were beautiful grays, blues and beiges, solids and stripes to choose from. Reuven and the boys quickly found what they wanted. One of the men walked us over to the tailor shop nearby and the tailor took everyone's measurements and with a few snips of his scissors, he marked where he would later cut and sew the cloth. We settled on a time we would come by the next morning. The tailor and the man who had sold us the fabric seemed very pleased that Reuven and the boys were outfitting themselves with traditional Egyptian clothing. They pointed out that having their *galabiyas* made here in Upper Egypt, they were getting the "real thing"—the authentic *sa'idi* cut, characteristic of the region. They tried to talk me into getting a *galabiya* too, but I declined as politely as I could, saying I would be buying something more feminine in Cairo.

The next day, we picked up the *galabiyas*, and after a delicious lunch at the same restaurant-hotel we had gone to the night before, we decided to make the hotel's back courtyard our "home base" for the afternoon. We would be taking a night train back to Cairo that night, and we had a few last minute errands, but the shade of the courtyard overlooking a canal was very inviting. We were all ready for a chance to just sit and read, sipping a cold drink in this lovely quiet spot away from the press of tourists and shops. The boys put on their *galabiyas* in keeping with the relaxed mood, and at one point Reuven and the boys left to get haircuts.

160

While they were gone, one of the men who worked at the hotel desk came out to the patio where I was sitting. He asked me where we were from and how long we were traveling. When he heard that we were living in Cairo for half a year, he had more questions, and we got into a whole conversation, some in Arabic, but mostly in English. It turned out that Rajab, whom I guessed was probably in his forties, had lived in Medinet Habu all his life, and was full of praise for the advantages of small village life.

"Everybody here gets along. When someone is sick, everyone goes to visit him. Christian or Muslim, it doesn't matter. We're all friends." He paused, and then added, "And if we had a Jewish neighbor, it would be the same."

"I'm Jewish, you know," I said, smiling, acknowledging what I was sure he had already guessed.

"I thought so. And really, it would not be an issue here. Personally, I want to go to Israel. Someday, I hope to go with my whole family. It is a dream. It's not safe today—too much violence. But someday, *Insha'Allah*, I hope we can go."

I had not met a single Egyptian who said he wanted to go to Israel. I couldn't help but be skeptical: was this a sincere lament on Rajab's part, or more likely, an effort to say something he thought I would like to hear? I had to acknowledge what he had said, but I would keep it simple.

"I hope you do get to Israel someday," I answered.

"For me, what's important is we all believe in one God-- the same God-- and we should respect one another," he continued. "This is what the Quran teaches." "I agree," I replied. "Like you, I believe there is one God, and Islam, Christianity and Judaism all look to the same God, just coming from different directions." We talked about how there is much more that is similar between the three religions than the differences, and both of us expressed regret that there is so much conflict today between religious groups.

"Often it's because of ignorance," said Rajab. "We must learn more about each other's religions. And we should learn from the past," he added. "Islam has always shown respect and tolerance for Jews and Christians, calling them People of the Book. For hundreds of years, Jews and Christians were able to live and practice their religions in peace in Muslim countries."

Rajab said this with pride. I was not sure how much I wanted to challenge him, but the issues were more complex, and the historical record more uneven, than his statement acknowledged. While Muslim rulers had often shown greater tolerance toward Jews and Christians than Christian rulers had shown to non-Christian subjects during the same periods, tolerance came at a price: clearly demarcated second-class citizenship and high taxes for *dhimmis*, religious minorities. Did I want to raise this issue of *dhimmi* status—with its stipulations that synagogues and churches could not be built as high as the mosques and Jews and Christians were not allowed to ride horses or camels, only donkeys, as a sign of lower status? And what about the passages in the Quran that expressed negative views of Jews? Didn't they contribute to the anti-Jewish sentiment we encountered? My thoughts went back to the young man we had met in the market our first day in Aswan.

But this conversation did not feel like the right place to raise these issues. I felt like I might be viewed as an unappreciative guest, and I did not want to challenge the pride Rajab had just expressed in the tolerance of his faith. Also, I was enjoying this amicable conversation and wanted Rajab to feel the same way, and I wanted to end on a note that would encourage him to have more such conversations with Jews in the future.

Out of the corner of my eye, I noticed a young Egyptian man walking in, but I gave him barely a glance. The next minute I heard him speaking to me in a familiar voice and I looked again. It was Noam! With his short-cropped Egyptian hair cut and his new *galabiya*, I had assumed he was another Egyptian working at the hotel. We both had a good laugh.

Reuven and I decided to take a short walk outside and find a local store where we could buy some snacks for train ride back to Cairo. On the way, I told him about my conversation with Rajab. We compared notes on the several talks we had each had recently with Egyptian Mus-

161

lims, and the pride we often heard expressed in Islam's general tolerance toward Christians and Jews. This was an important part of the historical record not always appreciated in the West. But I shared with Reuven my doubts and frustration in not knowing if what I was hearing reflected the true opinions of the person speaking, or simply what they thought I wanted to hear. "I know," Reuven replied, "I'm not sure how to break through that wall either. But we do the same thing with them. We want the other guy to know we're good people and that Judaism is a good religion. So we make choices about what we say too."

162

"That's true," I acknowledged, "but do you think it would be a good idea, in these casual conversations, for me to mention that the reality is really more complex, that both traditions—probably all religious traditions—have some texts that express positive views of the other, and others that express animosity toward the other?"

"I actually try to do that, even in casual conversations," said my husband, the religious anthropologist. "I like to say that in my study of history I've seen that different leaders tend to quote the passages from their sacred texts that support their point of view. Like other leaders throughout history, they turn to religion in order to motivate large numbers of people. So in times of conflict, leaders point to the more hostile and aggressive passages to justify their attitudes and actions, and at other times, they point to the passages that favor tolerance and peace, if that's the sentiment they want to express and encourage in others. I think it's important for people to see this, and to see that when leaders repeatedly quote verses from the Torah or the Quran that express hatred of the other, they create fertile ground for those attitudes to spread—like we saw with the guy in Aswan and his comment about the 'dirty Jews.'

"But I don't always go there," Reuven added, "only if I sense an openness." "That makes sense," I said, liking this suggestion. "I think I will try to do that too. And maybe I don't need to be so uncomfortable when I hear an Egyptian talking about how Islam teaches tolerance for Jews and Christians. I can actually see that as a choice in itself that reflects that person's desire for tolerance and mutual respect. That might make it easier for me to appreciate what the person is saying without feeling like I have to respond.

"And when I try and go a little deeper, I think I'll just make the point that each of our traditions actually has a range of texts with these different points of view, and that in the end, we all have to choose which verses and what values in our traditions we want to build on."

"Right. That's the real challenge," Reuven agreed.

By now we had completed our circle and were back at the hotel.

"Let's get the boys and find a place to eat before we head to the train station," I said, suddenly feeling pressed for time.

"Look--"Reuven said, grinning as he pointed to the boys playing cards at a table across the patio. Both of them were still wearing their *galabiyas*, and their bags were sitting on the ground next to them. "I think they're ready."

163

Visiting Abu Simel

Author's sons Noam and Amir in Upper Egypt

Chapter 7
Women and Literacy

الأم مدرسه اذا اعدتها اعدت شعباً طيب الاعراق

A mother is a school; preparing her is like preparing a good nation.
~Hafez Ibrahim, Egyptian Poet

FROM THE START, I WONDERED WHAT KIND OF FEMINIST
movement existed in Cairo. At the recommendation of Kathy and Maureen, I decided to visit the offices of ADEW, the Association for the Development and Enhancement of Women.

ADEW's office was in a small, nondescript office building on a busy city street. I was greeted by a friendly young receptionist and could hear the voices of several people working from different rooms. I met with one of their staff members, Ingie, a young Egyptian Muslim woman in her early twenties. We ended up talking for over two hours.

Founded in 1987, ADEW was the largest women's organization in Egypt, according to Ingie. She explained that most of the issues feminists were addressing in Egypt—early marriage, female circumcision, honor killings—all affected poor women to a far greater degree than more affluent women. Female heads of households in particular, were among the poorest, most marginalized and disadvantaged in Egyptian society. For this reason, Ingie explained, ADEW directed most of its efforts in improving women's education and employment opportunities to this segment of the Egyptian population.

ADEW grew out of a micro-financing project—a program issuing loans of very small amounts of money charging little or no interest—that was launched in Egypt in the mid 1980s, targeting Cairo's garbage collectors, the *zabbaleen*. This project—the first of its kind in Egypt—proved so successful in helping some of the poorest, most marginalized Egyptian men begin to step out of extreme poverty that the organizers wanted to expand it. Seeking a second target population they discovered a pocket of poverty that struck them as particularly pernicious: female heads of households in the poor sector. In addition to being poor, most of these women were legal non-entities with no legal rights. Many had never been granted even the most basic legal papers such as birth certificates and identity cards. Most had never attended school as children and could not read or write. Without legal documents, they could not vote or qualify for any government benefits. They could not register their children for school. These women were totally unaware of their legal rights and did not realize anything was remiss.

ADEW began working with government officials to simplify procedures for poor women to acquire legal papers. At the same time, they began to hold "legal awareness classes" in women's homes. These
classes were quickly followed by others addressing women's health issues and teaching literacy skills. ADEW found that by holding classes in women's homes, they minimized the chances of husbands and fathers objecting to their wives and daughters leaving the house to attend. By word of mouth, news of the classes spread and the numbers of participants grew.

Thousands of women, with ADEW's help, have acquired their legal papers and rights. But this problem persists, and in Cairo alone, several hundred thousand women are still in need of legal documentation. ADEW continues to work on this issue as one of its top priorities. It also offers micro-loans to women interested in starting their own businesses and organizes small groups for women to support each other's efforts, as has proven successful in other developing countries. Classes in literacy, health education, and leadership and communication skills also continue to be a priority for the organization.

Egypt suffers one of the highest illiteracy rates in the world: in 2005, 35 percent of the population could not read or write, putting Egypt on the list of the top ten countries of the world for illiteracy. For Egyptian women, the situation is even worse: for women and girls over the age of fifteen, that figure is 45 percent. And in rural areas, 85 percent of the female heads of households are illiterate. I could not wrap my mind around these numbers and the reality behind them, of so many women in Egypt today, still trapped in poverty, unable to even read or write. I also was shocked that so many young girls in rural areas were still being denied an education, even with public education available to all.

For many girls and women, the problems of legal status and illiteracy begin at birth. Especially in rural areas, parents often neglect to even register their daughters' births because the procedure is so cumbersome. As a result, girls often cannot attend school. Not everyone sees this as a problem. Even today, Ingie explained, parents often assume their daughters will simply marry and have children when they grow up. Why do they need to go to school? Even though public education is provided to everyone free of charge, children still need books and supplies. Who would pay for these, and is it really worth it for a girl?

There were other issues affecting women that ADEW also viewed as high priorities. In the 1980s, it was not uncommon for girls from Egypt's poor communities to be married off at the age of ten. Virginity tests at marriage, conducted by groups of neighborhood women, were still the norm. If a young woman could not demonstrate proof of her virginity at the time of her marriage, an honor killing by the men of her family would be expected. These problems all still persist, Ingie noted, despite the progress that has been made.

ADEW expanded its work with adolescent girls, because so many of these issues affected them directly. The main goal was for the girls to see they had choices about what kind of lives they would lead. Many of the girls they were first able to connect with were the daughters of the women who had already taken ADEW classes. The classes for girls covered the same basic topics of legal rights, health and social awareness, as well as leadership and communication skills. ADEW staff members counseled women and girls to advocate for each other –for their sisters and daughters along with themselves—to be able to stay in school and pursue their education for as long as possible before being expected to marry or work at a paid job.

ADEW employed roughly three hundred people full-time, most of whom were working directly with women living in and around Cairo. Because of the seriousness of the problems faced by women in rural areas, ADEW was also trying to expand its work in the Delta region north of Cairo, one of Egypt's primary agricultural areas.

On my way home I thought more about the women living in today's world, trying to survive and raise a family without knowing how to read or write. What kinds of jobs were available for someone who could not read? What was it like not to be able to read the signs and labels in the grocery store, let alone fill out a government form? Not to be able to read to your own children or help them with homework? Here, it seemed to me, was one place where the cycle of poverty started—and with the right efforts—perhaps could be stopped.

A few weeks later, all of this came to mind, when Mahabbah and I were in the midst of one of our long conversations over tea. We were talking about how difficult the economic situation was in Egypt, and how little money people actually earned. Mahabbah said that people like the men across the street working at the hotel generally made only about 300 LE a month, which translated to only sixty dollars. How could that be, I wondered out loud. How could you support a family, even in Egypt, on $720 a year? That was why they worked two full time jobs, she said laughing. It was true; I had wondered why Seif and Umar both worked two full time jobs, leaving them almost no time with their wives and young children. I also realized with some surprise that with what we were paying Mahabbah, she made more money working two days a week than the men earned in their full-time hotel jobs.

For the first time, Mahabbah spoke about her deceased husband. He had been a tailor doing piecework and did not bring home a regular paycheck. His pay was dependent on how much work was available that week at the shop and how many items he actually made. Some weeks were good and other weeks they had almost no income.

Seven years ago, at the age of thirty-seven, her husband had suffered a fatal heart attack. She was left with three children, then ages fifteen, eleven, and one. Mahabbah was so devastated by her husband's sudden death, she said, that all she could do for months was cry. She could not go out and get a job, she could barely take care of her own children. Without the help of a woman she had previously worked for as a full-time house-keeper and nanny, Mahabbah was not sure how her family would have survived.

Mahabbah told me that her father had also died young, leaving her mother with six young children. Mahabbah was ten at the time. They were so poor that there was only enough money for two of her brothers to go to school. Mahabbah and her other three siblings were expected to go out and earn money for the family as soon as they were able. Mahab-bah herself never went to school and never learned to read.

How was that possible, I wondered, in amazement. Mahabbah was helping me learn Arabic. She was a natural teacher, as Reuven and I had commented several times already. Her daughter was a teacher. Maybe I had misunderstood.

"These words here," said Mahabbah, motioning to the Arabic words on the page in front of me, "I can't read them."

With a start I realized that Mahabbah fit the exact profile of ADEW's target population: female heads of households. Women born into poverty, raised in poverty, who had never gone to school and could not read or write. It had not occurred to me when I sat in Ingie's office that Mahabbah might be one of these women.

I mentioned to Mahabbah that I'd heard about free literacy classes for women in Cairo. She nodded and said that this was an issue Mubarak's wife was committed to. She thought there might even be classes offered somewhere near where she lived. But right now she did not have time. She needed to work and she wanted to be home when her eight-year-old son, Muhammad, came home from school in the afternoon. That was more important. But her daughter, Aziza, had taught her some of the letters.

"You already know some of the letters? If you know the letters, you can read," I said. "Really, Mahabbah, it's easy if you know the letters." I pointed to one of the words on the page of my book from school and Mahabbah named the letters and the sounds they made. I went over with her the sound each letter made and showed her how easy it was to move from sounding out the separate letters, to gradually blending them together to make a word. We did it together a few times with one word, and then went on to another... and another. Sometimes I had to remind Mahabbah of the name of the letter or the sound it made. In other cases, it was only a question of saying the sounds out loud and gradually blending them together. Mahabbah was amazed that slowly, she could actually sound out some words. She wanted to keep going and try new ones. We were both having fun.

Why not spend time reading together whenever she came to our apartment to clean, I asked her. We could continue to spend some time speaking Arabic together, and we could also read together. It would be good practice for me too, I said. Mahabbah lit up. *Mumkin*, Maybe, she answered, *Insha'Allah*, with God's help. I could see she liked the idea.

And, if she could practice reading at home, a little bit every day, I told her, she would improve very quickly. Before she knew it she would be reading.

169

"Really?" Mahabbah asked in surprise. "Really," I answered.

After Mahabbah left, my mind was buzzing. It didn't seem possible that Mahabbah had lived her whole life without being able to read books or newspapers, or even street signs. It hurt me to think of the pleasure and employment opportunities reading might have opened up for her. I wanted her to have those opportunities.

Literacy had always been an issue I was passionate about. The first research paper I ever wrote was entitled "Slum Education." I was in eighth grade and I drew a large broken ladder on the cover. All through high school, I tutored younger children who were struggling in school and helped them learn to read. And most recently, in 1999, I started a literacy program at the high school where I taught in Los Angeles, linked to a citywide initiative. Through this program, interested high school students were matched with elementary school children two or more years behind in reading. They met with their child weekly, during the school day, and helped them learn to read. The program was an enormous success and by the end of each year, our high school students had helped another thirty or forty children learn to read. As a result of reading weekly with their high school "reading buddies," many of these children discovered a new enthusiasm for reading and for school in general. Do you like to read? I asked a girl a year before at the end-of-year party. "I LOVE to read!" she said as she proudly showed me the book her reading buddy had given her as a present. For the high school students too, helping a child learn to read was almost always a powerful experience. I knew of several who had decided to go into teaching as a result.

The most dramatic case of transformation that I witnessed in this literacy program had involved our own son, Noam, when he volunteered as a ninth grader and worked with a second grader named Rodriguez. On the day they met, eight-year-old Rodriguez was so shy he could not even say his own name loud enough for others to hear. He could not name most of the letters of the alphabet. Noam took Rodriguez under his wing. Each week he spent the first ten minutes just talking, drawing pictures, and playing games with Rodriguez. Then he would move on to games focused on learning the letters. But the first agenda item was the personal connection, and just having fun. The school librarian and I watched as this shy boy slowly began to smile and then to laugh at Noam's jokes and antics. Soon he was learning the letters his classmates had learned two years earlier.

One day we saw it happen. Rodriguez sat hunched over his book, concentrating intensely. "B-A-T" He slowly made the sound of each letter. Then, following Noam's encouragement, he vocalized the three sounds in sequence, closer together, and again, closer together. At Noam's instruction, he continued, trying to slur the sounds a little bit. Suddenly Rodriguez started flapping his arms up and down by his sides. He was so excited, he couldn't speak. I wasn't sure he was even breathing. "BAT!" he spit out the word in total delight. He looked up at Noam in surprise. "It says BAT!" "You got it!" Noam answered, hugging him and Rodriguez laughed, and pointed to the next word. Once again, Rodriguez slowly went through each of the steps, gradually moving the sounds of the letters closer together. Suddenly his arms started waving up and down again, and Rodriguez, with just as much astonishment as before, blurted out the word. "CAT!" The librarian and I looked at each other. We both had tears in our eyes.

I thought of that moment when I shared what had transpired that afternoon with Mahabbah with the boys over dinner. Noam was quiet. I knew he was thinking about Rodriguez, with whom he had worked for a full two years. He knew from his experience how learning to read could dramatically change a child's view of himself and the things he was capable of. He wondered out loud if the same thing might happen with Mahabbah even though she was already an adult. I had the same thought. We'll see, I said. As much as I was hoping, I wasn't even sure Mahabbah would be able to make the commitment to practice reading at home. I didn't want to set my expectations too high.

The next day at the Alexander School, before I sat down with Zayna for my Arabic lesson, I spoke with the director of the program and asked if she could suggest any books that would be appropriate for someone like Mahabbah to learn to read. The materials I was using were really not suited for someone who already spoke the language. Mahabbah needed something in *Fus-ha*, Classical Arabic, which was the true written language. The director told me that there were government-sponsored literacy classes all over the city and that they had created special materials for adults. She thought there was probably a school near where I lived where classes were offered and where I might be able to pick up a book for Mahabbah. She would try to find out.

Two days later, I was back at the Alexander School for another lesson with Zayna. The director had the name of a school in Maadi that held literacy classes for adults. She offered to buy the books for me and bring them the following week. I thanked her and told her I was happy to go to the school myself. She seemed very skeptical about my being able to find it, but I assured her I would be fine.

Later that afternoon, I asked the people working at the hotel across from our apartment, if they knew where the school was and they said it was nearby, but on a little street. They were not sure how to direct me and they suggested I take a taxi! Americans must generally be pretty wary of trying to find their way around on their own, I decided. But I knew how to ask directions, so I set out in the direction they pointed, with the name of the school in hand.

The walk took me through a different part of Maadi, and as usual, when I finally asked someone for directions, he insisted on walking me to the school. When we got there we learned that the school did not offer adult literacy classes after all, but the school next door did. Someone at the second school walked me to the program office. Yes, they taught adult literacy classes. The secretary was happy to give me the first two books and notebooks for Mahabbah. She would not even let me pay.

Looking through the books at home, I saw that some of the very issues Ingie had talked about were reflected in the first lessons. There were pictures of identity cards, and the opening story was about someone filling out the forms to get an identity card for her daughter. Subsequent pages discussed the benefits that came with identity cards for oneself and one's children. I couldn't believe that what had been an interesting theory a few weeks earlier was the reality I was now encountering first-hand.

When Mahabbah came the next day, she walked in with bags of fresh *aish baladi*— whole wheat pita bread she had made earlier that morning with her sister-in-law for their two families and for us. It was still warm with a fresh yeast smell and Reuven and I enjoyed a breakfast feast of the fresh bread with yogurt. Once the pita bread cooled I put the rest in the freezer. The boys would enjoy it for breakfast too and this amount would keep us supplied for at least a week.

I showed Mahabbah the books I had gotten for her and she agreed to read with me again later in the afternoon. When Mahabbah was ready, we sat down for tea, and I suggested that this time we read first, and then talk. Mahabbah was interested when she saw the topic of identity cards, and she proudly took out her card to show me that she had one. Then we started to read. She slowly sounded out the words and I helped her when she needed help. She was happy to go over the words and the first few sentences several times.

There was a page of exercises that involved reading and matching words and Mahabbah seemed to find them a fun challenge. She sounded out the words slowly—it was harder when they were out of context—and she proudly matched the words she could. She did not get discouraged when she made a mistake. I suggested that Mahabbah practice at home and that we would review these pages and go on when we saw each other on Sunday. Mahabbah answered that she would try to practice at home with her younger son Muhammad but not with her daughter Aziza. Her daughter was a great teacher, but she got too impatient with her, she laughed. But Mahabbah really liked the book and assured me she would try to practice with it. Then we had another cup of tea and Mahabbah asked me how life was different in Egypt and the United States. What did I like better about life here in Egypt, she wondered, and what did I like better about life in the States? I told her how much I appreciated Egyptian people's friendliness and warmth, and that this is something I much preferred about life here. And I said that there were many more classes for adults to learn how to read here than in the States, but in general I thought education was better in the States. Mahabbah was not surprised.

I shared with Mahabbah something Amir had told us over dinner the night before. Apparently his Arabic teacher had been complaining all along that he asked too many questions. That day, he had finally made Amir stand in the corner as a punishment for asking too many questions! I told Mahabbah that in the States, this kind of thing might have happened in the distant past, but that it would not happen today, because we *wanted* children to ask questions. As a teacher, I urged my students to ask *more* questions. Mahabbah understood and agreed.

I switched to a related topic and described how every day, Reuven and I heard full classes of children reciting their lessons by rote in the

173

school behind us. I thought large class size probably contributed to both these teaching styles, and Mahabbah agreed.

Mahabbah told me that her younger son was in a class of sixty children. I thought I had misunderstood and asked Mahabbah to repeat what she had said. But I had heard right. She explained that Muhammad could not concentrate in the class because of all the noise, and that he really could not learn much in that environment. So, every night he studied at home with five other children and a tutor. His older brother Omar had to do the same.

Mahabbah acted like there was nothing special about this. She explained that while Egypt boasted free public education, it was a bit of a misnomer. First of all, parents had to pay for books and even chip in for classroom supplies because what the government provided was simply inadequate. And if you wanted your children to learn anything, she said, you really had to provide them with private lessons. It was the only way children could learn enough to eventually qualify for the university and this was important to Mahabbah.

How much did the private lessons cost, I asked her. For her two sons together, 700 LE each month, I was astounded to learn. How could she afford it, I couldn't help asking, and she told me that she had two nephews she had helped raise who now helped her provide for her children by contributing 300 LE each month for the evening lessons. That left Mahabbah needing to come up with 400 LE each month, which was most of her earnings.

Then Mahabbah talked about Aziza, who helped Muhammad with his schoolwork in the evenings. Aziza was trained to be a middle school teacher but even after two years, she had not been able to find a job in her field. She was teaching kindergarten for now. In order to get a job, you needed *wasta*, Mahabbah said. *Wasta* meant connections, someone who could make a call for you and get you at least an interview and sometimes more than that. But Mahabbah had no such connections.

Aziza's situation was typical, I knew. Thousands of university-educated young Egyptians could not find work in the field they had trained for. The fact that Aziza had any job at all in education made her one of the lucky ones.

After Mahabbah left, I wondered if I had understood her correctly about the private lessons and I called our friend, Debbie, to see if she had heard of this practice.

"That's what everyone does," Debbie said. "And not only that, but guess who teaches these evening classes? The same people who teach in the overcrowded classrooms during the day. They get paid so little, they count on the private teaching to make enough money to live on. As you can see, this means teachers are not pushing to change the system. But it's a terrible system," she concluded.

Two days later I talked about it with Zayna, and she too confirmed that this was what people did. She added that it was no different once you got to the university. Classes were often huge, and teaching was so poor that students often relied on the assistance of private tutors to help them learn the material. Here too, it was often the professors themselves who, because of low salaries, turned to private tutoring.

175

"What if the government covered what it does now, but also charged low tuition in order to reduce class size and raise professors' salaries. Couldn't this eliminate the need for private classes?" I asked Zayna. She did not even pause for thought before she shook her head. "There's so much corruption," she answered. "Education in Egypt is a big problem." She thought the government might also support the present system because it forced people to focus so much energy on creating their own solutions to these problems that it kept them distracted from the broader societal issues. With the present system, the government could also claim that it was providing free university education and jobs to large numbers of Egyptians. The fact that salaries were so low that they did not cover even basic needs was in the small print, so to speak.

Similarly, rote learning was emphasized over critical thinking in Egyptian universities, not only elementary schools, according to our friends. An Egyptian woman I met, Nadia, who taught political science at one of the universities, said that most professors expected their students simply to memorize facts from lectures and readings rather than develop analytical skills and creative thinking on their own. While this type of education might be best for managing such a large population from a political point of view, wasn't it also severely limiting Egypt's ability to move successfully into the global world and economy of the twenty-first century, I asked. Nadia agreed. The lack of interest in critical thinking and analysis was something she found deeply frustrating and sometimes made her question her future as an academic in Egypt. She noted that in the sciences, more critical thinking was encouraged than in the humanities, and in private universities, the quality of education was generally higher than in the large public universities. But the vast majority of college students studied in the large public universities and that is where most of the jobs were too.

Over the week, I began to wonder if I had made a mistake getting so excited about Mahabbah learning to read. If she didn't want to work with her daughter—which I could understand—and she didn't want to take a literacy class, how would she find the motivation and discipline to practice at home on a regular basis? Reading with me twice a week for two months would not in itself be enough for Mahabbah to really learn to read. Maybe, despite our initial enthusiasm, it was asking too much.

The following week, Mahabbah arrived with a big smile on her face, and even before she took off her outer *galabiya*, she pulled out her new book and notebook. She showed me the two and a half pages she had filled in the notebook, copying the sentences we had read together the previous week. She was so proud. Then, still standing in the kitchen with all her layers of clothing on, she showed me how well she could read the pages we had read together the week before, and how well she could now do the exercises. She opened what looked like it was one of her son's schoolbooks that she had brought from home, slowly sounding out the words on the first page. I couldn't believe it. Mahabbah had practiced reading every day with Muhammad, she told me. She was so proud of the increased ease with which she could read what she had practiced. She wanted to go on in the book, and we sat down immediately and read the next several pages together. I encouraged her to practice at home, in exactly the same way she had, with this new material. Once again, I was really excited. In this first week, Mahabbah had actually exceeded my hopes and expectations, in both the amount of time she had put into working on her reading at home, and in her progress. Could she keep it up?

Two days later, my doubts were confirmed. Mahabbah had out of town family visiting in anticipation of a niece's wedding that would take place the following week. She had not been able to practice at all in the last two days. And she would be cooking all week, since she had guests and was expected to serve a big meal every night. But in another week, she assured me, she would get back to practicing her reading at home.

And two weeks later, Mahabbah made good on her promise. Once again, she showed improvement in her ability to sound out the words on the pages she had practiced. We moved on to read new material together, and I suggested that Mahabbah now experiment with reading ahead on her own at home, sounding out the words by herself, and then checking with Muhammad. She was a little skeptical, but said she would try.

Over the next few weeks, Mahabbah continued to make progress. There were ups and downs with the amount of time Mahabbah spent reading at home. It was not a question of her interest flagging. It was more that life kept interfering with the ever changing demands and challenges faced by a single mom with three children. Then her older son broke his leg and was bedridden. Mahabbah described how every few minutes Omar called down to her with a different request—he needed a glass of water, he was hungry, he needed his leg lowered, he needed his leg raised, could she please turn the light on? And so on.

But Mahabbah practiced when she could and she continued to make slow, steady progress. One day I showed Mahabbah a bottle of olive oil that two months earlier had prompted her to ask me what it was, since she could not read the label. She grinned at the sight of the bottle. Now she read it easily. I asked Mahabbah if she could read signs in stores and billboards she passed, as she walked and took buses through the city. Like me, she still found the fancy calligraphy styles on the billboards hard to read. But she was able to read street signs and bus destinations, and that made a big difference, she said.

One day in mid-June, Mahabbah spoke the words I had been hoping for: she had decided to enroll in a literacy class after we left Egypt. She had already made inquiries and there was a class that met near her home that would be perfect. "I really like this—I love reading!" she said. It was hard to know who was happier—Mahabbah or me.

178

Mahabbah Reading

Chapter 8
Getting Political

الناس أعداء الأشياء اللي يجهلوها

People are enemies of that which they don't know.
~Arabic Proverb

WHEN WE FIRST ARRIVED IN EGYPT, CONTROVERSY WAS
still raging over the political cartoons depicting the prophet Muhammad
as a terrorist that had appeared in the Danish newspaper, *Jyllands-Posten*,
a few months earlier, in September 2005. Large demonstrations had led
to violent riots and even loss of life in several countries including Afghanistan, Pakistan, Nigeria, and Libya. Death threats and rewards for
the killing of the Danish cartoonist had been issued by various radical
Muslim groups including the Pakistani religious party *Jamaat-e-Islami*,
the Islamist website *Ansar Al Sunna*, and al Qaeda.

Three weeks into our stay, thousands of Egyptian university students
demonstrated at Al Azhar University in Cairo and called for boycotts
against all the countries that had published the cartoons. Al Azhar University, the oldest university in the world and one of the most important
centers of Sunni Islam, is an institution that commands special respect
throughout the Muslim world. These demonstrations were not the first
Egyptian response to the cartoons. On the previous Friday, after prayers,
thousands of Egyptians had demonstrated throughout the country. And
at the African Cup soccer games hosted in Cairo, large banners reading
"We reject insulting our prophet Muhammad" were held up by fans. One
of Egypt's most popular players, Muhammad Aboutrika, roused cheers
from the stands when he wore a shirt that read "We sacrifice for you, our
prophet," even though he knew he would be dealt a yellow penalty card
for deviating from the required uniform.

In the West, the rights of free speech and a free press emerged again
and again as the core values that defined our view of the Danish cartoons
incident. But here in Cairo, respect for the prophet Muhammad and the
religion of Islam trumped free speech, and seemed to justify a strong,

even violent response. For many in Egypt and the wider Arab Muslim world there was no question—insulting the prophet and Islam crossed a line that could not be tolerated.

Coming from the West, I was startled by the angry and violent response. What I came to see was that our essentially different responses to the Danish cartoons was based on much more than whether we looked to Muhammad as our prophet. The cartoons incident revealed a deep cultural divide between societies that are built on very different core values. For the West, the starting point was freedom while for the Arab Muslim world it was honor. We all think we know what the words "freedom" and "honor" mean, but they actually mean different things in different cultures. Living in Cairo, we were constantly bumping up against honor codes we did not understand.

180

We encountered many situations that we found baffling at the time and only later understood as expressions of a radically different code of honor. One such case involved Muhammad, the young man who worked across the street with Umar and Seif at the hotel. We called him "Noam's friend Muhammad-from-across-the-street" to distinguish him from the other Muhammads we knew, including Noam's other friend with the same name who was in his Egyptian History class at school. Even though Muhammad had already finished college and was at least five years older than Noam, the two had become quite friendly and on a couple of different occasions had spent the evening together downtown, with Muhammad showing Noam around some of his favorite parts of the city. Noam often stopped at the hotel to hang out with Muhammad for a while on his way home from school. One afternoon, after stopping across the street, Noam walked in the door, letting it slam behind him.

"Muhammad wants to come say goodbye. He quit his job because his boss insulted his mother. He's really upset, but he wanted to say goodbye before he leaves." Noam was close to tears.

"He's quitting because his boss said something about his mother?" I asked. Knowing how scarce jobs were in Cairo, I was immediately concerned. "Has he thought about how hard it will be to find another job? Is this really final?" I asked.

"Muhammad is really upset. I don't think he's going to change his mind, but you can ask him. Can I tell him it's okay to come over?" I said it was fine, and a few minutes later, Muhammad was at the door. We invited him in and he sat down with us in the living room. His hand was shaking when he put out his cigarette.

We told him how sad we were to see him go, and asked him if there was any other way he could see to resolve the situation without quitting.

"There is no way. No way. I can't work there anymore. My boss said something very bad about my mother. It was a big insult, and I cannot forgive him for that," he said shaking his head.

"What did he say?" I asked.

Muhammad hesitated before telling us. "He was angry at me for coming to work late and we got into an argument and then he called my mother a dog. That's such an insult. I don't ever want to talk to him again and I can't work there anymore." He was near tears.

"But quitting your job seems to be something that will hurt you more than him. Isn't there anything else, anything you or someone else could say?"

"No, I cannot work there anymore," he repeated. "There's nothing anyone can say." We said goodbye and told Muhammad he would always be welcome in our home and we hoped to see him again soon. After he left, I was still confused about why he felt he had to quit over this. For Muhammad to quit his job over what seemed like a rather generic insult in the heat of quarrel struck me as an impulsive act and revealed a streak of immaturity I considered uncharacteristic of him.

"Maybe after he and his boss have had a few days to think about it, things will look different to them. Who knows, maybe his boss will apologize and Muhammad will come back to work after all," I said to Noam.

"Maybe," he answered. But he did not sound convinced.

In the end it turned out that Noam was right and Muhammad had quit for good. I was left baffled by this sequence of events that did not make any sense given my understanding of interpersonal relations. At the time I simply did not grasp the primary importance of honor in Arab society.

A few weeks later I read a book, *Understanding Arabs: A Guide for Westerners*, by Margaret K. Nydell, that shed new light on Muhammad's reaction to his boss's insult. "Honor" tops Nydell's list of basic values in Arab society: "A person's dignity, honor, and reputation are of paramount

181

importance and no effort should be spared to protect them, especially one's honor." Nydell's book helped me understand that without realizing it, I had been looking at Muhammad's behavior through a Western lens. The value placed on honor in this society created an entirely different way of seeing and interpreting events large and small.

Protecting the honor of one's family could demand much more than leaving a job. Israeli journalist Lazar Berman, reflecting on his experience serving as lieutenant in a unit of the Israeli army made up of Bedouin and other Israeli Arabs, writes: "In this culture, at its most basic, a man must strive to maintain his honor at all costs. He must fight, even lie or kill, to protect his honor and that of his family. Conversely, when a man fails to protect his honor, he is shamed. He may regain his honor by vengeance against those who shamed him, often through bloodshed." When I read these words, quitting a job over a perceived insult no longer seemed so extreme.

These explanations shed light on several other issues we had encountered, including a more profound dilemma involving honor that Noam had come home with a few weeks earlier, after a different conversation with Muhammad. On this occasion too, Noam had walked in with a determined sense of urgency.

"I need to talk to you," he said walking in, his voice stressed. Without even putting down his backpack, he came into the kitchen, where I was cooking dinner, and explained that he and Muhammad had been discussing some of the ways in which American and Egyptian societies differ. What a great topic, I thought to myself. I wondered what could have come up that put such an urgent tone in his voice.

"Do you know about honor killings?" Noam asked, the shock still evident in his eyes. I knew that an honor killing is a murder almost always committed by a male family member against a woman who is believed to have brought dishonor upon her family. This dishonor could be for any of a variety of reasons such as the woman having been the victim of sexual assault or refusing to enter an arranged marriage, but most commonly, it results from the woman's actual or suspected involvement in a sexual relationship before or outside of marriage.

"Yes," I answered. "It's hard to believe, I know. What did Muhammad have to say about it?" Noam took a deep breath.

"He explained that premarital sex is not accepted here like it is in the United States. That I kind of expected. But then he told me that a father will actually *kill* his daughter if he finds out she's having sex with someone before she's married. First I thought he must be talking about how things used to be. But he said it's the same today, and that practically everyone here agrees with it—whether they are Muslim or Christian or even secular. It has to do with family honor and parents feeling like they have to protect their family honor, even if it means killing their daughter—and – even themselves sometimes." He was shaking his head. "I can't believe it! I can't believe people still do this, it's crazy."

I told Noam that while honor killings were still sometimes carried out in Egypt, I was not sure they were as widespread as Muhammad had indicated.

"I'm sure there are also people and organizations actively trying to stop the practice, but I don't know how effective they are. I can try to get some more information," I told Noam.

A few weeks later I had the occasion to talk with a feminist political scientist, Nadia, who taught at a number of different universities in Cairo. I shared with her what Muhammad had said and asked how pervasive honor killings really were. She concurred with Muhammad: honor killings are still viewed by most Egyptians--regardless of religious background-- as necessary to maintain adherence to high moral standards. How frequently were they carried out? Nadia did not know, but was certain that they happened more than they are reported.

"I think there are maybe fifty cases a year that are reported, but I don't know for sure."

"Are they prosecuted? I asked.

"The men are rarely prosecuted, and even when they are, they are usually given only light sentences," she replied. Later I shared this information with Noam.

"Yup," he sighed, "this is definitely one way the United States and Egypt are different."

Now thinking about the reaction to the Danish cartoons in the Arab world, I could see how the high value placed on honor cast the incident in a far different light than did the context of free speech, coming from a Western perspective. If the need to protect family honor could obligate a man to kill his own daughter, the need to protect the honor of the prophet could certainly impose limits on free speech and freedom of the

183

press, and might well be seen as justification for violence. The frame of reference was completely different.

But some editorials and opinion pieces in the Egyptian papers also tried to meet the issue of free speech head on, and in so doing, introduced an additional argument when they charged that the Danish cartoons moved beyond any reasonable claims of freedom of the press by ridiculing and inciting hatred of Islam. That was the right note to strike for a Western audience. Hate speech was the perennial challenge to free speech in the West. More than one editorial argued that this attack was all the more infuriating in light of Islam's record in preaching respect for all religions. One such op-ed piece appeared in the International Herald Tribune. While the Arab press might express strong sentiments against Zionists and even Jews, the author continued, it never attacked Judaism as a religion, nor any symbols of the Jewish religion, or any other religion for that matter.

I had to wonder, was the author reading the same newspapers I was? How could he say that the Jewish religion was never attacked or insulted in the Arab press? Weren't the political cartoons in Egyptian papers that depicted Israel as an Orthodox Jew with the side curls and the long coat of a Hasid and a Star of David on his hat blurring of the lines between politics and religion, and between Israelis, Jews, and Judaism? To my mind the Star of David was a symbol of the Jewish religion as well as the Jewish people.

The more I thought about it, the more I questioned the very assumption that attacking a religion was worse than attacking the people who practice the religion. Were cartoons that depicted the Israelis as Nazis in relation to the Palestinians really less problematic than a cartoon ridiculing Moses would have been? Frankly, I found these cartoons even more problematic, as they demonized living human beings, making hatred the only reasonable response to a whole group of people.

We found that the demonization of Israel in the press was an almost daily occurrence, with the lines between Israelis and Jews constantly blurred. Inflammatory images of Israelis and Jews portrayed as the devil and as Nazis were regularly matched by equally incendiary words. Most of these appeared in government sponsored newspapers. We regularly read about Israelis engaged in a "holocaust" against the Palestinians in *Al Ahram's* weekly English edition, which also claimed that the Israelis

184

were "slaughtering Palestinian women and children." Many times I had seen cartoons and excerpts of articles from the Arabic press translated on the Web that I regarded as expressions of hatred with no basis in fact. *Al Akhbar* and *Al-Ahram al-Massai* even claimed a worldwide conspiracy of Jews existed that were intent on implementing *The Protocols of the Elders of Zion,* from the Zionist center, Israel, to pursue the long-term Jewish goal of ruling the world. During our first few weeks in Egypt, I was shocked. Then I came to expect it. But even so, certain days an image or ugly lie would catch me off guard and I would find myself startled and dismayed and angry all over again.

185

A few weeks after the demonstrations against the Danish cartoons, Reuven and I were walking through a central courtyard at the American University of Cairo. As we turned a corner we saw a large political cartoon blown up to poster size and placed prominently on an easel in the middle of a walkway where most students, faculty and administrators would pass. The cartoon depicted a conductor leading an orchestra. Each of the musicians represented a different nation, and all of them were straining and perspiring in their effort to follow the lead of the conductor. One of the players was belligerently refusing to go along with the conductor's lead: he was portrayed with a smirk on his face as he played, deliberately forcing a screeching sound out of his violin. This player, in contrast to all the other compliant nations of this orchestra, was Palestine, represented by Hamas. The conductor was a classically caricatured Orthodox Jew.

Was this conductor who so successfully controlled the entire orchestra, except for the rebellious musician of Palestine, supposed to represent Israel or the Jews of the world? Whatever the case, the cartoon was actively buying into and spreading the centuries-old canard that the Jews control the world. That this political cartoon appeared only weeks after the demonstrations against the Danish cartoon, was particularly unsettling. Was no one at the university but us struck by the parallel issues? The poster stayed up for a week. Literally thousands of people walked by, and apparently no one was troubled enough by the poster's antisemitic message to have it removed.

Again we were forced to wonder, what did the average Egyptian, university-educated or not, know about Judaism today? Frequently in downtown Cairo I walked by bookstores with *The Protocols of the Elders of Zion* (the famous forgery that attributed aspirations for world domination to the Jews) prominently displayed in the window. Apparently it was a best-seller. Several people had told us about the popular television series based on *The Protocols* that had aired the year before. It seemed preposterous that anyone would believe this stuff. But how many Egyptians ever heard a challenge to these ugly lies? With virtually no Jews living in Egypt, and daily attacks against Israel in the press, with the most outrageous claims made against Israel and the Jews, how many Egyptians would even think to question political cartoons such as the one displayed at AUC, or the slanderous depiction of the Jewish people in *The Protocols* and other books like it? This reality was so deeply disturbing that most of the time, we did not focus on it. But the appearance of this political cartoon in the center of the American University of Cairo—just weeks after the demonstrations against the Danish cartoons--brought up all of our feelings.

186

The Danish cartoons also prompted an interesting discussion in No-am's Egyptian history class that he shared with us one night over dinner. In discussing the incident itself, Noam's teacher asked the class if inciting hatred against a group of people should be grounds for imposing limits on free speech. When an Egyptian classmate asked for an example of such a case other than the Danish cartoons, someone suggested the use of swastikas to incite hatred. Another student asked, "What's the big deal about a swastika?"

Noam's teacher, Mr. Stevens, responded quietly. He told the class about the Nazis' efforts to eliminate the Jews of Europe, focusing on both their propaganda campaigns, and the different methods they used to murder six million Jews. Mr. Stevens mentioned other attempted geno-cides in recent history, but spent most of his time talking about the Ger-mans' attempts to wipe out Europe's Jews. Everyone listened quietly. It seemed to Noam that this was the first time most of his Egyptian class-mates had heard about the Nazis' war against the Jews at all. It was hard for Noam to remain silent, but he realized it would be hard for him to say anything without revealing he was Jewish. He decided that it was prob-ably more valuable that his classmates hear this information from their non-Jewish, Canadian teacher than from a Jew.

We discussed how unusual it probably was for Egyptians to learn about the Holocaust in school (a fact later confirmed by our ex-pat friends), and how AIS and other international schools had unique opportunities to expose young Egyptians to this chapter of recent history. Noam's classmates would probably react differently when they passed a bookstore with *The Protocols of the Elders of Zion* in the window, or heard Israel attacked for committing a "holocaust" against the Palestinians. Who knew, perhaps that day's discussion about free speech and its limits had planted an idea that would one day contribute to a class member's future efforts to shape Egyptian government policy. This kind of high school class discussion in Egypt seemed a potentially potent form of democracy education.

While attacks against Israel in the press were disturbing, it was even more difficult for us when extreme responses to Israel came up in our personal relationships. When Noam started telling his friends at school that he was Jewish, he encountered mixed responses. With certain friends, Noam was pleased to find his hopes for more thoughtful, challenging discussions about Israel were met. But when Ashraf, a Christian Arab, learned that Noam was Jewish, he almost immediately started to attack Israel. He said he had nothing against Jews for their religion but the fact that they supported Israel made Jews, along with Israelis, the enemies of Egypt.

One day Noam came home extremely frustrated after he and Ashraf had gotten into another heated discussion about Israel. Whatever question or idea he expressed, Ashraf had a ready answer. At one point, Noam realized that Ashraf was simply not open to the possibility of seeing things differently. I reminded Noam of the advice he'd been given before starting school--when it comes to discussions about Israel, listen don't argue.

"That's fine for class and for school in general, but with my friends I'm not willing to stay quiet any more." Noam spoke quietly and with conviction. "I am listening and really trying to understand their point of view. But I want to explain my point of view too. Nothing is going to happen to me—they're my friends. I know they probably won't agree with me and what I say may not change their minds at all. I don't care. But they don't even know there is another side. If they don't hear it from me, who will they hear it from?" I was moved by his confidence and clear assessment of the situation.

Meanwhile, Zayna and I were also talking more about Israel. She and I both came to these conversations with an increasing respect and affection for each other, along with a shared desire both to understand and to be understood. One day I brought along to class my *siddur*, the traditional Jewish prayer book. I showed Zayna some of the traditional prayers for the rebuilding of Jerusalem and a return to Zion. Zayna was genuinely surprised by the prayers themselves and the fact that they are traditionally said in each of the three daily services, as well as the prayer after meals.

From there we went on to talk about a wide range of issues relating to Israel and the Palestinians, as well as how Islam views Judaism. Zayna asked me if I see Jesus and Muhammad as prophets. I explained that I saw them as important teachers and spiritual leaders, but that I did not view them as my prophets.

188

"But why, if I can accept Abraham and Moses as prophets, why can't you accept Muhammad as a prophet?" I tried to explain that it is always easier for a new religion to accept past prophets than it is for an old religion to accept as true prophets the bearers of new revelation. Any claim of new divine revelation, by definition, is always threatening because it suggests the older religion is not good enough. The new revelation is seen by its followers as correcting and superseding what came before.

Zayna looked unconvinced. Then I asked "what if someone claimed to be a prophet and started a new religion today? Would Muslims accept him as their new prophet?" Now Zayna nodded slowly.

I told Zayna that I greatly appreciated Islam's respect for Judaism and Christianity as two other forms of monotheism. With Zayna I felt I could speak my mind, so I pushed ahead a little bit. I told her that I found it disturbing that while Islam taught that God spoke directly to Moses and Jesus, it also taught that Jews and Christians intentionally changed the revelations they had received from God. "What kind of people would do that? It's like saying Jews and Christians are not good people—they cannot be trusted." Zayna listened and nodded again. She was clearly thinking about what I was saying and seemed to appreciate what I saw as problematic.

When our conversation returned to Israelis and Palestinians, Zayna raised a key question: Did Jews' historical link to the land of Israel justify forcing Palestinians who had been living there for generations off their land? I told her that I found it deeply troubling that many Palestinians had lost their land, but I also noted that many Arabs had sold their land to Jews in the decades before Israel was a state. Zayna looked at me with a pained expression on her face.

"Selling your land, it's like this--" she said, dramatically drawing her finger across her own throat. "They had to have been really, really desperate. Or they never would have sold their land." I nodded. I did not have this direct experience of living on land that had been in my family for generations, but I could imagine it would be terrible, in ways unthinkable, to sell such land. I shared with her my understanding that in many cases the land had been sold by Arab landowners living elsewhere, perhaps not feeling such a strong attachment to this land, while the people living on the land, sometimes for generations, had not had a say in the matter. I told Zayna that it was also true that some land had been seized by the new Jewish state in 1948 when Palestinians were deliberately frightened, in some cases by Arab leaders and in other cases by Israeli soldiers, and fled their homes and villages.

189

I found myself thinking about the Zionist slogan I had learned as a child—"A land with no people for a people with no land"—and I felt sad and angry at the denial of the moral complexity of Israel's founding in my own education. I admitted as much to Zayna, noting that there were other Jews who felt the same way, and new approaches to Israel's history were being written, documenting more fully the displacement of the Palestinians. I came away from each discussion with Zayna with the sense that there was something profound in our efforts to listen carefully and to probe our own and each other's assumptions and accepted truths.

A week later, Noam came home with new questions. "Can you be friends with someone with whom you totally disagree about certain things that are really important to you?" he asked as we sat down to dinner. He and Ashraf had had yet another conversation about Israel. When Noam had tried to explain that because of the Holocaust, Jews had felt an even stronger need to have their own country, Ashraf interrupted.

"The Israelis are worse than Hitler!" he proclaimed. All their other friends groaned in response.

"I told him he didn't know what he was talking about if he could say something like that and I walked away," Noam concluded.

"That must have been painful," I said. "It was," Noam answered quietly. "I don't know if I can be friends with him if that's how he feels." We reminded Noam of his Egyptian history class discussion and how little most students here learned about the Holocaust, even at AIS. Ashraf's comment reflected ignorance as well as a deep prejudice fueled by the general culture. Ashraf had grown up here, in an environment where it was not unusual for Israelis to be portrayed as Nazis. Still, it was one thing to try and understand why someone would say something like this, and another thing to be friends with him.

"I don't think you have to be friends with someone who says things like that, Noam, even here in Egypt," Reuven said.

Noam nodded sadly. "You're right."

The next day, Noam came home smiling.

"Guess what? Ashraf apologized," he announced. "He realized he'd gone too far and said 'I thought about it and decided I don't really hate *all* Israelis. I just hate the ones who are doing bad things to the Palestinians.'" It wasn't everything Noam might have hoped for, but it was definitely an improvement, we all agreed. Noam felt confirmed in his decision to speak his mind with his Egyptian friends, even about Israel.

"I know people won't always agree with me, but I have to say what I really think. If the only Jew they know doesn't say anything, how can we expect them to know there is another side to the story?"

Tahir Square July 2011

190

Chapter 9
Winds of Change

حبّة تثقل الميزان

A single grain tips the scale.
~Arabic Proverb

"CHANGE IS IN THE AIR—YOU CAN FEEL IT. THE GOVERN-ment cannot simply continue with the status quo," my young friend Kareem remarked. He was referring to the growing numbers of Egyptians who were taking to the streets in late April in support of what was increasingly being called "the Judges Movement." The pro-reform judges had attributed the strong showing of Mubarak's National Democratic Party in the parliamentary elections of November and December 2005 to widespread election fraud. In response, the government initiated disciplinary proceedings against the most vocal of these judges. Now, more than two thousand judges in Cairo and Alexandria had joined in protest against these disciplinary hearings and hundreds of Egyptians were demonstrating in the streets in support of the judges.

Even before the elections, the pro-reform judges had pressed for legislation that would grant the judiciary greater independence from the executive branch of the government, arguing that only a truly independent judiciary could monitor elections and carry out its other functions with integrity. Many of these same judges now charged the government not only with election fraud, but also with intimidation and assaults on voters and even judges who had tried to properly supervise the elections. At the same time, they accused other judges of collaborating with the government in vote-rigging, and demanded a formal inquiry.

On February 15, the Supreme Judiciary Council stripped three top judges of their judicial immunity and charged them with "insulting and defaming the state." One of the accused, Judge Hisham El Bastawisi, told the Associated Press: "I'm appalled that they want to interrogate us for slander instead of investigating and questioning the judges who are accused of vote-rigging."

In April, the Minister of Justice called for disciplinary action against ten pro-reform judges. Most of the attention was focused on the disciplinary hearings scheduled for Hisham El Bastawisi and Mahmoud Mekki, the two deputy heads of Egypt's highest appellate court who had led the demands for a formal inquiry into the November parliamentary elections. The pro-reform Judges Club in Cairo started round-the-clock sit-in protests at their headquarters in support of the two judges, while activists organized civilian demonstrations outside. Out of eight thousand Egyptian judges—most of whom at least quietly supported the call for reform—roughly a third now stood in open dissent against the regime. Police beat up and arrested hundreds of demonstrators over the course of several days at the end of April, but each day, the number of demonstrators rose and the demonstrators proved more inventive in their efforts to elude the police, dispersing when the police appeared and reconvening a few blocks away and using cell phones to communicate with each other.

Fortunately for us, I had recently begun a friendship with Kareem, a 21-year-old Egyptian university student, who was able to interpret these events for us as they unfolded. As a teenager, Kareem had been one of the first participants in "Children of Abraham," a dialogue program for Muslim and Jewish youth from around the world. Ari Alexander, the co-founder and co-director of "Children of Abraham," who spent an evening with us at our home in Los Angeles shortly before we moved to Cairo, had spoken highly of Kareem and encouraged me to connect with him.

Kareem grew up dividing his time between his parents' home in England and his grandparents in Cairo. Even before his involvement with "Children of Abraham," he had participated in "Seeds of Peace," a summer program in the United States offering training in leadership and conflict resolution for Israeli, Palestinian, and Egyptian youths. Now finishing his B.A. in Cairo, Kareem was an ardent political activist involved in the closely allied human rights and free speech movements in Egypt. We frequently consulted him for his analysis of events taking place on the ground, as well as the broader contemporary political issues.

On one occasion Kareem's advice was particularly helpful. Zayna and I had been discussing the growing protests in support of the Judges Movement during class one day and she mentioned that she was think-

ing of going to one of the demonstrations. I had read about a panel discussion about the Judges Movement scheduled for the next day that I
thought I might want to attend as well. That night I spoke with Kareem.
Like many Egyptians, Kareem pinned great hopes on this judicial reform
movement, but he had reservations about our plans. The government
was proving increasingly aggressive in its efforts to stop the demonstrations and the Ministry of the Interior had just that day issued a new
warning explicitly invoking the Emergency Law. This law allowed the
government to take extreme measures to enforce public order, and while
it had been in effect since Mubarak took office in 1981, the government
announcement seemed to suggest that the police would be taking even
harsher steps against the demonstrators. Kareem advised that Zayna not
attend a rally now unless she had attended rallies in the past and had
experience dodging the police. "You have to know when to run," he told
me. He also had reservations about my attending the panel, which he was
certain the police would be watching and might disrupt. Both Zayna and
I decided to stay home.

Over the next several days, tensions continued to mount as the date
of the Mekki-Bastawisi trial approached. The trial had been postponed
several times. On May 10, in anticipation of the trial now set for the
following day, I heard that demonstrations were planned at the Midan
Tahrir traffic circle near the AUC campus. I was relieved when Reuven's
professor called to cancel their meeting.

In the end, three simultaneous demonstrations were staged in different locations downtown in an effort to confuse and diffuse the police. Hundreds of people marched through the traffic-congested streets
chanting "Oh freedom, where are you? Hosni Mubarak stands between
me and you!" Drivers honked their horns in support. Thousands of riot
police and plain clothed policemen broke up the demonstrations, beating
the demonstrators and half a dozen journalists. *Time* magazine reported
that cameramen from *Al Jazeera* and Reuters were beaten. The Muslim
Brotherhood reported that at least 350 of their supporters were arrested.

The protesters' courage was inspiring. Hanafy Mohammad Abdel
Salam, a demonstrator who was beaten by police was quoted in *Time*
magazine as saying, "I am sixty years old and retired. I have lived sixty
years without freedom, and my children, they have smelled only a whiff
of freedom. I can see that these judges are good people. We need to stand

with them, to let them know that the people are not yet dead, that there are still people who will speak out. I will help them even if I die."

While these demonstrations were erupting outside, there was also a lot of action at the courthouse. Three hundred judges attempted to enter the courtroom to observe the proceedings.

They were barred, along with the defendants' legal teams. Judges Mekki and Bastawisi boycotted the proceedings, demanding the release of arrested activists. The trial was postponed yet again.

When I talked with Kareem, he told me one of his best friends, Alaa Abdel Fatah, had been arrested by the police. He said Alaa might have been targeted because he was a blogger and activist in Egypt's Free Speech movement. Alaa was arrested on May 7, along with other demonstrators outside the courthouse where the trial of Mekki and Bastawisi was scheduled to take place. Authorities told Alaa's wife and parents that he was being held at the Tora prison, which was known for its harsh treatment of prisoners. Yet the prison guards denied Alaa was in the prison at all, preventing family members, Kareem, and Alaa's lawyer from being able to see him—not an uncommon practice, according to Kareem.

Kareem commented that several of the lawyers representing people who had been detained during these demonstrations had left Egypt in the last couple of days. "Why," I asked, "were they afraid they would be arrested too? And wouldn't this make it worse for them once they returned, if they said anything embarrassing to the Mubarak regime?" Kareem explained that the reality was just the opposite: by speaking publicly in Europe and gaining international exposure, the lawyers gained a degree of immunity that would protect them upon their return.

I did not realize, when Kareem was sharing all this, how well known a figure his friend Alaa was, but later I read several accounts of his arrest in the papers and on-line. There was even a website for people pressing for his release. Alaa enjoyed an international reputation as a blogger and Free Speech activist. He was credited with initiating the highly successful Egyptian blogosphere and had gained prominence when he won an award from the Reporters Without Borders just months earlier. For Egypt's young activists, blogging was a potent new tool they had seized upon as a vehicle for sharing and disseminating their ideas, and sometimes simply information about the next day's planned events. I hoped Alaa's new international reputation would contribute to his quick release.

Increasing numbers of people were looking to the Judges Movement with high hopes. I found my own hopes stirred by one particular op-ed piece I read in *The Daily Star*, the Lebanon-based independent English daily read all over the Middle East. Staff writer Rami G. Khouri argued that if the judges persisted in their demands, it might well prove to be the impetus for the change Egyptians had been waiting for. The high respect Egyptians had for judges, and the fact that the judges invoked principles that were key to the political reforms desired by so many Egyptians, combined to create a large following for the Judges Movement.

Khouri claimed the Judges Movement could well have an impact even beyond Egypt. Every important political trend in the modern Arab world had started in Egypt and then spread—from anti-colonial resistance, to nationalism, to pan-Arabism, to the Muslim Brotherhood, and modern Islamist politics. He noted that because of Egypt's more recent "slide into authoritarianism, mediocrity and marginality," its leadership role in the Arab world was sometimes forgotten, but could still reassert itself. Khouri expressed the hope that like Poland's independent trade union, Solidarity in 1980, the Judges Movement could become the rallying point for the nation and send out ripple effects beyond the country's borders throughout the entire region. 195

While I saw some of these trends Egypt had heralded in the past, especially the growth of the Muslim Brotherhood and Islamist politics, as highly problematic developments for Egypt and the Middle East, the Judges Movement represented something altogether different. The judges' demands for an independent judiciary and adherence to the rule of law was a dramatic call for true democracy in Egypt. If this movement could succeed in galvanizing the Egyptians to push for broader democratic reforms, maybe Khouri was correct, and we would see ripples for democratic reform spread through the region. It was an exciting possibility.

The disciplinary hearing of Mekki and Bastawisi finally went forward on May 18. To the surprise of many, instead of disbarring the two senior judges as had been feared, the panel cleared Mekki and only reprimanded Bastawisi, who had suffered a heart attack the week before and was still in the hospital recovering. At the same time, however, the government cracked down even more strongly on the demonstrators. Tens of thousands of police were mobilized and the city center was sealed off to put a halt to the demonstrations. The Muslim Brotherhood said that police picked up 500 of its members, including two of its leaders, but the Ministry of the Interior put the figure at 240. Where would the movement go from here, we wondered, along with everyone else.

Over the next month, news of the Judges Movement receded from the pages of the newspapers, but many people were still being held in prison, among them, Kareem's friend Alaa.

As the events around the Judges Movement were unfolding through the late spring, Reuven and I continued to seek out opportunities to meet and socialize with Egyptians. Through Dorothy, an American ex-pat Reuven had met at the university, we found out about a group of Muslims and Christians who were starting an interfaith dialogue group in Cairo. The group—mostly people in their forties—had been communicating by email for several weeks and decided they wanted to start to meet in person. For their first meeting the group had arranged to take a *felucca* ride together on the Nile and talk over a picnic dinner on the boat. After checking with the other participants, Dorothy invited us to join the group for this first get-together.

The group seemed to be evenly split between Muslims and Christians and consisted mostly of couples with a few single people too. Other than Dorothy, we were the only non-Egyptians. If anyone was uncomfortable about two American Jews joining them for the evening, they did not show it. People were friendly but we were not made to feel the center of attention in any way.

As I looked around the boat, I noticed that none of the women wore the *higaab*. I found this interesting, since the *higaab* was so common in Cairo, that I sometimes found myself assuming that a woman without her hair covered must be Christian. I wondered if the Muslim women here were mostly secular, or feminists, or simply more Westernized than most of the Muslim women I had met until now.

Several people said they worked for USAID or different NGOs. One of the Muslim women, Haniya, worked for the World Hunger Organization on a project assisting farmers who had relocated in Upper Egypt in and around Aswan. It was interesting to learn of these efforts to assist farmers in the area we had so recently visited.

Haniya described herself as a "liberal Muslim." I was immediately intrigued. For years I had been struck by the fact that virtually all the Muslims I met whom I thought of as "liberal" in religious belief and practice in fact described themselves as "secular." The option of being religious but in a non-traditional way, seemed to be in an experimental stage of development in the Muslim world, still searching for a language. I asked Haniya what the liberal Muslim community was like in Cairo, and she answered that she was looking but had not yet actually found a community she felt comfortable in. She preferred to pray at home and did so daily.

Haniya mentioned that many people were now writing about liberal Islam. Websites and blogs offered a safe arena to explore new ideas, not as public as attending a class, "where you never knew who might be watching," she said, and it allowed like-minded people to connect over large geographic areas. Here too in a religious context, the Internet offered new opportunities for discussing ideas that might be threatening to the establishment.

I asked Haniya if she was ever uncomfortable not wearing the *higaab* in Cairo, since it had become so widely practiced, and she shook her head no, saying that in her circles of work, family, and friends, not wearing the *higaab* was acceptable. A few people made comments, she admitted, but then she laughed. "People who know me, know to leave me alone about this."

One of the participants was Talal, a gay Christian man who was an opera singer. His partner was in the States teaching at a university, and Talal hoped to join him there eventually. He was full of praise for America, and several of the others gently poked fun at what they termed his naiveté, while others seemed outright impatient at his pro-American leanings. But Talal was unrepentant. For him, the United States offered true freedoms that were only paid lip service in Egypt.

Another Christian man, Jaafar, wanted to talk with Reuven and me about Israel. We were there to talk about religion, not politics, and we tried to avoid this discussion.

"What is the moral justification for the existence of Israel?" Jaafar pressed on. With some reluctance, Reuven answered him, reviewing the historical link of the Jews to the land of Israel and the beginnings of modern Zionist movement in response to the long history of antisemitism. He tried to explain the need that Jews felt for a state of their own when their rights could so easily be revoked elsewhere.

"Does any of this justify taking land away from the Palestinians?" Jaafar asked angrily. We acknowledged the problems of two peoples with historic claims to the land, but Jaafar kept at it. He was unwilling to acknowledge any Palestinian or broader Arab responsibility for the ongoing conflict between Israel and the Palestinians, or the failure of negotiations thus far to produce a Palestinian state. Jaafar was also highly critical of Israel's military buildup, seemingly unaware of the fact that in challenging Israel's right to exist as a nation, he was pointing to the very reason Israel needed to have a strong military.

198

Only when I mentioned that the United Nations' vote to establish Israel as a state in 1947 had been a vote establishing two states—a Jewish state and a Palestinian state—and that it was not the Israelis but all the Arab countries that rejected the plan and declared war, was Jaafar quiet. Either he did not have a good response or he did not trust his memory enough to defend the Arab rejection of the U.N. plan.

Walking home later, Reuven and I revisited our conversation with Jaafar. We found it particularly disturbing that a well educated, liberal, Christian Egyptian who was obviously interested in interfaith dialogue, was so strongly opposed to Israel's very existence. No one else on the *felucca* ride had joined the conversation we had with Jaafar, though several had seemed uncomfortable with his tenacity, and we were left wondering where the others stood. Would we ever meet Egyptians who accepted the fact of Israel's existence and were ready to move on?

Aside from the unpleasant exchange with Jaafar, Reuven and I liked most of the people we had met and we invited Talal and a Muslim couple about our age, Safiya and Isaam, to join us for Shabbat dinner the following week.

While baking *challah* and cooking dinner on Friday afternoon, I realized that perhaps because we had met Talal, Safiya, and Isaam in the context of an interfaith dialogue group, I felt no anxiety wondering how they might feel about our being Jewish and joining us in our home for a Shabbat meal. In fact, I was looking forward to the evening much as I would in Los Angeles where, when we met people we liked with whom we thought we might want to be friends, our first inclination was to invite them for Shabbat dinner.

Talal was the first to arrive. We sat down in the living room and relaxed over cold drinks. Talal spoke enthusiastically about an opera he had attended the previous evening that he had thoroughly enjoyed. When Safiya and Isaam came, Safiya wanted to see the apartment so we showed them around. Safiya and Isaam especially liked the small garden in the back.

Over dinner, we were delighted to learn that our three guests had grown up together in Maadi—Safiya and Isaam had known each other since they were eleven. They quickly fell into reminiscing about the Maadi of their youth.

"Maadi was a little town then, a village really," Talal began. "I sometimes feel sorry for the children growing up here today. When we were children, it was the perfect place to grow up. There was just one of everything—one grocery store, one butcher, one stationery store, one vegetable market—and, very important—one bike repair shop. In those days, bicycles were the main mode of transportation. We all got around on bikes."

Safiya and Isaam had both grown up speaking French at home. Safiya's mother was Belgian and Isaam's grandparents were from France. Talal's family was from Lebanon. All three represented the cosmopolitan background of Egypt prior to Nasser's nationalization campaign of the 1950s. Isaam worked for USAID on water projects and Safiya was an architect. Their son and daughter, who were spending the night with their grandparents, attended the same school as our boys, although Noam and Amir didn't recognize their children's names.

Our guests had never seen a Shabbat evening meal before and we enjoyed sharing our various Shabbat traditions with them, such as starting the meal with blessings over the wine (or in this case grape juice, since we had Muslim guests) and bread. After the destruction of the Temple in Jerusalem in 70 C.E., we explained, the Rabbinic sages transferred some of the sacred Temple rituals to the home, so all meals, but especially Shabbat and holiday meals, took on an added sacred dimension. Before gathering at the sink to wash our hands, we explained how hand washing before the blessing of the bread and sprinkling salt on the bread ritually connected the breaking of bread to the offering of Temple sacrifices.

Reuven and I talked about the Jewish practice of saying blessings before and after eating as expressions of gratitude and our guests told us about similar practices in their traditions. Isaam was especially interested in comparative religion and he had lots of questions about Jewish history, beliefs, and practices. He asked us to recommend a good English translation of the Hebrew Bible as well as other Jewish books he hoped to purchase for his own study.

We felt so comfortable with our guests, who were in many ways our counterparts—university-trained professionals with a liberal approach to their religious traditions and an interest in the faiths of others—that I regretted we had not met them earlier in our stay. Since our remaining time in Egypt was short, we would try to make the most of these new friendships. Safiya and I made plans to meet again a few days later.

200

Safiya and I met at Café Greco in Maadi around noon and wound up spending more than three hours together, talking about our children and our families of origin as well as our current religious leanings. Safiya had grown up in what she calls a secular family. I asked her how she was affected by the growth of Muslim conservatism in Egypt.

"If someone wants to be more religious, that's fine, but they shouldn't impose it on anyone else. I really resent it when there is pressure on me from outside to be more religious," Safiya said. In the last two years, however, Safiya and her husband had become more involved in a Sufi community. They were attracted to the more spiritual and mystical aspects of Islam, which they found in Sufi teachings and practices. They both attended weekly women's and men's Sufi prayer groups and she tried to pray five times a day. Their community had originally met as a mixed group of men and women, but, as Safiya explained, "the government does not like large religious gatherings, so we meet now in two separate groups of men and women.

"We meet in people's homes one night a week, and maybe twenty women come. Personally, I don't mind meeting in separate groups," she added. "I really like to pray and chant with just women."

Safiya drove me home and on the way, we started talking about American foreign policy.

"Since 9/11," she said suddenly, "the United States has really been at war with the Arab Muslim world."

"Where do you see that?" I asked, taken aback.

"You see it everywhere!" she answered. "*Masalan*," she said, (using the Arabic term that means "for example"), "look at what the Americans are doing in Iraq, in Afghanistan, and about Iran, Sudan, and Egypt..."

"Egypt?" I asked. "America gives more aid to Egypt than to almost any other country." The fact that Safiya's husband worked for USAID contributed to my surprise at her comments. Were these feelings typical of even Egyptians who were themselves the direct beneficiaries of American aid?

"That's true, but not everyone thinks American aid is good for Egypt," she responded. "America gives aid in ways that are good for America, not always for Egypt. And foreign aid creates its own problems. We become dependent on that aid." I agreed that foreign aid could be something of a mixed blessing, fostering dependence even as it provided the means for important programs. But I told Safiya that in my experience, Americans were not hostile to Egyptians, the original point Safiya had been making.

"I don't see any connection between American reactions to what is happening in Iran, Sudan, and Iraq—they are all totally different situations raising very different issues. I don't think Americans see them as connected at all."

"But they are all Muslim countries that America is fighting against," she insisted. "And there's a lot of prejudice against Muslims and Arabs in the United States, isn't there?"

"I think there is a lot of fear... and ignorance," I said. "There is certainly a lot more fear since 9/11, and as a result, more prejudice. I probably should know more," I admitted. Safiya told me about an Egyptian friend living in Boston who complained about the increase in prejudice and hostility she had experienced since 9/11. She had told Safiya that security lines at airports had become particularly humiliating. I wanted to hear more about her friend's experiences, but at that moment we saw Amir and Noam walking toward our apartment building from where the school bus had dropped them off. That meant Safiya's kids would be arriving home too.

"Well, I guess we won't solve all the problems of the world today," I said, opening the car door and reaching over to give her a good-bye hug, despite my sadness at this sudden turn of the conversation.

"No... that will have to wait for the next time we see each other. I hope I did not offend you by raising these issues. It was so good to spend time with you like this. I really hope we can see each other again soon!" she responded, kissing me on my right cheek and my left.

Later that night I found myself still thinking about this last part of my conversation with Safiya. I was still trying to wrap my mind around Safiya's view that American foreign policy in the Middle East expressed the deeper reality of America being at war with the Muslim world. We were at war with Islamic extremism, but not the whole Muslim world. Where I saw different actions and policies on the part of the United States, Safiya saw a general trend. I found it stunning and very difficult to connect this view with my own sense of American policy evolving in distinctive ways in response to the different circumstances of each country in the Middle East. Sadly, I guessed that Safiya's view was probably not so uncommon in the Arab Muslim world. Even if it was untrue, as I believed it was, this view probably served as a lens for many Arab Muslims looking at American behavior at home and in the Middle East. When Safiya heard about particular instances of prejudice and hostility against Muslims in the United States, this would reinforce the image she held of my country, while for me, they would stand as exceptions to what I see as the true America.

I felt like I had hit upon something about the power of the narrative we each carry around. New evidence was always interpreted in the light cast by that narrative: if it resonated with the narrative, it reinforced it. If it conflicted, we tended to see it as an exception, or even of questionable veracity. In this way, without even being aware of it, we tended to dismiss contrary evidence that could pose a challenge, and at times a corrective, to our narrative. And in times of greater polarization and fear of the other, this tendency would be even stronger. Thinking about the challenges I found myself experiencing in these conversations was helping me understand why it was sometimes so difficult for people on different sides to really hear each other.

The festival of Shavuot began later that week, and we invited our Jewish friends, Debbie and Steve, along with Kathy and Paul, our first hosts in Cairo, for a special dinner to celebrate the holiday commemorating the giving of the Torah at Sinai. Amir also invited his friend Khalid from school. We had hoped that Steve's wife Musheera and their children would join us too, but they were back in the States for a brief visit.

It is an Ashkenazic tradition to eat dairy foods on Shavuot, so for the first time in my life, I made cheese blintzes from scratch with the boys. With the help of a recipe I found online, and a very patient vendor at the market where I tasted all the white cheeses, trying to find one that might work as a substitute for farmer's cheese, our blintzes proved a mouth-watering hit. Maybe we did not have a Torah scroll or a minyan of Jews with whom to celebrate the giving of the Torah, but we would celebrate the holiday with a sense of at least culinary authenticity!

Dinner felt festive. Flowers from Steve adorned the table and Kathy and Paul had brought a good bottle of wine. Over dinner, our guests compared notes on their experiences in the NGO world of Cairo. Paul shared some his recent frustrations working on a large educational reform project he had thought held great promise. Over tea and cheesecake, another classic holiday treat, courtesy of Debbie, we participated in the Shavuot evening tradition of studying texts together. Reuven shared a selection of texts he had collected that dealt with "chosenness" in the Jewish and Christian traditions. We wondered together if this concept of chosenness was intrinsic to monotheism, or if it had roots in a tribal world view in which each tribe had its own local god who favored them. We also discussed whether it was possible for our faiths to balance a sense of special closeness with God with a genuine respect for religious diversity.

As we were talking, I thought about the fact that once again, we had people of all three monotheistic traditions at our table. At one point, Khalid excused himself to go pray. He asked Amir where he should wash his feet and Amir showed him to the one bathroom that was properly equipped. The blend of genuine affection and respect, together with the desire to learn from each other that was shared around the table, seemed to answer that question affirmatively. It was exhilarating to be able to share a meal, with our differences, in this way. I hoped the kids felt it too.

But towards the end of our meal, the conversation shifted to the subject of Arab antisemitism. Kathy and Paul both challenged Debbie's view of Arab criticism of Israel in the newspapers and television as being antisemitic.

"If I criticize Israel, am I antisemitic too?" Kathy asked with some emotion.

203

"You have every right to criticize Israel. I sometimes do as well," Debbie responded. "But there are different kinds of criticism, different tones of critique. Over time, I have come to see a lot of the Arab criticism as another form of antisemitism. There's such hatred, with a level of demonization that goes way beyond criticism. And when the discussions move so quickly from critiquing policy to questioning the right of Israel to exist as a state, there is something else going on."

Kathy disagreed and after some more discussion, we decided to let it rest as a point of disagreement. I was a little sad that the discussion had taken this turn and had grown so heated, but at least everyone had been comfortable enough to speak their minds and to listen to each other's points of view. We came away from the discussion agreeing to read the articles others had mentioned. This seemed to me a more constructive outcome than most of the other discussions about Israel I had had in Egypt.

Recent conversations about religion and politics in Egypt made me eager to run some of my impressions and questions by Kareem. He had been very busy with final exams but now that his exams were over we arranged to meet for coffee. I met him at my favorite Café Greco, and we ordered our coffees and sat down. Kareem complimented me on my Arabic.

"It's great that you are pushing yourself to speak," he said. I told him how friendly I found people in general, and how encouraging they were of my efforts to speak. "But I still have to ask people to slow down and repeat themselves all the time," I admitted. "And for real conversation of course, I have to use English too, or it's hard for me to go beyond simple ideas."

I knew that Kareem was interested in Sufism, and thinking of Safiya and Isaam, I asked him if this was a typical choice of Egyptians involved in the pro-democracy movement.

"Some people are attracted to Sufism as an alternative to the more conservative and often politicized Muslim communities," he said. "But you see Muslims of every stripe in the free speech and pro-democracy movements. And you have people attracted to Sufism for purely religious reasons too. I'm attracted to it because it emphasizes the spiritual aspects of Islam without the politics. And unlike mainstream Islam, which is focused on the individual, Sufism emphasizes being part of a community, an intense prayer community, and I love praying and chanting in community that way," he said, "*Masalan*, listen what happened to me last week."

Kareem was under so much pressure with final exams and papers during the last few weeks, he had not been able to attend his community's regular prayer services. As a result, he had been feeling less connected to his prayer community, while at the same time feeling that he needed that connection more than ever. He spoke to his *sheikh* about this. The next Saturday night, to his surprise, his *sheikh* called to see if he and some members of his community could come to Kareem's apartment for a prayer and meditation session.

"It was so nice!" he said with a big smile. He described the *zikher*, the chanting of God's names, and it was clear that it was both the quality of the prayer and chanting, together with the fact that his community had reached out to him in this way, that had so moved him. 205

Moving on to politics once again, Kareem had some insights I found helpful. He noted that even educated Egyptians were not always particularly sophisticated about politics and tended to see things in "very black and white terms." He talked about his own early experience in "Seeds for Peace" as waking him up to the need for wider reading and the need to question the version of events he generally encountered in the Egyptian press.

"I didn't know that the October War was not an unequivocal victory for Egypt," he told me. "When I was first heard Israelis talking about that war, presenting me with facts I knew nothing about and could not answer, it was a terrible experience. I was ashamed of my ignorance. That's when I started asking more questions." We agreed this was not a problem confined to Egypt. I told Kareem about Noam's experience, hearing from an Egyptian classmate that Egyptians viewed the 1973 war as *their* victory, and about our visit to the October War Panorama Museum. Even though we were troubled by the grossly distorted view presented there, it had made us all conscious of the power of a national narrative and of our own narratives' hold on us, in ways that we are sometimes unaware.

"This is exactly why the Free Speech Movement is so important in emerging democracies," Kareem replied. "We need to promote the free exchange of ideas. That's the only way forward."

I knew from previous conversations that Kareem was in favor of a two-state solution to the Israeli-Palestinian conflict. I shared with him my frustration that even here in Egypt, a country with whom Israel had a peace treaty and diplomatic relations, every conversation I had about

Israel moved quickly beyond Israeli policies on the settlements, or a Palestinian state, to the question of Israel's right to exist. If a Palestinian state were created that had reasonable relations with Israel, did he think the view of Israel in the Arab world might change?

"Absolutely, that would make a big difference," he answered without hesitation. "Jerusalem is also an important issue. If Jerusalem were under international control, that would help a lot too. There would still be Arabs who would prefer to see the map of the Middle East without Israel, but they would not feel the same justification for attacking Israel's right to exist. "I have to admit," he added, "I get really depressed about the Israeli-Palestinian issue—and that is not really my nature. But I don't see a resolution of the problems coming any time soon. We have a saying in Arabic—'not war and not peace.' That's how I see the Israeli-Palestinian issue. It could be worse, we should remember that. But it could also be better."

"*Insha'Allah*, God willing," I agreed.

"*Insha'Allah*," he responded.

In the month following the ruling against Judges Bastawisi and Mekki, there was a quiet but real crackdown by the Egyptian government on both journalists and bloggers. As Kareem had explained to me, increasing numbers of Egyptians were turning to blogging as a safe haven for the free flow of information and debate about controversial issues. Unfortunately the government had clearly observed the same facts and had come to the opposite conclusion: blogging posed an evident threat to the government's attempt to control the flow of information.

Every few days, online news sources such as *Al Jazeera* and *The Christian Science Monitor* carried reports by human rights organizations about the arrests and extended detentions of journalists and bloggers. There were accusations of torture and even sexual abuse. Several pieces lamented the government's arrest of six bloggers, including Kareem's friend, Alaa Abdel Fatah. I found a new website devoted to Alaa, with brief updates and emotional appeals for his release. Alaa had been in prison for more than a month now and I hoped that at least he was safe and would come to no harm.

Meanwhile, the eagerly anticipated film version of "The Yacoubian Building," a novel by one of Egypt's best known writers, Alaa-al-Aswany, about the widespread corruption experienced at all levels of Egyptian society, finally opened in Cairo. I had finished reading the book in English and Reuven was reading it in Arabic, with the English translation by his side. Everyone was talking about it, and Kareem actually saw the film three times in ten days, each time with different friends. The newspapers were full of talk about the film as well, and not just in the film section. "The Yacoubian Building" spared no words or images in depicting the destructive effects of corruption on individuals and on society as a whole.

The night Reuven and I went downtown to see "The Yacoubian Building," we were too late—it was sold out. We finally saw the film the following week and we found it to be even more powerful than we had expected. As Kareem had remarked, there had been other books and films that dealt with corruption in government and business, but this one focused on its destructive effect on individuals and society with particularly striking personal portraits and narratives. The personal stories it told reflected the untold suffering of countless individuals and the destruction of their hopes for the future.

One of the film's narratives revolves around high school sweethearts whose lives soon take them in radically different directions. Taha, the son of the doorman of the Yacoubian Building, excels in his high school studies, but his dream of entering the Police Academy ends abruptly when he is dismissed from his interview by generals who look down on his father's lack of professional standing. He enrolls at a Cairo university but grows increasingly alienated when shunned by the wealthier students and eventually joins a militant Islamist group, with tragic consequences. Meanwhile his girlfriend, Buseyna, lives with her mother and siblings as squatters in a storage room on the roof of the Yacoubian Building. Forced to work to support her family, she immediately finds her new employer demanding sexual favors. To her great disappointment, not only her friends, but even her mother expects her to give in to just enough of her boss' demands, while protecting her virginity, to keep her job.

Another one of the film's interwoven narratives involves a homosexual relationship. This proved to be the film's most controversial element. Some people were even demanding that the film be banned. Others expressed frustration that so many Egyptians were focusing on the homosexual relationship and not dealing with the film's more central theme of corruption in politics and business and its impact on people's lives. But I was impressed by

207

the number of articles that suddenly appeared on the subject of corruption in the pages of the daily newspapers. It looked to me like "The Yacoubian Building" was having a profound impact, at least for the moment.

An article in *Al Ahram* reported on a seminar on corruption that had been sponsored by the opposition party, Kifaya. It actually began with an extensive quote from "The Yacoubian Building" and noted that the novel "uncannily reflects the stories of corruption that are now seeping out of the corridors of power and into the press via reports released by opposition groups such as Kifaya, the Egyptian Movement for Change." According to this article, a popular independent newspaper, *Al-Masry Al-Youm*, had launched its own anti-corruption campaign with a series of "daring" articles exposing the links between Egyptian political and business elites.

208

That they were talking about the problem openly was the good news. But another article detailed Mubarak's efforts just the week before to pass legislation that included jail terms for journalists who raised questions about the financial integrity of public officials. Only at the last minute had Mubarak withdrawn this contested clause. The new legislation remained problematic as it permitted the arrest of journalists for certain publishing offenses and fined others so heavily that the question of the viability of small opposition papers had been raised.

Which way was the pendulum really swinging?

Ever since my conversation with Haniya on the interfaith group outing, I wondered about how Zayna felt about wearing the *higaab*. She said she would be happy to discuss it after class and joined me for a coffee at a café.

"I wear the *higaab* so people will focus on who I am inside, what kind of person I am, not how I look," she explained. "So many people are focused on 'What does she look like? Does she have a nice body?' That is not how I want people to relate to me. Islam teaches that men should have respect for women and the *higaab* is part of that.

"I know that there are people who say just the opposite," she continued. "They say that Islam gives women a lower role, but that is not Islam, it is the wider culture we are part of. Islam teaches respect for women and rights for women.

"Another reason I wear the *higaab*, and for me the really important reason, is that the *higaab* is something like prayer. When I put on the *hi-*

gaab it reminds me of my connection to Allah. It reminds me how I want to act, how I want to be in the world."

I found this a beautiful idea. Zayna and I agreed that the greatest spiritual challenge is not how we behave during times of prayer but in the course of daily life, when interacting with other people. I mentioned that for Jews, wearing a *kippah* (Hebrew for yarmulke or skull cap) had perhaps a similar purpose: to remind people—traditionally men—of being in the presence of God. I shared with Zayna how much I liked hearing the slow and soothing chants of Quran recitation that wafted through the market from CD players in the small shops up and down Road Nine as I did my errands. I welcomed the chanting as a reminder to slow down and take a breath, to be patient and treat people around me with kindness instead of just pushing ahead to get my errands done as quickly as possible. Zayna nodded.

209

But if this indeed was the purpose of *higaab*, I wondered out loud, why was it only for women? Was there anything equivalent for men? Zayna did not know. While I could certainly appreciate this added benefit of wearing the *higaab*, it did not change the problematic aspect of requiring women to cover their hair as an expression of modesty. I thought of married Orthodox Jewish women who also covered their hair with wigs, scarves, or hats, often for the same reason, and my objections to what I had always regarded as overly stringent rules of modesty for women.

Now that I had been living in Cairo for over four months, I was beginning to notice my own attitudes and thinking on certain subjects changing. One striking example was with regard to this issue of modesty. While I was still opposed to women having to cover their hair, on other issues of dress I was becoming more conscious of modesty. Increasingly I found it disturbing to see women who were obviously foreigners wearing short sleeves and on occasion, even sleeveless tops. Didn't they know that was not how people dressed here? One day, I caught myself thinking how much more attractive women actually looked in long pants and long sleeves. I shook my head in surprise, but that was genuinely how I felt.

One day in early June, I met Reuven downtown near AUC and we decided to grab a bite before heading to the market to buy some gifts. We went into a fast food restaurant near the university and ordered *Alexandrias*—cooked beans served in pita bread with chopped tomatoes, peppers, and onions—a little bit like a good chili! I noticed three American men, probably in their twenties, standing around a small raised table in the middle of the restaurant, eating. They were wearing shorts and sleeveless tank tops, their biceps bulging. They stood with their feet set wide apart, chomping on their sandwiches, talking loudly to each other. They seemed totally oblivious that their dress and even their body language was grossly out of place here. The young men exuded an arrogance that was embarrassing to me as a fellow American. I watched as one of them took a big bite out of his sandwich and swallowed it down with a gulp of coke. Where did they think they were? I was indignant.

But lest it sound like I was about to don the full *burqa* (black full body and face covering) myself, I also had moments that pushed me completely in the other direction. As the weather was growing hotter by the day, I was increasingly amazed to see women running around the outdoor track at the health club still totally covered in traditional garb. Often this meant not just one but several layers of clothing: long pants and a long-sleeved tunic blouse, followed perhaps by a skirt and vest before the final layer of *galabiya* and *higaab*. How could women run, wrapped in all these clothes, I wondered, and not suffer a heat stroke?

One morning that was hotter than most, I pushed myself to go for a run at the Naadi. As I was warming up for exercise, I was surprised to see a woman rounding the track, completely covered in a *burqa* with only the tiniest of slits for her eyes. She was even wearing long sleeved black gloves, so no skin would show. I was sweating in my shorts and T-shirt. I could not begin to imagine how this woman must experience the penetrating heat of the sun beating down on us, fully cloaked in black.

I had recently noticed that most of the women wearing the *burqa* were young, in their twenties. I wondered once again what thinking motivated this choice in attire that seemed to deny any individuality in presentation of self. Not even the woman's face was allowed to show. In this heat, physical discomfort seemed an unfair accompaniment of modesty; men, even in uniform, were now walking the streets in short sleeves, or at least light colored and lightweight cottons. I knew women had all kinds of reasons for wearing *higaab* and assumed the same was true with regard to the fuller black garb. But try as I might, I could not help but see the *burqa* as an oppressive custom, pressuring women to cover up as if their physical bodies and their sexuality was something to be ashamed of. I resented that it turned every woman into an almost formless "black mountain" gliding anonymously through the streets. It made me want to wear short sleeves in protest.

As spring turned into summer, and our departure date of July 26 was set, I was also conscious of all the things I'd miss once we were back in the States. One day Mahabbah came with fresh spinach to make *sabaneh* for us one more time before spinach went out of season. *Sabaneh* was my favorite Egyptian dish and I wanted to cook it with Mahabbah one more time in the hopes that I would be able to make it back in Los Angeles without Mahabbah by my side.

While we were browning the onions and garlic, Mahabbah mentioned that the garlic was a local variety, much sweeter than the imported garlic that is in the stores most of the year. She and her mother and sister each bought enough fresh garlic when the crop first came on the market to last the whole year. She described how they braided it and hung it on the wall in the kitchen in a decorative way, and then would simply reach up for it when they were cooking, as they needed it, bulb by bulb.

"How much did you buy this year?" I asked.

"Twenty."

"Twenty what?"

"Twenty kilo." Twenty kilo… that was forty pounds!

"You bought twenty kilo of garlic?" How could anyone use forty pounds of garlic in a year, even if it was divided among three households?

But Mahabbah seemed to read my mind.

"I bought twenty, my mother bought twenty, and my sister bought twenty." Mahabbah burst out laughing when she saw my surprise. "You think it's too much?"

Later that day, at the end of my Arabic class, Zayna asked me about a Hebrew newspaper I had folded up in my notebook. I had actually brought it to show her. It was *Du-Et*, a supplement to the regular Israeli newspapers that was written by both Israeli Jewish and Arab journalists and was published four times a year in both Hebrew and Arabic editions. This was a project my cousin and I had both been impressed with on our recent visit to Israel, and had decided to support with funding from the family foundation.

I explained to Zayna that the goal of the project was to provide Israeli Jews and Arabs with each other's points of view that they rarely had

211

opportunities to read in their regular newspapers. I showed her an article I found especially interesting: two full pages side by side, with parallel accounts of the historical development of Palestinian and Zionist nationalism, written by an Israeli Arab and an Israeli Jew, respectively. I only had the Hebrew edition with me, so I knew Zayna would not be able to read it, but even the graphic layout of parallel narratives made the point.

"It looks really interesting. I wish I could read it," said Zayna. I told her I would try to get her a copy of the Arabic edition, which had been inserted in Arab newspapers in Israel.

Zayna wanted to hear about other projects that our foundation supported in Israel that were designed to increase the number of Israeli Arab journalists working for major Israeli newspapers. I mentioned a one-year course for Israeli Arabs offered by Ben Gurion University together with the Israeli newspaper, *Haaretz*, with plans in the works for a follow-up internship program in television and print media. Zayna nodded when I described the need for the programs.

"Did you know that yesterday the Israeli Prime Minister Olmert addressed the Congress in the United States?" Zayna responded. "I read on the Internet that he spoke about one American child who had been killed in Israel by a terrorist attack and there were members of Congress crying—for one child!" She held up her finger for emphasis. "And yet, on the same day, Amnesty International released a report about Israeli human rights abuses of Palestinians and American human rights abuses in Iraq that involved the killing of many innocent people! Only those people were Arabs. These two things were happening at the same time! What should people like me, living in the Arab world, think?"

It was difficult for me to answer Zayna. Even though Judaism, Christianity, and Islam all teach that every human life is infinitely precious, all too often people act as if this teaching only applies to their own group. Zayna was upset that Americans and Israelis seemed to care so much about their own children and so little about Arab children.

"I understand how you feel," I told Zayna. "I feel the same way when Palestinians and Islamists carry out acts of terror in Israel and the West, while people in the Arab world cheer them on. But isn't there a difference between acts of violence where the intention is to kill as many civilians as possible, like blowing up a bus, and conflicts where, despite efforts taken, civilians are killed?" I knew that I was treading on risky ground, but I felt I had to make this point.

"Yes," Zayna replied cautiously, "but these are cases that Amnesty International identified as human rights abuses."

I told Zayna that I would look for the Amnesty International report online, but I had a hard time believing these claims to be true, based on what I knew about American and perhaps even more, Israeli policies. I had often read and heard from Israelis I knew about the efforts taken by the Israeli Defense Forces to avoid civilian casualties. If these events had in fact occurred, I would view them as exceptions to the norm, while for Zayna, they would reinforce what she believed to be the norm. I thought about my recent conversation with Safiya, and I realized that this too was an example of how our narratives affect how all of us take in new information.

Still I agreed with the connection Zayna was making between a human tendency to dehumanize the other, and the subject we had just been discussing—how important it was to learn about the narrative of the other in situations of conflict. Without this understanding, people were more likely to accept negative stereotypes about the other that could lead to the acceptance of violence against them.

"I think it's hard for people to make the effort to see both sides." I said, coming back to our first topic. "We know there are always two sides, at least, to any story. I think of it sometimes like this," I said, holding up my two hands with my fingers spread wide, and then moving them together so that the fingers of my two hands interlocked to form a single panel.

"We need the two sides together to make a whole. But in reality, most of us really understand only one side. And we tend to forget there even is another side, as though our half were the whole story."

Zayna explained this was why she liked to read the Spanish and English language news analysis on the Internet. She wanted to better understand Western perspectives on events in the Middle East and around the world and was glad she had studied both Spanish and English at the university. I said that I hoped that when I was back in the States I would continue to seek out different sources of information and different points of view on political developments in the Middle East.

"That's why I think what you and I are able to share with each other is so important. For me, this was the best part of my coming to Egypt—as well as beginning to learn Arabic and learning how much harder I need to work to see the side of the story that is missing for me."

Zayna relaxed and smiled a warm, appreciative smile.

On June 20, to Kareem's great relief, his friend Alaa Abdel Fatah was freed from prison. But other protesters who had been arrested during the Mekki-Bastawisi disciplinary hearings were still being held. Now the government initiated a trial against three journalists accused of publishing a list containing the initials of judges who reportedly colluded with authorities in falsifying the Parliamentary election results. On the opening day of the trial, the courtroom was packed with journalists and legal and civil rights activists, chanting slogans demanding that the corrupt judges be tried instead of those attempting to expose corruption. The trial was postponed until September.

Meanwhile, the pro-reform judges were launching a campaign against the draft of a new law intended to regulate the judiciary. This bill ignored almost all the judges' recommendations for greater judiciary independence and in fact included new constraints on the judges. The Cairo Judges' Club was considering holding sit-ins and partial work stoppages to voice their opposition before the bill, already approved by the cabinet, would reach the floor of the People's Assembly for a final vote. Anticipating that the bill might be endorsed, the judges were already planning to call for wider public efforts to overturn the law.

By the end of June, however, the Judges Movement was no longer front page news. For now, people's hopes for a popular revolt galvanizing around the Judges Movement had not materialized. But we assumed that the government crackdown was only a temporary setback and had not destroyed the people's hopes for change. Only time would tell.

Chapter 10
Israel's War with Hezbollah

اللوم يأتي قبل السيوف

Blame comes before swords.
~Arabic Proverb

STANDING ON LINE IN THE AIRPORT OUTSIDE OF NAIROBI, 215
Reuven, the boys, and I were getting ready to board a plane and return to
Cairo, having spent a fabulous week on safari in Kenya. We had decided
a family safari was an adventure we couldn't miss, seeing that we were already in Africa, and we were right. The boys were already recalling the exciting parts, like watching migrating herds of wildebeests plunging across
a river and managing to avoid the lurking crocodiles. I tried to hold onto
favorite memories too, like the haunting beauty of the undulating grasses
of the plains stretching endlessly before us, our experience of camping out
with chimpanzees and elephants as our neighbors, and meeting members of
some of the different indigenous tribes of Kenya. It had been a great adventure in every way, with one of the surprises being that Reuven and I loved it
as much as the boys, for whom we had thought the trip was intended.

Now we were returning to Cairo for the final ten days of our Egyptian sojourn. The four of us were comparing notes on the things we still
wanted to do and the people we wanted to see one more time before we
left Cairo.

"I want to have *kusheri* at least five more times!" said Amir.

"I'll probably have it every day for lunch, and I want to have it for
dinner as a family at least once or twice," Noam answered. "Me too!"
Amir seconded the motion, jumping around our carry-on bags.

The line started to move forward. Suddenly we heard the words "Israel" and "Hezbollah" as larger than life images of two young Israeli soldiers appeared on the large screen television up to our right. Before we
could make out what was being said, the images of the Israeli soldiers
disappeared and were followed by film clips of artillery attacks and air
strikes. The announcer was making references to southern Lebanon and

Gaza, various northern Israeli towns, and Hezbollah and Hamas. What could have happened?

Shortly before our trip to Kenya, on July 25, 20-year-old Gilad Shalit, a staff sergeant in the Israeli army, had been kidnapped by Hamas in a cross-border raid into Israel and was being held captive in Gaza. Israel had responded swiftly with air attacks against Hamas. We knew about this before our trip, but we had not seen a newspaper or heard a single news report while we were in Kenya.

From what we could piece together from the news and fellow passengers, on July 12, Hezbollah, the militant group of Shi'a Muslims based in Lebanon, fired missiles into several northern Israeli towns from Lebanon as a diversionary tactic, crossed the border into Israel and ambushed an Israeli border patrol, killing three soldiers and kidnapping two others—the young men whose pictures we had just seen on television. Israel attempted a rescue operation in which five more Israeli soldiers were killed. Hezbollah followed up with additional rocket strikes into Israel and Israel responded with artillery, air and naval strikes into southern Lebanon. All this had just happened in the last twenty-four hours.

We suddenly went from savoring the last days of our family travels to anxious questions about what exactly we were returning to as we headed back to the Middle East. We wondered what this would mean for Israel. How far could Hezbollah hurl their Iranian missiles into Israel from southern Lebanon? And what level of attack would Israel go to in order to stop Hezbollah? Could this be the start of another war?

I also wondered what the sudden escalation of conflict might mean for us in Cairo. For five and a half months we had lived in the midst of a society hostile to Israel, even in peacetime. How far would the anti-Israel leanings of the Egyptians carry them in their response to these events? I felt a sudden wave of sadness, wondering if we might feel unexpected relief to be leaving Cairo in another ten days. For now, all we could do was board the plane, hoping that efforts were already underway to reduce the level of violence between Hezbollah and Israel.

Late that night, as we walked into our apartment in Maadi, we were immediately enveloped by the pungent aromas of fresh-cooked food. A whole feast awaited us in the kitchen, with several pots of food still warm on the stove, and rice pudding, another family favorite, in the refrigerator. Mahabbah had been at work and the apartment was sparkling. "Mahabbah is something else," said Noam, looking at the dishes she had prepared for us with admiration. We were all too tired to eat anything, but it was clear that there was a wonderful Egyptian meal for us to look forward to the next day.

First thing in the morning, Reuven went out and returned with a couple of newspapers and some fresh bread and yogurt for breakfast. Lucky for us it was Thursday, the day when *Al Ahram's* English weekly came out. Two huge headlines dominated its front page: "Enter Hizbullah" (a variant spelling of Hezbollah) and "Israel Attacks Lebanon," and the rest of the paper was almost entirely devoted to the unfolding conflict in Lebanon and Israel, with reports and assessments about the situation in Gaza as well.

We were eager to dive into the papers, but no sooner had we sat down to tea and breakfast when Mahabbah came to the door to welcome us home. She seemed very pleased with how much we oohed and aahed about the food that had greeted us the night before. We put aside the newspapers and invited her to join us for tea and breakfast. She wanted to hear about our trip and we wound up watching the videos from our safari together. At first I felt pangs of discomfort in sharing pictures of a trip like this with Mahabbah, something she couldn't possibly do with her children. It widened the gulf between us in a way I found uncomfortable. But Mahabbah didn't seem to have a problem with it. She laughed along with us at the chimpanzees' antics, and took as much delight as we did in the mother elephant spraying her baby, and large herds of zebra grazing together with wildebeests. Mahabbah shared with us all the Arabic names for the animals, and we tried to learn a few of them.

Later, over a second cup of tea—just the two of us this time—Mahabbah told me that she had been experiencing spells of sudden weakness and would be having some tests on her liver the following week. I was concerned about Mahabbah's health in general. She was seriously overweight and I knew she had diabetes. Like so many Egyptian women her age, she struggled with this and other health ailments exacerbated by a diet high in carbs, sugar, and fat. While Mahabbah had talked to me before about trying to control her diet, I sensed she had very limited success in this area, partly because of her children's and her own preference for the regional dishes she had always made for them.

She also shared with me the fact that her daughter's wedding date had been moved up to October, which also made her anxious. It sounded like everyone was afraid of the groom's father who had announced the week before that he wanted the couple to get married in October. Mahabbah didn't see how she and her daughter could save up enough money in the next month or two to buy all the kitchen things and dining room furniture that Aziza was expected to bring into the marriage. While the groom's family was providing the apartment itself and the rest of the furnishings, for Mahabbah, the kitchen and dining room furnishings were still a tall order. This had been the primary reason for the delay in setting a date all along. I had heard of engagements here breaking up over these arrangements to provide for the new couple. I told Mahabbah that a friend of a friend of ours coming to live in Maadi in September to work for USAID and she was interested in having Mahabbah work for her. I also mentioned that Basima, the owner of our apartment who first introduced us to Mahabbah, had also assured me that Mahabbah could work for her again after we left. Mahabbah seemed very pleased that she would be able to continue working with no significant drop in her income. As long as she stayed healthy, I thought to myself.

Mahabbah explained her connection to Basima. She had actually worked for Basima's mother's best friend, Madame Aziza, for many years, and that she was still close with this woman and saw her regularly at her home. Before Mahabbah was married, she lived in with Madame Aziza and had taken care of her children and household responsibilities for thirteen years. Even after she was married, she continued to work for Madame Aziza until her own daughter, Aziza, was born. It suddenly occurred to me to ask, "Is Aziza named after Madame Aziza?"

"Yes," Mahabbah smiled, "and I named my sons after Madame Aziza's sons."

Throughout our conversation, I wondered if Mahabbah might be subtly seeking our help both with regard to her health issues and her daughter's upcoming wedding. I was sure that Madame Aziza provided Mahabbah with some ongoing financial assistance. I had learned by now that this was one of the ways people like Mahabbah survived. While we

218

were in Cairo only short-term, it might well be that this was her hope, if not exactly her expectation of us. While we were not wealthy, and we did not live like we were wealthy, we could certainly help. I had some ideas, but wanted to talk them over with Reuven before I said anything.

After Mahabbah left, I talked with Reuven. As far as Aziza's wedding, I thought we should plan on giving Mahabbah a generous gift of cash when we left in another week and a half, and she could use it for the things that she still wanted to buy Aziza. Reuven also agreed that it was a good idea for Mahabbah to be seen by our doctor and have whatever tests he recommended. I would explain to the doctor that Mahabbah would not be able to afford seeing him on her own, and that this was for a diagnosis only and the ongoing care would be under the supervision of her own doctor. I had made a similar arrangement a few months earlier for Mahabbah's daughter, who had been out of work with severe pain in her back and legs, and it turned out, was suffering from arthritis. It had been helpful at that time to get a clear and trusted diagnosis and recommendations for treatment. I called the doctor and arranged for an appointment for Mahabbah for the next day.

219

It was already afternoon and I still had not gotten to read the newspapers, but I decided to first call our ex-pat friend Debbie to find out the latest news from her. Debbie always followed the news closely in connection with her work at her NGO and she had already read several news updates online. Early that morning, she said, Israel had attacked the Beirut International Airport, putting all three runways out of commission. Israeli officials were insisting that even though it was Hezbollah that had launched the attacks against Israel, Lebanon had to bear the responsibility for these incursions into Israel as the sovereign state of which Hezbollah was an active part. The reality was that Hezbollah participated in the governing coalition, even holding seats in the Lebanese parliament, so its rogue actions had far-reaching consequences. While Israel's response seemed perfectly reasonable to us, article after article in *Al Ahram* criticized the Israelis for a military response out of proportion to the attacks in both Lebanon and Gaza. Already over 50 Lebanese civilians had been killed, the paper reported.

But the articles did not say anything about Hezbollah's continuing rocket attacks into Israel. In the online edition of *The New York Times* I later read that according to an Israeli official, Hezbollah fired over 120 Katyusha rockets and mortar shells into Israel on Thursday, killing two and injuring over 100 Israelis in Nahariya, Safed, Haifa, Carmiel and over twenty other Israeli towns. Thousands of Israelis had fled their homes and were camping out in bomb shelters, or the casualties would have been much higher.

Several articles in *Al Ahram* raised the question whether Hezbollah and Hamas had coordinated their attacks on Israel, since Hamas' kidnapping of Gilad Shalit had occurred only three weeks earlier. A senior member of Hezbollah's leadership, Ali Al-Fayad, told *Al Ahram* that there had been no active coordination, but that Hamas and Hezbollah shared the same strategy of kidnapping Israeli soldiers on Israeli soil in order to exchange them for Arab political prisoners being held by Israel. He also noted that their parallel actions had now forced Israel into a weaker position by having to fight on two fronts. Hezbollah's Secretary General Hassan Nasrallah also hinted at some kind of linkage between the Lebanese and Palestinian plans when he suggested that Israel should begin simultaneous negotiations with Hezbollah and the Palestinians for the release of prisoners.

Joseph Samaha, a Lebanese journalist and editor-in-chief of the Lebanese newspaper *Al-Akhbar*, expressed his opinion that most Lebanese supported Hezbollah's actions, in large part because of Israel's recent attacks on Gaza: "The Palestinian crisis only gives greater legitimacy to Hizbullah's action," he commented in an *Al Ahram* article. "The brutality of the Israeli re-invasion of Gaza has struck deep in Lebanese society, and it has engendered genuine anger among the majority of the country's citizens." But other Lebanese journalists suggested the country was more split between support for Hezbollah and anger against it, for bringing the intense Israeli attacks upon their country and destroying all hopes for the summer tourism that so many Lebanese depended on for their living.

I remembered the summer of 1982, when Israel, in response to a steady stream of deadly attacks by the PLO against its civilians both in Israel and abroad, invaded southern Lebanon in order to drive out the PLO fighters who had established their base of operations there. What was supposed to be a short campaign called "Peace in the Galilee," succeeded in forcing Yasser Arafat and the PLO to withdraw from Lebanon by September. But

Israel's routing of the PLO came at a price—high casualties on both sides and a prolonged involvement in Lebanon. Bad blood between Christian and Muslim factions, and the involvement of Syria and Iran, made Lebanon a military and political quagmire that proved to be far more difficult for Israel to extricate itself from than anticipated. Israel was finally able to withdraw to an eight-mile security zone in southern Lebanon in 1985 and withdrew its military presence in Lebanon completely in 2000.

Meanwhile, Hezbollah, the Shi'a group founded in 1982 in response to Israel's invasion, took over where the PLO left off, attacking Israeli troops first in Lebanon and then in the security zone. Over the next decade, Hezbollah absorbed other militias and emerged as the single most powerful militia group in southern Lebanon. Since the 1990s, Hezbollah's growing influence in Lebanon included entering the political process and gaining representation in Parliament. Yet Hezbollah persisted in its rogue military actions against Israel with cross-border attacks on northern Israeli towns and military posts.

The elimination of the State of Israel was one of Hezbollah's primary goals since its founding. Claiming that Israel is an illegitimate state, its leaders declared "an open war until the elimination of Israel and the death of the last Jew on earth." While Hezbollah's leaders have said the organization distinguishes between Zionism and Judaism, the group repeatedly referred to the Jews as the "enemies of mankind" and as "conspiratorial adversaries" intent on destroying Islam and Arab cultural identity to advance their own ends. Originally trained by Iran's Revolutionary Guards, Hezbollah continued to receive military training, weapons and financial support from Iran.

Now, twenty-four years after the invasion that led to the uprooting of the PLO and to the birth of Hezbollah, Israel was again invading Lebanon, provoked by Hezbollah's attack and the kidnapping of its soldiers. Clearly, this attack demanded a response, but what combination of military and political action could most effectively stop Hezbollah without drawing Israel again into a Lebanese quagmire? What course of action would Israel pursue and with what success?

Friday morning, things continued to heat up. Israeli missiles struck the headquarters and home of Hassan Nasrallah, Hezbollah's senior military and political commander. Less than an hour later, Nasrallah's voice was heard in an audiotape on Lebanese television, threatening to send missiles into Israel's northern port city of Haifa and towns further south.

Nasrallah's words were greeted with heavy celebratory gunfire that rang out across the Lebanese capital. Likewise, according to *Al Ahram*, sentiments in Egypt were "jubilant" as hundreds exchanged mobile text-messages welcoming the speech of "the Arab hero in the region." Three thousand Egyptians came out to demonstrate their support of Hezbollah and protest Israel's incursion into Lebanon at the Al Azhar mosque downtown. They seemed unperturbed by the thousands of Egyptian police in full riot gear, lined up as they were every Friday, their presence a silent warning to Egyptians not to get too carried away after the Friday sermon.

222

Despite the demonstrations downtown, I pulled myself away from news reports to meet Mahabbah at the doctor's office in another part of Maadi that afternoon, as we had arranged. Our friends Kathy and Paul had originally referred us to Dr. Shenouda., an Egyptian doctor whom they had been seeing for years. He listened carefully to Mahabbah when she described her history with diabetes and her current ailments and asked lots of questions. Dr. Shenouda was very patient and wrote out orders for several tests he wanted her to have. He also mentioned that there was an excellent lab right near where I lived that would be convenient for Mahabbah.

While Mahabbah was getting dressed, I asked Dr. Shenouda if he was going away on vacation. He looked pleased to tell me that he was actually going to Los Angeles for a week to participate in the next stage of a medical research project that he was working on together with Israeli and American doctors, investigating the causes and possible treatments for childhood diabetes. I told him how happy I was to hear there was such a project, and that he was involved in it. Why aren't more things like this in the newspapers? I wondered silently.

When Mahabbah reappeared, we talked about going to the lab on Sunday morning, when Mahabbah would be at our home next. Outside the doctor's office, we embraced and said our good-byes, and both of us went to our respective homes to cook the evening meal.

Our young friend, Kareem, who had kept us well informed during the most intense days of the Judges Movement, joined us for Shabbat dinner that night, as we had arranged before our trip to Kenya. I thought he looked tired when he came in, but his eyes lit up when he saw that we were having a mixed vegetable dish with eggplant, zucchini, peppers and tomatoes.

"Wow, is this Turkish?" he asked. "It looks and smells just like a Turkish dish my mother makes that I really love." My cookbook called it "Spanish Vegetables," so this was clearly a case of the Mediterranean blending of food cultures and tastes across borders. This was Kareem's second Shabbat dinner with us and he seemed immediately comfortable with us, though that had been true the first time he came as well.

Over dinner, we talked a little bit about our trip to Kenya, but it quickly became clear that what was really on all our minds was the outbreak of violence between Hezbollah and Israel. About certain things, we were in full agreement: Hezbollah had acted irresponsibly by crossing into Israel and kidnapping two Israeli soldiers, provoking an almost certain Israeli military response and a new cycle of violence. But Kareem was more focused on the intensity of the Israeli strikes into Lebanon. The attacks on Beirut especially troubled him. Kareem loved Beirut—he had very good friends there and had visited many times over the years, and he was deeply distressed by the rapid escalation of the conflict and what he considered Israel's disproportionate use of force.

"Of all the countries in the Arab Middle East, Lebanon is the one that holds the greatest hope for increased democracy and openness," Kareem said. As he saw it, Beirut had just reached the point of a new prosperity and the extensive destruction that had taken place in the last 48 hours would set it back for years. He was even more concerned about the loss of life and what he called "the terrorizing effect" of the violence on Lebanese civilians. He feared that the Israel's use of force in Lebanon could end up quashing the nascent democratic developments in Lebanon by shifting the focus from developing democratic institutions to bolstering their military capacity.

Kareem thought there was sad irony in Israel's actions because the Lebanese themselves had recently begun to question the value of Hezbollah's military presence in Lebanon, especially in light of its participation in the government: "How could the Lebanese continue to allow Hezbollah to have a military presence alongside the Lebanese military? It's crazy!" he said. "But now, what's going to happen? The Israelis are

223

hoping with their attacks to persuade the Lebanese to dismantle the military wing of Hezbollah, since it was Hezbollah's actions that brought this new war upon them. Instead it's going to do the opposite and push the Lebanese to support Hezbollah's right to defend itself in the face of Israeli aggression." I wondered what the Lebanese thought about Hezbollah's deliberate policy of planting armaments and men in the midst of civilian areas, intentionally drawing Israeli fire to those areas, but given how Kareem was feeling, it did not seem like the right time to raise the question.

224   Kareem was so troubled by the conflict that he was leaving for Beirut on Sunday to see for himself what was happening and to do some reporting for two different blogs for which he occasionally wrote. Reuven and I both expressed our concern for him heading straight into a war zone, but he seemed pretty firm about his decision. He also shared with us an interesting Egyptian reaction to the Israelis' attacks on Lebanon and Gaza. He claimed that mixed in with Egyptian anger at Israel's disproportionate use of force in its attacks on Lebanon and Gaza, there was also a bit of envy: "Looking at Israel's response to the kidnappings, some people are saying things like, wouldn't it be nice if our government cared that much about the life of every citizen?" Kareem told us, "but you won't read that in the papers."

The evening passed quickly, as we moved on to Kareem's personal plans for the year. He was hoping to do some more writing and continue his involvement in the free speech movement, and the following year, go to graduate school in economics or public policy, probably in England. I was glad to hear that Kareem was planning on pursuing his studies. It was easy to imagine him someday teaching in a university setting or some kind of research institute. When it was time for Kareem to go, we all hugged him good-bye and wished him a safe trip to Lebanon—and back home again.

Sunday morning, after meeting Mahabbah at the lab for her tests, I continued walking down Nine Road to meet Safiya for coffee at one of her favorite cafés that happened to be right near our apartment. On my way, I thought about how happy I was that Reuven and I had connected with Safiya and her husband from the interfaith dialogue group. This would probably be our last chance to see each other before we left Cairo and I had been looking forward to it. When Safiya arrived, we greeted each other warmly and sat down inside, grateful for the air conditioning on this stiflingly hot afternoon.

Even though we started out comparing notes on how the school year had ended for our kids, but we quickly moved on to the reports of continuing violence in Lebanon and Gaza.

"The worst part of it is how many people are getting killed—the tragic loss of life on all sides," Safiya said. On this point I certainly agreed with Safiya, but beyond this, it turned out that there was very little on which we could agree.

"But the casualties are much higher among the Lebanese and Palestinians than among the Israelis," Safiya said with rising emotion in her voice. "The United States has really betrayed the Arab world. It just lets Israel do whatever it wants, first in Gaza and now in Lebanon." She added that all her friends felt the same way.

Safiya was unwavering in her belief that Israel harbors expansionist plans to take over lands beyond its current borders—even beyond the borders of the lands taken in 1967. When I questioned her belief, she answered: "What about Israel's plans to expand its borders from the Nile to the Euphrates?"

"No one in Israel is talking about expansion into Egypt. The debate in Israel isn't about expansion—it's about what portion of territories occupied since the 1967 war are negotiable and could be given up for a Palestinian state."

Safiya remained unconvinced. "But isn't that what it says in your Bible, that Israel will conquer all the land from the Nile to the Euphrates?"

"The only place I've ever heard that expression was in Egypt," I responded. "I've never heard any Jews talking about Israel expanding to 'the Nile and the Euphrates,' and I've never seen that phrase anywhere in the Bible. Actually, there are several different places in the Torah that describe the land God promised to Abraham and his descendants with different borders, but even if one verse did use that language, I have never heard it singled out by Jews as the intended borders for a Jewish state."

Safiya still looked doubtful, and we moved on to a different issue.

"Why do the Jews even need a Jewish state? And why in Palestine?" Like so many people in Egypt, it quickly became clear that Safiya saw Israel's existence as a Jewish state as a foreign imposition in the region

225

that by definition would involve the displacement of Palestinians from their homes.

"What if Israel and the Palestinians were to achieve a peace agreement that resulted in a Palestinian state alongside Israel?" I asked her.

"Even then, it would have to be a very small state, so many people would still not be able to go back to their homes," she responded, waving her hand to dismiss the idea. "That wouldn't solve the problem. But why did the Jews decide to establish a country for themselves in Palestine? Why not somewhere else?" she asked.

I was a bit taken aback. Had she really never heard or read that Jewish roots went back to this very land? Later it occurred to me that if Safiya thought the phrase "from the Nile to the Euphrates" was from the Bible, wouldn't she know that according to the Bible, the Israelite nation was centered in that region too, in what is today Israel? Had she never heard of David's Kingdom, or Solomon's Temple, or the Israelite nation?

"There was nothing random about the location—this is the land where Jewish history began, where Jews once had sovereignty, and the place we have always longed to return to," I said. "Since the Second Temple was destroyed almost two thousand years ago by the Romans, Jews have prayed for their return to this land that was once theirs." Safiya's face registered a complete blank; she was clearly unfamiliar with anything I was saying. How could a university-educated Egyptian woman who had such strong opinions on the subject have no awareness that Israel was the historical homeland of the Jewish people?

Our conversation moved on to Hezbollah's attack on Israel and I brought up the kidnapping of the Israeli soldiers that triggered this crisis.

"Hezbollah is just reacting to the situation in Gaza and the West Bank," Safiya asserted with conviction. "Israel is responsible for killing so many Palestinians, something had to be done. It's a Holocaust, like what Germany did to the Jews," she said.

I felt my heart sink. It was bad enough to read such statements in the paper. But hearing them from someone I considered a friend was altogether different. I thought of Noam's encounters with his school friend Ashraf, when he had asked us, "Can you be friends with someone with whom you totally disagree about certain things that are really important?"

"How can you say that, Safiya?" I asked. "Not every situation of conflict—even if people are getting killed—is a Holocaust. The Holocaust against the Jews was a case of systematic genocide, with the intention of literally eliminating an entire people. Palestinians are definitely suffering, and yes, even dying. We don't disagree about that. But do you really think Israel is trying to murder all the Palestinians, so there are no more Palestinians in the world?" Safiya looked ready to say yes, but remained silent. Maybe this is what she really thinks, I realized.

"I know that in the newspapers and on television, Israel is blamed for all kinds of things— Israel is portrayed as evil, as a monster—but do you really believe everything you read and hear in the news? Isn't a lot of it propaganda, a kind of diversion tactic for the government so people won't focus too much on the problems inside Egypt?".

"I don't just rely on Egyptian news," Safiya said, looking slightly hurt. "I listen to BBC and European news too." Now it was my turn to look skeptical —not that Safiya listened to BBC, but that their news reports would refer to Israel committing "genocide" or a "holocaust" against the Palestinians.

"You say Israel isn't conducting genocide against the Palestinians? What about the Separation Wall?" Safiya asked.

"How is the Separation Wall part of a genocide?" I tried to stay calm.

"It's keeping people from their fields, their work," she answered.

"That's the same as rounding people up and gassing them?" I asked, no longer able to mask my incredulity.

"If they can't work they starve," she answered. "People are dying. Lots of Palestinians have died."

"I agree that many Palestinians are suffering economically because of the Separation Barrier," I said, switching to the term I was used to, since parts of the Barrier actually consisted of high fencing as opposed to a concrete wall. "But no one is starving and this is not part of a systematic plan to kill all the Palestinians. This is *not* a genocide," I said emphatically, though I had to watch my tone. Safiya wouldn't hear a word I was saying if I didn't calm down.

"I don't see the Separation Barrier as a long-term solution either," I added. "Neither do most Israelis. But I do think it's important to remember why the Israelis built it. They built it to keep Palestinian extremists from coming into Israel and killing a lot of innocent people on the buses and streets of Tel Aviv and Jerusalem. Every country has the right and the responsibility to defend its citizens.

"The Separation Barrier has greatly cut down the number of terrorist attacks on Israelis within Israel. But I also understand the Separation Barrier is very problematic, especially in certain places, where it imposes severe restrictions on many people who have no intention of attacking Israelis and are just trying to live their lives. In several cases, Israel's Supreme Court has ruled that the Barrier needs to be moved because of its economic impact on certain communities, like where it separates people from their orchards and fields."

Safiya again looked skeptical. I wasn't sure there was anything left to say. I was feeling increasingly frustrated with what seemed much more than a parallel narrative based on a different way of looking at the same facts. Several times I felt we were crossing the line into what amounted to inflammatory statements with no basis in fact, the result of deliberate attempts to spread hatred. What allowed such lies to take root was probably ignorance, but once planted, could they even be answered with facts?

We both admitted it was hard for us to talk about Israel and Palestine because of our strong disagreements. Both of us felt sad because we really valued our new friendship. Of all the people I had met in Egypt, Safiya seemed the most like me—middle-class, educated, even a member of an interfaith dialogue group! And our kids went to the same school.

"Maybe I said too much… I don't want to offend or hurt you," said Safiya suddenly. She looked genuinely concerned. "This is partly why we're living in Egypt," I said. "I want to hear how you see things, how you see Israel and other issues too. It's difficult to talk about, I agree, but it is also important."

This was all true, but inside I was actually hurting more than I let on. This had been such a painful conversation, but I didn't want to admit to Safiya how upset I really was. I was afraid that if I let down my guard and shared my true feelings I would end up crying. Tears in themselves were not the problem. But I didn't want Safiya to hold back from sharing her true views with me, even if they were difficult for me to hear. And though we would be leaving in a week, I had hoped this friendship would continue. Because of the level of our sharing on previous occasions, I still valued this relatively new relationship. I wanted it to be possible for us to be friends, even with our different views. So I held myself together as best I could, admitting the conversation was difficult but not revealing the full extent of my feelings.

We moved on to other topics. I talked a little bit about our time in Kenya and Safiya described her family's plans to visit her father in Alexandria for two weeks later in the summer. Then we hugged each other warmly and both said how much we hate goodbyes. Safiya said she would call me before the end of the week to see how our last week had gone and we could say goodbye then. I liked the idea. Neither of us wanted to end on the emotional note of our political disagreements.

Walking home, I could feel how tense my body was. What, under other circumstances would have been another long conversation of personal sharing and getting to know each other, had turned into one of the most painful and difficult discussions I had had in the last six months. I was exhausted and confused. I had come to Egypt wanting this—wanting to take advantage of this opportunity to hear and better understand others' perspectives, even when they challenged everything I believed. But in this case, what I had encountered was not just a different political perspective, but what I considered some of the most baseless and hateful accusations against Israel I had read and heard these last six months. And as difficult as it was to read in the paper, it was far more disturbing to hear it from someone whom I viewed as a new friend. Why didn't Safiya question any of these anti-Israel slurs she had repeated? Was this an unreasonable expectation on my part of her, or of any Egyptian?

When I got home, after checking my emails, I decided to look up the phrase "from the Nile to the Euphrates" on the Internet and see if it did appear in the Bible. I had heard this claim about Israel's expansionist intentions before when talking to Egyptians, and as I had told Safiya, I had never heard Israelis refer to it. But I was curious to see if I could find some discussion of relevant Biblical verses by contemporary Israelis.

As I thought, the Bible never uses this phrase "from the Nile to the Euphrates" in discussing the future borders of Israel. But in Genesis 15, God makes a covenant with Abraham and promises to Abraham's descendants the land from "the Egyptian River" to the Euphrates. I could see how one might assume the phrase "the Egyptian River" referred to the Nile, but since there were many Biblical verses that did mention the Nile by name, why wouldn't the Nile be mentioned by name here too?

The well-known medieval Jewish commentator, Ibn Ezra, offers the brief comment that the verse refers not to the Nile but to the Shihor

River. Later scholars assume he had in mind the same Shihor River identified in Judges 13 as the border of the land that God intended for the Israelite nation. In Joshua 13:3, God said Joshua still needed to conquer land then occupied by the Philistines and the Gerushites, to the Shihor river "before Egypt," effectively establishing that river as the Israelites' southern border. This made much more sense as a border for the Israelites than the Nile River running through the middle of Egypt.

Not so surprisingly, my Internet search for discussion of the phrase "from the Nile to the Euphrates" led to a wide variety of anti-Israel and antisemitic websites, but not a single Israeli or Zionist proponent of the phrase. The phrase and the accompanying claim seemed to be spoken only by Israel's enemies intent on portraying Israel in an inflammatory manner. I could not find a single reference to Israeli Jews, or any other Jews for that matter, calling for expansion to these boundaries. But the phrase "from the Nile to the Euphrates" repeatedly led me to two other blatantly incorrect beliefs about Israel that, despite all evidence to the contrary, continue to be widely accepted in the Arab world. The first assertion was that the Israeli flag indicated its secret expansionist intentions in a kind of code. According to this claim, the blue stripes on the top and bottom of the Israeli flag represent the Nile and Euphrates Rivers and symbolize the Jews' "true aspirations" to conquer all the land between those two rivers, including much of Egypt, all of Jordan, and some of Syria and Iraq. Yasser Arafat was among those cited online as having repeatedly made this claim.

But the actual facts are well documented and quite different. The design of the Israeli flag went back to 1897, when the "Flag of Zion" with this same design was officially approved at the Zionist Congress in Basel in 1897. In fact, the stripes of blue were intended to recall the stripes on a traditional Jewish prayer shawl, the *tallit*. Some of the secular Zionist leaders, including Herzl himself, had expressed opposition to the religious reference in the design of the flag. But this was the design and intended symbolism that won the day at the Zionist Congress, and in 1948, the white flag with two blue stripes and a Magen David in the middle became the official flag of the State of Israel.

The second erroneous claim, also expressed by Arafat among others, was that this same phrase "from the Nile to the Euphrates" could be found prominently displayed on an inside wall of the Knesset, pointing to Israel's "true" expansionist vision.

Once again, this was more than simply a "different" parallel narrative. These were blatant lies, intentionally spread by people whose sole purpose was to create the false impression of Israel's expansionist designs, feeding into Arabs' fears and fanning their hatred of Israel.

Especially if one heard it often enough, claims of Israel's plans to expand "from the Nile to the Euphrates," like claims of a planned Israeli "genocide" or a "holocaust" against the Palestinians, could apparently come to be accepted without much questioning.

Later that evening I shared my frustration with Reuven. While I certainly still saw the value in talking with people here to understand better how they viewed Israel, I was finding myself increasingly upset when I encountered what seemed to me to be blatant lies with no other intent than to spread hatred. Did rational discourse stand a chance against the deliberate spread of fear and hatred? At moments like this, I told him, I had my doubts.

"Look," Reuven said, "I've been hearing the same kind of things at the university this week, and it bothers me too. But didn't we come here to gain some understanding of where this society is at? We knew from the start it was unlikely that we would have any kind of impact here."

"I know," I said to Reuven, "but these conversations do raise questions about how this kind of ingrained and pervasive anti-Israel sentiment can be worked with in any way. I don't mean just by us, but by anyone. Rational discourse is all about getting to the basis behind our different points of view. When Zayna and I talked about how the Palestinians lost their land—was the land taken or sold, was it legal, was it moral—there was a meaningful discussion. Whether we came out agreeing or disagreeing at the end, we both came away with more understanding of each other's points of view.

"But what do you do when what you encounter is not just another way of looking at the same facts, but something different—some conspiracy-type theory where the other person won't be persuaded by any facts, because their view is based on a claim that doesn't require concrete evidence. In fact, their claim is actually impervious to contrary evidence, because it is based on "secret" information—like the Israelis have their eyes on conquering all the land from the Euphrates to the Nile, or that Israel's flag is code for these expansionist designs. It's like some of the worst antisemitic lies about Jews, like the notion that a cabal of rich or power-hungry Jews is running the world. What can you do with something like that?"

"You're right. That's a real problem, and it's not just here," Reuven pointed out. "Conspiracy theories are everywhere—like our neighbor, Bill, and other Americans who believe our government was behind 9/11 as a pretext for going to war in Iraq. We had the same problem talking with him—it was almost impossible to have a rational discussion about it."

"But I still wonder if something could be done to help generate a more rational discussion of the issues with different points of view. I mean, for someone like Safiya, who bought into these lies, not out of malice, but because they are all around her. Do you know if there are websites being developed by anyone in Arabic from an Israel-friendly perspective? One that analyzes some of these claims and misconceptions?"

"That's an interesting idea," Reuven agreed. "I don't know if there is anything like that, or if anyone is working on that kind of project. There are all sorts of challenges, of course. Any site offering such a perspective would be suspect. But it would be great to have it out there as a resource, that's for sure."

It was already late and Reuven started to get ready for bed, but I stayed up for a long time thinking about how a website like this might look and who might conceivably be interested in creating it.

When I met Zayna for class the next day, of course we also talked about the situation in Lebanon. As I anticipated, Zayna was very angry about the action Israel had taken against Lebanon and Gaza. She focused mainly on the many civilian deaths, including the well-publicized case of a family of nine on the beach in Gaza. "The Arab people will not forget this," she said firmly, looking at me directly with great emotion. I told her I too had a heavy heart at the loss of life on both sides of the conflict. When I asked Zayna her opinion about the role of Hezbollah in Lebanon, she responded, "Most Egyptians really like Hezbollah. Hezbollah is fighting for the Palestinians and the rights and the dignity of all Arabs."

"But what kind of authority does Hezbollah have to launch an attack like this when they are part of a sovereign country and government with a national army of its own? Doesn't that matter?" I asked. She did not respond and I decided not to press further. Turning back to the Arabic lesson, Zayna taught me the command form, which, as with other verb forms, proved to be very similar to the Hebrew construction. Once more I felt the tragedy of the conflicts raging between Arab and Jew all the more striking. Sitting together studying Arabic for the purpose of my being better able to talk to Egyptians and other Arabs, suddenly seemed to me a hopeful act in itself.

Later in the afternoon, Reuven and I went downtown with Amir so he could meet his friend Khalid for a movie. We had decided to relax in a café near the movie theater while we were waiting, and Reuven bought a newspaper before we sat down. With Reuven's encouragement and a little bit of help, I tried my hand at sounding out and translating the headlines.

"Mubarak Makes Statement…" I was slow, but I could actually do it, I realized with some excitement: "… critical of Hezbollah."

"That can't be right," Reuven said, pulling the newspaper closer to him, as I finished the first headline. I was puzzled, but had to agree. There was no way Mubarak could be condemning Hezbollah for their attacks against Israel. I must have missed something. Every single Egyptian we had spoken with, from our friends to the taxi drivers and shopkeepers in our neighborhood, applauded Hezbollah's actions and sharply condemned Israel. Reuven read the headline again. "I don't get it," he said, shaking his head. "That's what it says."

Reuven continued reading and translating aloud. Mubarak apparently had made a public statement the day before criticizing Hezbollah, and he was not alone in his condemnation. After an emergency summit meeting of the Arab League in Cairo, the leaders of Saudi Arabia, Jordan, and several Gulf states together with Egypt, had all expressed criticism of Hezbollah for starting the conflict in an irresponsible manner.

We were amazed. We had read so many articles over the weekend condemning Israel's actions in Gaza and Lebanon. Were these more moderate Arab leaders speaking out now because of American pressure to do so, or because they saw Hezbollah's rogue action as a threatening precedent for their own countries? Or, was it that they saw in Iran, clearly the force behind Hezbollah, a danger they felt they could no longer afford to ignore? Iran was the most powerful Shi'a dominated country in the region, Reuven explained, and Egypt, Saudi Arabia, and Jordan were all primarily Sunni. The rise of Hezbollah in Lebanon would shift the balance of power in Lebanon toward the Shi'a Muslims, and toward Iran and Syria. Any of these issues alone might be a factor. Whatever the case, we were happily surprised to read that several Arab leaders were placing responsibility for the conflict with Hezbollah.

At the same time, we couldn't fully cast aside our initial puzzlement. For how long could Mubarak take a stand like this, so at odds with the vocal position of his own people? We assumed this was the same for the leaders of Jordan and Saudi Arabia.

Just then we saw Amir and Khalid come out of the theater and we waved. It was time to head back to the Metro and make our way home.

As we continued to talk to people, the view on the street, from our admittedly small sample, appeared to remain unanimously in support of Hezbollah and condemning of Israel. Mubarak's voice seemed at odds even with other voices in his own government. Debbie told me later that evening, that she had heard a spokesperson from the Ministry of Foreign Affairs claim in a Nile TV news report that Israel had itself engineered the abduction of the Israelis soldiers in order to create an excuse to attack Hezbollah in Lebanon. The spokesperson went on to blame Israel for the gap between the Arab street and the government. As ludicrous as these claims seemed, many if not most Egyptians would probably accept them at face value.

The Lebanese War continued to be our constant shadow as we tried to prepare for our own imminent departure. One day as I was doing some errands on Road Nine, I stopped to buy a bottle of water at a small shop. The small, slightly stooped, older woman working there had a beautifully wrinkled face and real warmth in her eyes.

"You are American?" she asked me in Arabic. I answered affirmatively in Arabic and she said something about how terrible it was that so many people were getting killed in Lebanon, shaking her head for emphasis. Did her choice of topic have anything to do with my being American, I wondered, or was Lebanon just on her mind? I told her I was very upset too, that so many people were being killed, but that Israel was defending its own people against Hezbollah's attacks, and was trying to do what it could to minimize killing Lebanese civilians. Now that Mubarak and some other Arab leaders had been publicly critical of Hezbollah, I felt more comfortable speaking up on Israel's behalf.

"President Bush must say 'No more war' to Israel," the woman concluded, her tone friendly, not angry. I saw the connections now: for this woman, as for many Egyptians, the U.S. and Israel were such close allies that the U.S. could and should put pressure on Israel to stop fighting. Even if Mubarak was critical of Hezbollah, the Egyptians I encountered did not appear ready to question their support of this militia group that they regarded as the defender of the Palestinians and Arab dignity.

This whole conversation took place in Arabic. I had not been able to say everything I wanted to say, but I thought I had understood most of what the woman was saying, and I was able to express some of my thoughts too, albeit in very simple language. 235

I continued on to a jewelry store further up the street, where a few days earlier, Reuven had bought a small silver cup and arranged to have it engraved with the words "Yom Shabbat" in Arabic. Now that we were getting ready to leave, we were being more open about the fact that we were Jewish. When I walked in, Mahmoud, the owner, had a newspaper spread out on top of a glass display case, with full pages clearly devoted to what was happening in Lebanon, complete with photos and maps. "There are such terrible things going on here," he said, clearly upset, shaking his head.

"This is the next step in the plan to create a new Middle East," he told me. "You know, they have a twelve-year plan to redraw the map of the Middle East. Well, this is just the next step."

"Who is 'they?'" I asked. Did he mean the Israelis, or the United States? He shrugged with the hint of a smile.

"I've noticed that many people here believe in conspiracy theories," I commented.

"Yes," he said, "a lot of people here see it this way."

Mahmoud showed me an article in the paper, in which the author had collected quotations from Israeli leaders through the twentieth century that purportedly demonstrated their commitment to drive out Palestinians in order to make a homeland for the Jews. I wondered if the quotations were all accurate, but I could not read the statements, so I couldn't make any comment. I was struck by the fact that Mahmoud did not express anger, though he may have felt angry. His expression and his words reflected deep sadness and even resignation. At one point he said, "I cannot talk about it anymore. I am too upset."

I told him I understood. I thanked him for his help, and told him that I was returning home with several pairs of earrings—like the ones I happened to be wearing—that I had bought in his shop, and these were among my favorite things I was bringing home from Egypt. Mahmoud seemed pleased, and told me he hoped we would see each other again when we came back to Egypt.

While I was taking every opportunity I could in conversations like these, to bring up the fact that Israel's attacks were in response to Hezbollah crossing the border and killing and capturing Israeli soldiers, people almost always responded, "But Hezbollah was just reacting to the Israeli violence against Palestinians in Gaza." They saw no justification for Israel's attacks, just like it was my tendency to view Hezbollah's attacks as unjustified, even if they claimed they were a response to the Israeli violence in Gaza. Similarly I was quick to point out that the Israeli attacks on Gaza had certainly not started the conflict but there, too, had been in response to the kidnapping of an Israeli soldier and a steady stream of rocket attacks fired into Israeli towns from Gaza. It was clear that on the question of which side was responsible for the current conflict, the answer depended in large part on how far back you took the story. Or rather, it was the other way around—how far back you took the story depended on who you saw as ultimately responsible for the conflict.

In addition to the Egyptian press, we followed the developments in Lebanon and Israel through online news websites like *The New York Times, The Jerusalem Report*, and *Haaretz*. On Wednesday, a senior Israeli commander claimed that Israel had destroyed 60 percent of Hezbollah's arsenal, and that Hezbollah itself had fired 2000 rockets and missiles into Israel, also reducing its arsenal of weapons. Israel had also closed the airport, seaports, and routes connecting Lebanon and Syria, in an effort to prevent Hezbollah from re-arming with supplies from Syria, Iran or any other source.

I was curious how our Israeli friend, Elie Antebi, who was the Consul General in Alexandria and originally from Lebanon, saw the situation. I called him to say goodbye and asked him what he thought about what was going on. Elie had lived in Beirut into his mid-teens, so his connection to the city and region was particularly strong. He was saddened by the Israeli attacks and the level of destruction, but he also clearly understood Israel's reasons for responding with air strikes into Lebanon. He said the Israelis had no illusions about achieving anything through military action in Lebanon, but viewed it as a necessary first step that would hopefully lead to negotiations. Eventually he believed that there would have to be international peacekeeping forces to prevent Syria and Iran from continuing to destabilize Lebanon. It was very much in Israel's interest, he noted, for Lebanon to be a stable, healthy, thriving society.

Elie also seemed to understand both the positions of the Egyptian "street" and the government. He felt that Mubarak was sincere in his efforts to play a positive mediating role, but he thought it would be difficult for him, as well as other moderate Arab leaders, to maintain a position for very long that put them at odds with their own people. "The longer the fighting continues, the more difficult it will be for the more moderate individuals to maintain their minority point of view," he concluded.

I couldn't help wondering: even if Israel's use of military force was morally and politically justified, what would be the long-term cost? How many of those still in the moderate camp would now be moved to join groups more openly hostile to Israel? Might this be the case with our friend Kareem?

Mahabbah walked into our apartment Thursday morning, three days before we would be leaving, balancing two pots of *mahshi*, one upon the other, on top of her head. She lowered them carefully and after making a tomato sauce for them, allowed them to sit on a low flame to finish cooking. Within minutes the whole apartment smelled of cabbage, zucchini, tomatoes, garlic and olive oil. Mahabbah knew how much we all loved *mahshi*, and seemed to take special pride in the fact that she had introduced us to this Egyptian specialty. She also was a wonderful cook—and she wanted us to have one more meal of her *mahshi* before we left Egypt. I told Mahabbah that she was giving me a double gift because it meant we would be able to have a special Egyptian meal for our last Friday night dinner—and with dinner already cooked I would be able to go downtown with Reuven on Friday to enjoy the day exploring a part of Cairo we had not yet seen.

I had been trying to figure out how we could possibly still see a museum of contemporary Egyptian art as well as another smaller art museum. Now that would be possible. While the *mahshi* was cooking, Mahabbah insisted on making us all breakfast—another Egyptian dish we all especially like, *shakshouka,* made with eggs scrambled into well sautéed, finely chopped onions, garlic, tomatoes, and peppers. It was delicious, and the boys made me promise to make it for them "Mahabbah's way" back in Los Angeles. I said I would do my best, but they should know, it probably wouldn't be quite the same as Mahabbah's. I told Mahabbah what the boys were saying, and once again, she seemed pleased that we all enjoyed her cooking so much.

238

When we sat down to read together, Mahabbah found it even easier than previously to sound out new words. It was clear that she was beginning to discover the power of being able to read whole sentences with new information on her own, not just reading to develop the skill. At several points she laughed in excitement at what she was reading.

"Look—I just read all this!" she said, sweeping her hand over the page proudly.

Mahabbah and her daughter had found a literacy class for adults at a school right near where she lived. She was planning to start a class there the following week.

"After I learn to read well, I am going to start learning English," Mahabbah said proudly. "Muhammad is learning English in school now, and he said he can help me." Muhammad was eight, and had also been helping his mother with reading. It was a thrill to realize that learning to read was not only opening up new possibilities for Mahabbah to participate more fully in her surroundings and culture, and help her son with homework, it was dramatically changing how she viewed herself and her own potential. My private fantasy was that someday Mahabbah would be teaching a literacy class like the one she was about to begin. She was a natural teacher, that was clear from how she helped me learn to speak Arabic. And what could be better for an adult trying to learn to read, than having as an instructor someone like Mahabbah, who for so much of her adult life had herself experienced the frustrations of not knowing how to read?

We also talked about Mahabbah's health, and how she was planning to take better care of herself. As I had before, I expressed my concern that more than anything else she could give her children, Mahabbah needed to do her best to stay healthy. Mahabbah laughed. Don't worry about me, she said. I will do better. Lots of vegetables. Not so much *mahshi*, like Dr. Shenouda had said.

Dr. Shenouda had called to say that the test results had come in and that Mahabbah had a slightly compromised liver but not anything terribly serious. The main thing Mahabbah needed to do was to better control her diet and exercise if at all possible, in order to control her weight. This was key to her health. He also wanted her to take calcium and certain vitamin supplements. The only problem was that these are kind of expensive for Mahabbah, so I decided to buy her a few months' supply, which I gave to her now.

When it was time for Mahabbah to go, it was clear that neither of us wanted to say good-bye. She asked if she could come by on Saturday afternoon, and we agreed on a time we would all have tea together.

After Mahabbah left, I walked up Canal Street to the Alexander Language School for my last Arabic class with Zayna. I had been anticipating this good-bye for days already. It was bittersweet from the start. We reviewed the different forms of verbs and read a dialogue together a couple of times, and then switched parts and read it again. We talked a little bit, and then, sadly, it could no longer be avoided—it was time to say good-bye. I told Zayna that studying with her and getting to know her had been one of the most special parts of my six months in Egypt. She seemed both pleased and a little bit embarrassed. She said she had never had a student like me, and it had been a special experience for her too. I gave Zayna a gift-wrapped box containing a leather handbag, which as I told her, was just a small expression of gratitude for the gift of language she had given me. She accepted it shyly and thanked me. We both got teary as we hugged each other and kissed each other back and forth, right cheek and left cheek twice each, and then I left.

I was still feeling quite emotional as I walked home. I was so grateful for what we had shared, and so sad to be saying good-bye to Zayna, unsure if and when I would see her again. This felt like one of the most unusual and precious friendships I had known, with a woman just a few years older than my own daughter. Zayna had introduced me to more than Arabic. In a number of different ways, she had been my personal entry port into Egypt. Our conversations about Islam and Judaism were rich for both of us. And our discussions about Israel and Palestine, while very difficult at times, had also felt like a rare and important opportunity for both of us to ask questions that we could ask very few people, to learn from each other, and to be able to say what was on our mind, and feel like we were being heard.

For me, the end of my last Arabic class spelled the end of our stay in Egypt. It also meant the end of my formal study of spoken Arabic, at least for a while. I hoped I would be able to find a way to continue speaking and learning Arabic back in Los Angeles, but honestly, I did not know if that would be possible. I took my time walking home, savoring all that these last months studying with Zayna had meant.

240   On Friday, the tenth day of fighting, the Israel military called up several thousand reserves and moved more tanks to the northern border, suggesting the possibility of Israel launching an expanded ground war in Lebanon. At the same time, intensive bombing raids into southern Lebanon continued and the Israeli Air Force showered Hezbollah-dominated areas in the south with leaflets urging residents to move north of the Litani River. Hundreds of thousands of people lived between the Israeli border and the river twelve miles to the north. Israel was clearly trying to prevent civilian casualties, even as it was apparently considering an expanded ground offensive targeting Hezbollah rockets and launchers that were deliberately placed in and near villages in southern Lebanon. Seventy percent of the population had already left, according to local estimates, and more people were leaving every day.

Also on Friday, Hezbollah continued to send a stream of rockets and missiles into northern Israel, targeting the port city of Haifa and nearby towns. Ten people were wounded in Haifa when a rocket hit their apartment building.

While growing concerns were being voiced in Lebanon about the humanitarian costs of an extended war, and anti-war demonstrations were being organized in Tel Aviv, a survey published on Friday in the popular Israeli newspaper, *Maariv*, said that 78 percent of Israelis were satisfied with the performance of Prime Minister Ehud Olmert, and 95 percent believed Israel's military response was "justified and correct."

Meanwhile, in Gaza, Israel was continuing attacks against Hamas targets. The Palestinian Prime Minister, Ismail Haniya, called again for an exchange of Palestinian prisoners for the Israeli corporal, Gilad Shalit.[1]

1   IDF soldier Gilad Shalit was released October 2011 in exchange for

U.S. Secretary of State Condoleeza Rice was planning to travel to the Middle East on Sunday, the day we were leaving. There was speculation that she would be testing the waters for a diplomatic solution to the conflict between Israel and Hezbollah. With suggestions that the conflict might well intensify over the next few days, we were eagerly following the news in the Egyptian, Israeli, and American press.

Since this was our last "real" day in Cairo. Reuven and I went downtown as planned to see the contemporary Egyptian art museum. We also bought a few last minute gifts, and did our best to finish packing before Shabbat, since we would have only a few hours after Shabbat before we had to leave for the airport. 241

As I was packing, sorting through the books and pictures and scarves I had accumulated over these last six months, I found myself wondering, what had it all meant? There was no question, even with the challenges of the last ten days, I felt more connected to a people and a place that six months ago I had felt were antagonistic to everything I held dear, because we had lived here, because of some of the friendships we had made. But in some ways, it was even more painful that we were in fact so divided by the different ways we saw the world and sometimes each other's people. I had experienced from the inside what it meant to seriously grapple with another society's narrative of history and issues of political controversy, and it was not easy. I was coming away from the experience humbled and more deeply troubled by the gap that separated our peoples and the implications this held for Israel, and indeed the whole world.

At the same time, I felt that there was still hope in our ability to connect with each other as human beings, and from there, to grow to better understand each other, even where we disagreed. These six months, including the last ten days, confirmed for me how essential it was that as communities and individuals, we reach out to connect in meaningful ways with people who hold perspectives different from our own. I was clearer about the difficulties, the discomforts, and yes, the limits of this path, but also clearer about the necessity and potential power of our efforts. More than ever, I was aware that ignorance and hatred existed on all sides, and that hatred could sometimes rise up like a tsunami and wipe out the peace builders' efforts in a moment. But I also knew that

---

1,000 Palestinian prisoners released by Israel.

there were individuals and groups still working for peace and greater understanding between our peoples, and it is with these people that I wanted to join my best efforts. For me, I knew, it could never be a choice. I could never give up on this hope.

Before we knew it, Friday night had arrived. When we lit candles and sat down in the living room for our last Kabbalat Shabbat, a Sabbath evening of singing and prayers, I thought back to our first Shabbat in Cairo six months earlier, when we had sat together in the living room of our hotel quarters across the street behind closed curtains, with our whole Egypt adventure before us. Thinking back to how it had felt when we were just starting out, not knowing anything about the neighborhood, before we had met any of the people who would become our good friends, it seemed much longer than six months ago.

Listening to our four voices all blending and harmonizing as we sang the prayers, it was clear that our Shabbat time as a family had turned out to be especially meaningful for all of us in these last six months. In ways we had not anticipated, Shabbat had proved a little Jewish oasis for us, even without a Jewish community in which to celebrate. In just one week, we would be back at in Los Angeles, at Shabbat morning services surrounded by two hundred other Jews. I was sad to be leaving, but with a bit of a start, I realized I was also starting to feel excited to be going home.

Sitting on the airplane at 5:30 in the morning, waiting for take-off, I closed my eyes and allowed my mind to wander. The men who were sitting across the aisle from me were speaking Arabic and at one point I realized that even without concentrating, I understood certain expressions and phrases. That surprised me. While I was still far from fluent, Arabic was a language that I had come to love and that was now part of me. I felt a connection to the men sitting across from me, instead of being separated by the foreign sounds of their speech, as I had on the way over. I settled in, happy in the knowledge that this was something I was taking with me, even as I was leaving friends and places that had become part of my life.

Author's favorite spice shop, an important memory of Cairo.

Author, husband Revuen Firestone and sons Amir and Noam
at the airport leaving Egypt.

Chapter 11
The Return

تأتي الرياح بما لا تشتهي السفن

Winds do not blow as the ships wish.
~Arabic Proverb

RETURNING TO CAIRO ONE YEAR LATER FELT ALMOST like coming home. Reuven had been invited to give a public lecture on July 4, 2007 at Ain Shams University, one of Egypt's most prestigious institutions of higher learning, and we were back in Cairo for one week.

His topic— "The Origins of the Chosen People Idea in Judaism, Christianity, and Islam"— was announced in Arabic and English on the black and white posters throughout the campus. It was an ambitious topic, and one he would never have broached in a mosque, even had he been invited. But here at Ain Shams University, he had been assured by Mohamed Hawary, a good friend and colleague who had issued the invitation, that it would be perfectly fine in this academic setting to discuss the topic in reference to the three monotheistic faiths.

Reuven was giving this talk as an American Jew in one of the most respected universities not only in Egypt, but the Arab world. I felt the thrill of opening night as we walked up the stairs of the lecture hall. I was also excited that my Arabic teacher, Zayna, herself a graduate of Ain Shams, had asked to attend the lecture and would be waiting for me inside.

Reuven's talk proved to be one of the best I had ever heard him give. As always, he elucidated complex ideas without oversimplifying them. I could not remember ever having been more proud of him and his academic work. Zayna also was impressed. She murmured expressions of her interest and approval intermittently through the lecture. A translator by training, she told me at the conclusion that the ongoing translation of the lecture from English to Arabic had been thorough and clear.

But from the outset, the question and answer period that followed the lecture seemed to get off on the wrong foot. Thanking Reuven for his wonderful talk, Mohamed mentioned that Reuven was not only an academic scholar of Islam, but also a rabbi. Mohamed, a scholar of Judaism who was also a believing Muslim, shared this fact out of pride in his long-time friend and colleague, but the comment seemed to evoke other emotions in the audience.

246   The first questioner expressed dismay that he had come to hear an American professor only to learn that Reuven was a rabbi, and therefore he could not believe a word he had said. The second questioner asked Reuven whether he believed Abraham had offered Isaac or Ishmael as a sacrifice, to show his submission to God's will. Reuven calmly explained that this was a point of disagreement between Muslims and Jews, reflecting the different accounts in the Torah and the Quran: Jews regarded Isaac as the intended sacrifice, while Muslims believed him to be Ishmael. Reuven also noted that the Quran did not explicitly name which of Abraham's sons was intended for sacrifice. While the early commentators of Islam had been divided on the subject, within two hundred years, virtually all Muslims had come to believe that the intended sacrifice was Ishmael.

But even that response did not satisfy the audience. Almost every subsequent questioner returned to this issue, asking Reuven about his personal beliefs on the matter and evoking surprise and even some embarrassment on Zayna's part. "What—Ishmael again?" she exclaimed after the fourth or fifth time the question was asked.

Finally the questions ended. Mohamed escorted us and Zayna to the Faculty Club where we relaxed together over an elegant lunch. Afterwards we sat with several graduate students in Jewish Studies who wanted to discuss their dissertation research with Reuven. The hostile comments and questions receded into the background. It had been, we agreed on our way back to the hotel, an exhilarating, if at times disquieting, day.

Two days later, our friend Elie Antebi, Israeli Consul General to Alexandria, called Reuven with a clipped message: "Get hold of *Al-Musry Al-Youm*," he said, referring to "The Egyptian Daily," Egypt's most popular newspaper. "There's an article about you on the front page." Standing on a small side street in downtown Cairo, with a cacophony of horns blaring from all sides, Reuven perused the newspaper's headlines. "There it is," Reuven said to me, "*Jewish Rabbi Attacks Islam* –right on the front page—I can't believe it." He pointed to the article on the right hand side of the page, and I slowly sounded out the headline in Arabic. "Thank God there's no picture of you," I said. "Very funny," Reuven answered. But I was serious. As a steady stream of men passed by us on the street with barely a glance, I was grateful for our anonymity.

This article would not be missed. It was Friday morning, when the most widely read "weekend" edition of the newspapers came out, like Sunday papers in the States. Friday was also the day when every mosque was filled to overflowing. Riot police standardly assembled every week in full garb outside the largest mosques downtown, just in case an imam roused his crowd of followers to take to the streets.

Our two teenage sons, Noam and Amir, were stunned that their father, who was increasingly becoming known in the United States for his work in Muslim-Jewish dialogue, as well as his scholarship on Islam, had been accused of attacking Islam.

The boys and I moved closer to Reuven as he read and shared with us the key points of the article. "They say I advocated the chosenness of the Jews and attacked the idea of chosenness in Islam...that I criticized the Quranic verse that describes the Islamic people as 'the best brought forth to humanity.' When did I do that?" he asked no one in particular as the furrow in his forehead deepened. "Here, one professor says I acknowledged Jewish racism and the fact that for Jews, chosenness is based on race. And another professor accuses me as an 'academic rabbi' of only coming to Ain Shams to 'publicize my goods!' This is incredible." Reuven shook his head in disbelief. "The article only quotes the people who challenged me in the Q & A. It doesn't say anything about what I actually said. It's infuriating!"

The cell phone rang again. "You made the front page with similar headlines in at least two other papers," Elie reported. Reuven jotted down the names of the papers and thanked him for the update. "I want to see those papers too, but first I have to call Mohamed," he told us.

Mohamed already knew about the three articles. He was surprised and angry that this had gotten into the papers with no one interviewing him or checking the facts in some other way. He also felt very badly that his statement at the end of the lecture that Reuven was a Jew and a rabbi had provoked such a negative reaction.

Mohamed updated Reuven with more news: in response to the articles, twenty members of parliament had already come together and demanded that the speaker of the People's Assembly of Parliament call an emergency meeting of the Education Committee to determine who was responsible for the convening of the seminar. They were also calling for the firing of the minister of higher education. The acting president of Ain Shams had asked Mohamed to write an official report that the University could send out immediately to all the newspapers and to the Minister of Foreign Affairs and other interested parties in the government. Mohamed was trying to finish that report now.

As Reuven hung up, the phone rang again. It was a graduate student in Jewish Studies at Ain Shams who introduced himself as Muhammad Aboud. He had very much enjoyed Reuven's lecture and was very upset at the response in the papers. He was also a journalist, he explained, and he wanted to interview Reuven and write a counter-article for *Al Karama*, a well-respected weekly newspaper that would come out on Monday. Could he come to our hotel later that night? It was Friday night but we immediately said yes.

At about 10 p.m., Muhammad Aboud together with another young man with a camera, joined us in our hotel apartment. As we sat down together in the living room, Aboud's first words were apologetic.

"I am sorry you are having this kind of experience in Egypt. It is very unfortunate," he said sadly. Reuven agreed and expressed appreciation that Aboud was taking the time and interest to interview him and write an article that would present a different picture.

"I liked your lecture a lot, and what they wrote is simply not true. Someone has to set the record straight." Aboud explained that he planned to stay up late and finish the article so it could meet the morning deadline and appear in Monday's paper.

We sat down in the living room and after a few minutes of informal conversation over tea, Muhammad Aboud addressed more pointed questions to Reuven about the content of his lecture, and his efforts to increase understanding of Islam in the United States. His companion took a few pictures as they were talking. After about an hour, Aboud stood up to go.

"I am taking my Orals tomorrow morning for my Masters degree," he told us, "so I need to go home and write this, and then maybe catch a couple of hours of sleep. But don't worry—I will finish the article tonight. It's very important to me." We were even more appreciative of Muhammad Aboud's efforts in light of his exams the next day. We went to bed wondering what he would write, and what the response might be.

Apart from the lecture, our week back in Egypt proved a time to reconnect with friends for all of us. Noam and Amir both spent most of the week on their own with their friends. I saw Zayna and Mahabbah for some part of the day, almost every day, and Reuven and I also managed to see everyone else we wanted to see. We stayed at the hotel across the street from where we had lived, in the same apartment we had stayed in when we first arrived in Cairo. A year later, Umar and Seif were still working at the hotel and Imad was still the building manager of our apartment building. They were all excited to see us and exclaimed about how much Amir and Noam had grown. We had dinner with Maureen and Hamdi, and Kathy and Paul a couple of different times over the week. Unfortunately, our friends Safiya, Kareem, and Debbie, were all traveling the week we were in Cairo.

249

It was especially good to see Mahabbah and Zayna and hear how they were doing. Mahabbah was working two days a week and continuing to attend a literacy class as regularly as she could. Her youngest son, Muhammad, had completed a good year in school, and Omar, her older son, now out of high school, was sometimes working odd jobs, looking for something more steady. Aziza and Amir had gotten married and Aziza was still teaching kindergarten. Mahabbah continued to be a bit worried about her older son, Omar, who was having trouble finding steady work, but otherwise she seemed very content. Zayna now had a paying part-time job as a translator, and was still teaching at the Alexander School. She was very happy with her work, although she would have liked to have more paid work as a translator.

Zayna told us that she and her father had finally finished Reuven's book, *Children of Abraham: Introduction to Judaism for Muslims*, which we had given her a year earlier when Reuven received the first copies of the Arabic translation. She and her father had read the book slowly, Zayna said, finding it of great interest and discussing it together as they went along. "To think that I read a whole book about Judaism—and one written by a rabbi—years ago I would have said it was impossible!" she said with a smile.

Mohamed Hawary came by on Saturday to tell us that the next night, he and the acting President of Ain Shams University would be interviewed on national television, on Egypt's most popular evening talk show. He hoped that this opportunity to speak directly to a wide Egyptian audience would enable a speedy resolution of the "crisis" that had erupted in response to Reuven's lecture. Sunday would be our last night in Cairo, and we already had tickets for a special outdoor concert of traditional Arab music with Maureen and Hamdi and all our kids. We did not want to change our plans, so we would miss the interview on television, but Reuven and Mohamed agreed to speak together later that night.

When they did talk late Sunday night, Mohamed felt very good about how the interview had gone. He was confident that this chance to set the record straight before such a large national audience would put the matter to rest.

The next morning, Mohamed came by our hotel with *Al Karama* in hand. He was very pleased with the long article that Muhammad Aboud had written, and as Reuven looked it over, so was he. There was a large photo of Reuven. I knew Mohamed and Reuven would play down any risk, and might even make a joke of it, but I had to ask.

"If a photo like this had come out on Friday, I would have insisted we leave Egypt the same day," I admitted. "But between last night's program and this article, what do you think—are we safe walking on the street until tonight when we leave?"

"And I thought I might have to look for a new job. Maybe in Los Angeles," Mohamed laughed. "But now I think we will not see any more trouble."

And indeed, our last day in Cairo on this visit proved happily un-eventful. We left Cairo very pleased to have reconnected with most of our friends, still trying to digest the response to Reuven's lecture, but encouraged that serious efforts had been made to set the public record straight about the content of Reuven's lecture, and that at least some se-rious discussion of the meaning of academic freedom had resulted from the newspaper attacks. Ironically, the press drama ended up bringing Reuven's ideas to thousands of Egyptians, far beyond the 150 people who had attended the public lecture itself,

And the articles kept coming after we left. One piece that appeared in *October Magazine* a week later, sharply critiqued Egypt's national newspapers for publishing incendiary front page articles that could well have incited violence, without checking the facts. The author enumerated all the major claims made in the initial provocative articles, contrasting them point by point, with the actual facts, and called on journalists and parliamentarians alike to be more responsible in the future. Again, we felt that as the events continued to play out, what was initially a disturbing eruption of antisemitic intolerance and fear mongering, had prompted not only a sound defense of Reuven and his ideas, but also a very public discussion about the value of free academic discourse and the role and responsibility of the press within a society. We came away from our week's visit feeling a mix of disappointment and appreciation for the complex reality of Egyptian society.

Later we would look back at the defense of academic freedom and the calls for responsible journalism as positive signs that the hunger for freedom and the reformist sentiment were very much alive in Egypt. It would take a few more years, however, before these stirrings for more expansive freedoms would find their moment, and when that happened, Tahrir Square would hold the world at rapt attention.

Mohamed Hawary and Reuven Firestone in Tahir Square

Woman on metro with colors of Egyptian flag painted on her face.

Epilogue: A Post Revolution Visit

أول الشجرة بذرة

A tree starts with a seed.
~Arabic Proverb

On January 25, 2011 Tahrir Square erupted in protests with over 50,000 Egyptians demanding that Egyptian President Hosni Mubarak and his regime step down from power. Inspired by the success of young people demonstrating in Tunisia in bringing down their government with non-violent mass protests, a group of young Egyptians who had been looking for the right moment to launch a large-scale public protest against Mubarak's regime saw their chance, and with their strategic use of Internet networking, including Facebook and Twitter, succeeded even beyond their dreams. At first tens and then hundreds of thousands of Egyptians from every walk of life—men and women, Christian and Muslim, religious and secular, rich and poor—came together to protest the regime's rampant corruption and failure to combat the problems of extreme poverty and lack of economic opportunity. Eighteen days later, on February 11, 2011, a weakened and confused Hosni Mubarak gave in to the demands of his people and resigned, turning over the power to govern Egypt to the Supreme Council of the Armed Forces (also known as "SCAF," or the "military council").

253

Reuven and I returned to Cairo in July 2011, six months after the youth-led revolution had taken place in Tahrir Square. We had closely followed the events leading up to and following Mubarak's dramatic fall from power and we were eager to hear how our friends had been affected by the revolution and how they viewed its future.

During the week of our visit, protesters were back in Tahrir Square, calling on the military council to respond more quickly and fully to the original demands of the revolution. With Zayna, my Arabic teacher, and Mohamed Hawary, Reuven's colleague from the university as our "guides," we walked among the demonstrators in Tahrir Square. Zayna counted herself among the active protesters. She had participated in the January protests and since then had joined and become actively involved in the Socialist Popular Alliance Party. For the last two weeks, she had spent every evening in the square, going there straight from work and returning home only to sleep.

The square we encountered was a heady blend of demonstration and celebration, both a protest event and a freedom festival. Posters, banners, and Egyptian flags were everywhere. Recorded and live performances of songs about the uprising mingled with recitations of poetry composed for the revolution. Half a dozen stages were set up around the square, which was located in the middle of downtown Cairo. Ordinary people with microphones in hand argued for their ideas about how to remake Egypt. Zayna led us to some of the more interesting spots and explained the content of songs and speeches as we went along.

One man slowly walked by, holding up a handmade map of the Nile River with its branch-like tributaries labeled to represent the "Family Tree" of Christians and Muslims through the ages in Egypt; its caption read: "We are all one family." Several people stopped to take pictures and talk with the man. Large posters with photographs of young men killed in the early protests called for justice. People strolled about, pausing to read the posters and hand-written manifestos and listening to one speaker for a while before moving on to another. Groups of people in twos and threes were engaged in animated discussions, while roving artists offered to paint the red, white, and black stripes of the Egyptian flag on people's faces.

The crowds around us reflected the diversity of Cairo. Many were wearing baseball caps or T-shirts with political slogans. There were women with their hair uncovered, others in *higaab*, and even a few women fully covered in black *burqas*, with tiny slits for their eyes that allowed only for uncertain navigation in the crowds.

I found it striking to see people engaged in meaningful political discourse after so many years when indiscreet public statements could have landed them in prison or worse. And while there was plenty of disagreement about how best to move the country forward, there seemed to be a shared commitment woven through the music and speeches and art—a shared, insistent call for justice. The speakers and singers were united in their demands for the martyrs' killers to be brought to trial and for prosecuting the corrupt officials whose greed most Egyptians believe was responsible for the extreme poverty and stagnant economy that plagued their society.

Still I was a little bit surprised that Zayna, who was quite religious, had become involved in one of the socialist parties. She explained that after months of searching for a group working against religious and sectarian discrimination, she found an excellent group working on these issues in the socialist party. She went to one of their meetings, liked what she saw, and became an active member. I was very moved that Zayna had chosen to be involved in this kind of work. I didn't want to ask, but I couldn't help but wonder if our friendship and wide-ranging talks about Judaism and Islam had contributed to her interest in fighting religious discrimination in Egypt.

Zayna was quite enthusiastic about how much had already been accomplished by the revolution and she was optimistic about the future. She also realized that the most important institutional and structural changes would take time, and that people were impatient for change. Many Egyptians simply did not understand the kind of changes that were necessary, she said, and they expected to see change immediately. In particular, they wanted to see more jobs and higher salaries and they would measure the success of the revolution by these criteria.

Sure enough, when we visited a few days later with Mahabbah and her older son, Omar, they confirmed what Zayna had told us. In Mahabbah's small but brightly painted apartment, located in a densely populated working class part of Bassatine, Reuven and I listened to their views of these momentous events. Both Omar and Mahabbah said they had supported the revolution, but they were frustrated by the fact that there were now even fewer jobs and less money. With tourism way down, many sectors of the economy had taken a direct hit, which gradually affected virtually every level of society. A series of strikes had also contributed to the disruption of services and production of goods. "*Mafeesh shughl, mafeesh fuluus*—no work, no money," Mahabbah said repeatedly, holding up her empty hands. Omar explained that even before the revolution, his work as a tailor had been sporadic at best; typically he would find a job working a sewing machine in a small women's clothing factory, but after two or three months, he would be out of work again. Since January, however, he hadn't been able to find any work at all. Mahabbah and Omar also had mixed feelings about the behavior of the protesters in relation to Mubarak. There was no question, they wanted Mubarak out, but they did not want their former leader to be humiliated. "He was like our father," Omar said. "We should still show him respect."

255

Like most of our friends, Mohamed Hawari had participated in the protests in January and February and he too was very supportive of the revolution, but he expressed a more sober assessment of the short-term future than most of the people we encountered. In his view, the Egyptian people had much to learn and there were certain misunderstandings about the meaning of freedom and democracy that would have to be corrected. For decades, Egyptians had seen people in power making all the decisions. Now, for the first time, the people had power and some thought this meant that they should be able to make *all* the decisions. In every sector people were demanding a voice, sometimes justified, and sometimes not. University students, for example, were suddenly demanding that the university fire professors who were not charismatic lecturers. It would take time for the Egyptian people to learn how to handle the democratic process and new freedoms effectively, he said. Nevertheless, Mohamed felt optimistic about the future because of the new sense of both possibility and responsibility people had already gained from the revolution.

Even more than Mohamed, our artist friends Maureen and Hamdi expressed great enthusiasm for how much had already been accomplished and how empowered Egyptians felt as a result of the events of last six months. They told us about significant changes they saw in the media and the arts, noting that more independent newspapers and television stations were functioning and there was increased interest in reading the news both in print and online. They attributed this interest to greater freedom of expression, claiming it made a difference not only in what was being printed, but also in people's general level of engagement.

We left Egypt in late July, enthusiastic about the revolution's prospects, but in the weeks and months that followed, the news out of Egypt raised a number of red flags of concern, starting with Egypt's relationship with Israel. On August 18, 2011, Palestinian militants carried out attacks in southern Israel near the border with Egypt, leaving eight people dead before fleeing into Sinai. Israeli forces pursuing the attackers fired into Egypt, killing five Egyptian soldiers. Enraged Egyptians took to the streets in Cairo, protesting the killings and demanding a tough response from their government. With thousands of protesters gathered in front of the Israeli embassy cheering him on, a young man shimmied up the flagpole and replaced the Israeli flag with an Egyptian one. While Egyptian and Israeli officials tried to work out their differences, the young man who had removed the Israeli flag at the embassy was celebrated on YouTube and Twitter as a folk hero.

Three weeks later, on September 9, tensions sharply escalated again when 3,000 Egyptians armed with hammers, axes, and steel rods attacked the Israeli Embassy. Egyptian military and police security on site made no attempt to stop the protesters as they attacked and breached a new security wall and then the embassy itself. In the end, six Israeli security guards trapped inside had to be secreted out to safety (with the help of a direct intervention by President Obama with the Egyptian authorities). The six guards, as well as Israel's ambassador and the rest of the diplomatic team, were evacuated back to Israel. The incident set off new alarm bells about how the Egyptian Revolution might impact relations between Egypt and Israel, including the peace treaty that had been in force since 1979.

Another set of concerns claimed the headlines in early October 2011 when the worst violence against Coptic Christians in decades erupted in Cairo. Coptic Christians had organized a march in Cairo to protest the burning of a church, and thousands of liberal Muslims had joined them. The march from Shubra to Maspero started out peaceful but turned violent when Egyptian security forces arrived, deliberately driving their armed vehicles into the crowds and firing live ammunition indiscriminately. Later conflicting reports claimed that Muslims armed with sticks and knives joined the fighting on both sides. The massacre left 24 people dead and over 300 wounded in the worst instance of sectarian violence in Egypt in sixty years.

As soon as I heard the news I tried to reach Zayna, because I knew there was a good chance she would have been among the marchers. Zayna wrote back that she had indeed marched with her Christian and Muslim colleagues and friends from Shubra to Maspero, even though she was sick with the flu. Once they arrived in Maspero, her friends convinced her to leave and go home. Just as she was crossing the street, Zayna saw military vehicles arrive, then heard intensive gunfire. She fled, and later learned that her friend Mina Daniel, a young Coptic man, had been killed in what she described as "a military massacre with the help of thugs." Zayna ended her email: "We feel so sad, broken, and beaten."

In the days that followed, the military denied responsibility and claimed the shots fired had come from the Copts themselves. Many

Egyptians expressed anger at what they recognized as an all too familiar tactic of the military—to foment violence and chaos among the Egyptian population in order to have an excuse to clamp down and extend their hold on power. The following Friday, five days after what was already being called "Egypt's Bloody Sunday 2,000 Muslims and Christians protested the violence in Maspero by marching from Al Azhar Mosque in downtown Cairo to Abbasiya Cathedral, where the funerals for the victims of the previous Sunday's violence were held, and then on to Tahrir Square. Marchers shouted, "We are all Mina Daniel," referring to Zayna's friend.

258   These attacks against Coptic Christians, who constitute about ten percent of Egypt's population, did not begin with the revolution. In fact, just weeks before the revolution, on New Year's Day in 2011, a church burning in Alexandria resulted in the deaths of 33 people. Coptic Christians had suffered discrimination for decades under Mubarak's rule.

From the start, Coptic Christians embraced the cause of the Egyptian revolution with enthusiasm that included hopes for greater religious tolerance in a future democratic, pluralistic society. But at the same time, fears of growing Islamist influence have raised the possibility that the revolution could usher in a government even less tolerant of its Coptic minority than Mubarak's regime. Since March, almost 100,000 Copts have left Egypt, with thousands more still trying to leave out of fear for what the future might hold for their community.

Finally, as Egyptians were moving toward their first post-Mubarak parliamentary elections in November, new signs of the military's unwillingness to give up its substantial economic and political power emerged. The military council announced a further postponement of presidential elections, and called for the continued independence of the military budget and operations from the oversight of any future civilian government. Egyptians across the political spectrum responded with anger and renewed protests. When the military attempted to crack down on protesters with violence, Egyptians again bridged their differences and took to the streets by the tens of thousands in angry opposition to the military.

The first parliamentary elections, held in November, were notably successful in bringing out large numbers of voters and proceeding peacefully, but confirmed early concerns about the Muslim Brotherhood's singular advantage going into the elections and raised new ones: in the first rounds of parliamentary elections and all that have followed, not only the Muslim Brotherhood but also the ultra-religious Salafi parties consistently won even more votes than anticipated. While it is still unclear with whom the Muslim Brotherhood will seek to form a coalition—the more liberal secular parties, or the Salafis—there is no question that the Islamists will have a definitive role in shaping the new government and constitution of Egypt.

Some critics have claimed that what we have seen in Egypt is not a revolution at all, but simply the fall of a dictator, with the military that stood at the foundation of Mubarak's regime still in control. They are quick to point out all the dangers—how the self-proclaimed fledgling revolution could be hijacked by the military, or the Muslim Brotherhood, or both. But this claim underestimates the significance of what was accomplished in the popular uprising that began in Tahrir Square and quickly spread to other Egyptian cities, in the peaceful ousting a powerful dictator of over thirty years, and in the people's calls for the establishment of a true democracy in Egypt, with free elections and the accountability of elected officials, protection of minority rights, and individual freedoms of speech and political assembly. Led by their youth, Egyptians of all ages and religious and political persuasions, suddenly saw possibilities for change and hope in their lifetime, and that they could have a voice in shaping the new Egypt. Tahrir Square, in the protests during the day and the discussions, music, and poetry of the nights, provided Egyptians with a taste of their own power and potential. And while the revolution is far from complete, for the first time in their lives, Egyptians are participating in real, unrigged elections, with large voter turnout and without violence or claims of corruption.

The new hope and sense of possibilities was a palpable change we saw and felt when we were in Cairo this summer. Not only in Tahrir Square, but on the streets of Cairo and on the Metro, visiting with our friends, and talking to strangers. Not from everyone, and not without reservations. But even with all the uncertainty and continuing hardships, the general emotional tone had shifted from resignation and frustrated cynicism to hope and eagerness to consider new possibilities. The Egyptian people are allowing themselves to imagine a different future for themselves and their children. They have experienced and witnessed the power of people taking to the streets and raising their collective voice and succeeding in winning concessions, not once but repeatedly. These are changes the Egyptian people are not going to be ready to give up so quickly. This is the heart and the hope of a true Egyptian revolution.

But revolutions are not accomplished overnight. Even a brief look at history can help us be more realistic about how long it takes for true revolutions to take root and flower. The French Revolution, usually identified with the year 1789, actually took over ten years—and included a Reign of Terror—before it took hold, and arguably, required two additional smaller revolutions in 1830 and 1848 to succeed. The American Revolution of 1776 also spanned almost a decade between the initial rejection of British rule and the signing of a treaty with Great Britain, and with twelve years between the signing of the Declaration of Independence in 1776 and the ratification of the American Constitution we consider the foundation of our democracy in 1788.

Concretizing the revolutionary changes in Egypt will take years and it would be naive to expect the way forward to be studded with only achievements and no setbacks. There are sure to be rough patches along the way, especially in the short-run, as the powerful military attempts to hold on to its control and emerging political groups jockey for power in a new government. But the last few months provide ample evidence that setbacks also are not the end of the story, and they do not have to derail further democratic progress. They can even serve to remind people of their purpose and galvanize them to move forward again with clearer resolve.

Given the events of the last year, I have many concerns for Egypt together with hope and even cautious optimism for the long-term possibilities. The challenge of establishing a democratic system that has sufficient checks and balances to insure that the rule of law can resist the manipulation of powerful groups is enormous. This is especially true for a country in which people are just beginning to participate in a democratic political process and where most political parties are now forming for the first time. Add to that the staggering economic challenges facing Egypt, a country of 82 million in which the average family income comes to one dollar a day, while many can't find any employment at all; where over a million Egyptians graduate from university each year with few job prospects; and where the major industry of tourism, along with foreign investment, have all but ground to a halt in the last year. In the short-run, I worry that the intractable economic troubles of Egypt will defy quick solutions and Egypt's new leaders will face rising frustration and anger from the Egyptian people. I worry that these leaders may turn to old patterns of scapegoating to deflect public anger. Intermittent eruptions of violence against Coptic Christians and baseless accusations against Israel have been such strongly imprinted reflexes in Egyptian society that it is hard to imagine that we won't see attempts to use these same tactics in the future.

I am concerned that the widespread anti-Israel sentiment in Egypt that predates the revolution will continue to escalate. Israel faces multiple challenges because of the current unrest in Egypt, including the growing threat of terrorist cells taking refuge in Sinai and the transport of weapons to Gaza through Sinai. How the Muslim Brotherhood support of Hamas will affect internal Palestinian politics, and in turn the prospects for future negotiations between Israel and the Palestinians, is also a big question. At the same time, it is hard to imagine that the future Egyptian leadership will have any real interest in escalating conflict with Israel. To the contrary, we have heard public assurances from the military council and from the top leaders of both the Muslim Brotherhood and the Salafi party that they intend to honor the peace treaty between Egypt and Israel. And despite the clear challenges Israel faces in relation to Egypt and the changes throughout the region, there are also opportunities in the short- and long-term for partnership with Egypt in business, as well as medical research and scientific development. I believe that in the long-term, real democracy in Egypt, with freedom of expression and a free market, offers Israel a better chance to develop a relationship of mutual benefit with Egypt than what existed under Mubarak.

I also have concerns about how far the military will go in its increasingly brazen efforts to hold on to its power. Reasserting the need for the Emergency Law, raiding independent media outlets, and harassing pro-democracy groups—these are disturbing signs of the military's interest in preserving its own power. There is also an increasing tendency to blame "foreign hands" (read: the United States) "for inciting the current unrest for their own gain."

But even with all of this, I am hopeful and even guardedly optimistic about the long-term possibilities for Egyptians establishing a democratic government. I believe the Egyptian people's discovery of their own political voice and power will help ensure that no single group will be able to hijack this revolution. If tens of thousands of Egyptians are willing to confront the guns and even tanks of the interim military government to protest their inaction, their new policies, and their repressive tactics, they will be willing to do the same with the Muslim Brotherhood or any other group. The Egyptian people's experience of bridging their differences to successfully oust from power their dictator of thirty years, and even more important, the Egyptians' new experience of hope for a different future for themselves and their children, is not something they will be willing to give up so easily. We can expect to see protesters continue to use this "people's veto" as needed, to keep the revolution on course.

262

One example of the effectiveness of the people's veto power was the Women's March on December 20. In the midst of several days of large public protests against the military regime and escalating violence against the protesters, videos began being circulated that showed soldiers beating, stripping, and kicking female demonstrators in Tahrir Square. Shocked and angry Egyptians announced a Women's March of protest against the military. Over 10,000 women came out to march, surprising even Egypt's feminists. The marchers included women of all ages, secular and religious, with young mothers carrying babies, and women who were demonstrating for the first time. Before the march ended, the Supreme Council of the Armed Forces had reversed themselves, offering a statement of apology to women for "the violations that took place during the recent events" and pledging that legal action would be taken "to hold whoever is responsible accountable." The march helped end the military's escalating violence against both female and male protesters that had claimed fourteen lives in five days and reaffirmed the important role women can play in Egypt's continuing revolution.

From the first days of protest in Tahrir Square there have been concerns about what role the Muslim Brotherhood will play in post-Mubarak Egypt. Can Egypt create a democratic state with the protection of individual and minority rights that is informed by Islamic values and in some cases, Islamic law? How might growing Islamist influence in government affect foreign policy, including Egypt's peace treaty with Israel and relations with the United States and the West?

Concerns center on the question of what the Muslim Brotherhood's true agenda is. The Muslim Brotherhood, first established in Egypt in 1928, is the oldest and one of the largest Islamist organizations in the world. It existed for years as the main opposition organization in Egypt and several other Arab countries. While the group has officially renounced the use of violence to achieve its goals, it has spawned several groups that continue to use violent means. It has maintained relations with Hamas, which was founded as an offshoot of the Egyptian Muslim Brotherhood in 1987 during the first Intifada against Israel. And Brotherhood leaders, in writing and in speeches, have continued to openly express their often virulent anti-Israel views.

Over the last several months, Muslim Brotherhood leaders have repeatedly said they are committed to building a democratic society in Egypt, and are not interested in creating a theocratic Islamist state. They have also said they intend to abide by Egypt's peace treaty with Israel. But both in and outside Egypt, political analysts debate whether or not such statements by the Muslim Brotherhood can be trusted. There is concern that the Muslim Brotherhood could be using such statements to allay fears now, while the elections are underway, and that once in power, they will impose their long-held views to create a government based on Islamic law.

Can leaders of the Muslim Brotherhood be taken at their word? Especially in light of their history, the Muslim Brotherhood needs to be carefully watched. Like all political groups, their actions will reveal where they stand more than their proclamations.

But at the same time, we need to be open to the possibility that the Muslim Brotherhood is indeed different from what it was a generation ago. It is important to note that the most radical elements within the Brotherhood have left to join or form new *jihadi* groups. This breakaway phenomenon resulted from and contributed to the Brotherhood becoming more moderate in the last few decades. Some of these individuals and groups have been quite vocal in their condemnation of the Brotherhood for "selling out" and even "collaborating with the enemy" to achieve their political goals.

The Brotherhood's success in the polls together with the unexpectedly large vote won by the ultra-religious Salafi party raises real concerns about the impact of the Islamists enjoying such clear dominance going into the first post-Mubarak parliament. In addition, I am particularly concerned about the Brotherhood's sometimes too cozy relationship with the military. But I am also curious about how the shift from the opposition to the center of power will affect the Muslim Brotherhood in the months ahead. When they are responsible for the economic, political and social well being of the country, what impact will this have on their policies? Can they afford to alienate the West and lose the infusion of funds they so desperately need from the United States, the European Union, and the International Monetary Fund?

264

I am reminded of a piece I read in the newspaper when the Judges Movement was raging in Egypt during the spring of our time living there. The writer, Rami G. Khouri, noted that every important political movement in the modern Arab world had started in Egypt, from anti-colonial resistance to Arab nationalism, to pan-Arabism, the Muslim Brotherhood and modern Islamist politics. Egypt's new efforts to create a form of government reflecting democratic principles and Islamist values could well prove an important model for other countries in the region. The importance of the experiment being launched in Egypt cannot be overstated, for the eighty-two million people who live in Egypt, for the rest of the region, and in some sense, for all of us.

When I read the latest updates about Egypt, I inevitably see the faces of my friends, scenes I encountered in Cairo or other parts of the country, the faces of people I passed on the street or stood with while riding on the Metro. For me, no news story about Egypt is just about a people in a distant country, but about a people with whom I continue to feel a true bond. I am tremendously grateful for my experiences living in Egypt, and especially the friendships I formed and have been able to maintain. With a heightened sense of how much is at stake, because of my experience of living in Egypt, I fervently hope that the Egyptian people's dreams of a better future for themselves and their children—and the potential for far-reaching change unleashed with the protests in Tahrir Square in January 2011—will be realized in the months and years ahead.

Appendix
Fourteen Arabic Proverbs

The Arabic language is rich in its poetry and proverbs. These are ones that are particularly meaningful for me.

265 الكلمة فى فمك ـ أنت سيدها، خرجت من فمك ـ هى سيدتك

Acknowledgments:

Al-kilma fi fumak inta sayyidha, kharagat min fumak, hiya sayyidatuk

While the word is yet unspoken, you are master of it; once it is spoken, it is master of you.

Prologue:

رحلة الألف ميل تبدأ بخطوة

Rihlat al-alf mil tabda' bikhatwa

A journey of a thousand miles begins with one step.

Chapter 1

صدِّق ما تراه، ونحي جانباً ما تسمعه

Saddiq ma tarahu wanaḥi janiban ma tasma'oh

Believe what you see and lay aside what you hear.

Chapter 2

يوم عسل ويوم بصل

Youm 'asal wayoum basal

One day honey, one day onions.

Chapter 3

التكرار يعلّم الحمار

It-tikraar yi'allim il-ḥimar

Repetition teaches even a donkey.

Chapter 4

راح الخيط والعصفور

Raḥ al-kheyt wal 'asfur

Both the line and the bird have gone.

Chapter 5

كل يوم في حياتك هو بمثابة صفحة في تاريخك

Kull yom fi ḥayatak huwa bimathabat safḥa fi tarikhak

Every day of your life is a page of your history.

Chapter 6

أكتب على الرمال الأشياء السيئة التي فُعِلَت لك، ولكن أكتب على قطعة
رخام الأمور الحسنة التي حدثت لك

*Uktub alal-rimal al-ashya' assayyi`a illi ḥadsat ma`ak wuktub ala qit`at
rikham al-umur al-ḥasana illi ḥadsat ma`ak*

**Write the bad things that are done to you in sand, but write the good
things that happen to you on a piece of marble.**

Chapter 7

الأم مدرسه اذا اعدتها اعدت شعباً طيب الاعراق

Al umm madrasa; izza a'dadt-ha a'dadt sha'b tayyib al-a 'raq

A mother is a school; preparing her is like preparing a good nation.
~Hafez Ibrahim, Egyptian Poet

Chapter 8

الناس أعداء الأشياء اللي يجهلوها

Annas a`da' ilashya' illi yighaluha

People are enemies of that which they don't know.

Chapter 9

حبّة تثقل الميزان

Habba tithaqqil al-mizan

A single grain tips the scale.

267

Chapter 10

اللوم يأتي قبل السيوف

Al-lom ya'ti qabla ssyūf

Blame comes before swords.

Chapter 11

تأتي الرياح بما لا تشتهي السفن

Ta'ti riyaah bi-ma la tastahi sufun

Winds do not blow as the ships wish.

Epilogue

أول الشجرة بذرة

Awwali shagara bizra

A tree starts with a seed.

Author's Bio

Ruth H. Sohn is a rabbi, teacher, and writer. A graduate of Yale University, she received rabbinic ordination from the Hebrew Union College-Jewish Institute of Religion in New York. Sohn teaches and directs a mentoring program for rabbinical students at the Hebrew Union College in Los Angeles, and teaches adults in both local and national venues.

Sohn's articles have appeared in *The Reconstructionist, Reform Judaism, The Baltimore Jewish Times* and other Jewish newspapers. Her essays can be found in numerous anthologies including *The Torah: A Women's Commentary*, ed. by Tamara Cohn Eskenazi and Andrea Weiss (URJ Press), *Dancing on the Edge of the World*, ed. by Miriyam Glazer (Jewish Lights) and *Reading Ruth: Contemporary Women Reclaim a Sacred Story*, ed. by Judith Kates and Gail Reimer (Ballantine Books).

The author has a longstanding interest in the Middle East and Arab-Israeli relations, having lived in Israel as well as Egypt, and having traveled in Jordan and Turkey. She and her husband have three children and live in Los Angeles.

270

With the collaboration of:

Gaon Institute
A 501 c 3 organization
www.gaoninstitute.org

CPSIA information can be obtained at www.ICGtesting.com
Printed in the USA
BVOW01s1211140914

366735BV00003B/87/P